GUILLA ANTIGUA ATLANTA AUCHTERARDER AUSTIN
BANGKOK BARBADOS BARCELONA BAUX DE PROVENCE
BIG SUR BOCA RATON BOSTON BOTSWANA BRESCIA
BO SAN LUCAS CAIRO CALCUTTA CANCUN CANNES
SBAD CARMEL CHARLESTON CHESTER CHIANG-MAI
US DALLAS DANA POINT DELHI DRESDEN DUBLIN
FLORIDA KEYS FRANKFURT GENEVA GREAT BARRIER
LS INTERLAKEN ISTANBUL JACKSON JAIPUR JAMAICA
LA KONA LA JOLLA LAS VEGAS LAUSANNE LENOX
NE MADEIRA MADRID MALDIVES MANCHESTER
HOBRA MAUI MAURITIUS MELBOURNE MELTON
RLO MONTREAL MOSCOW MT.TREMPER MUNICH
IS NEW YORK NEWPORT BEACH OKAVANGO DELTA
PETER ISLAND PHILADELPHIA PHOENIX PORTOFINO
NCHO MIRAGE RANCHO SANTA FE RANTHAMBHOR
SAINT-JEAN-CAP-FERRAT SAINT-TROPEZ SALZBURG
RANAC LAKE SARDINIA SCOTTSDALE SEATTLE
LA SINGAPORE SNOQUALMIE S BARTS
ST. THOMAS STOCKCROSS STO SYDNEY
COS TUSCANY UDAIPUR VANCOUVER VENCE VENICE
WIESBADEN WINDERMERE ZERMATT ZURICH

# Valerie Wilson's World

## The Top Hotels & Resorts

### Valerie Ann Wilson

Publisher and Editor-in-Chief
Valerie Ann Wilson

Editor
Nancy Perelli DePalma

Associate Publisher
Joseph R. D'Alto

Authors
Valerie Ann Wilson and Nancy Perelli DePalma

# Author's Acknowledgements

Valerie Wilson's World...The Top Hotels & Resorts could not have been possible without the dedication and enthusiasm of many talented individuals. I am extremely grateful to all of the hotel general managers, senior executives at hotel companies and the numerous management teams for supporting my project and providing me with materials and terrific photography. Special thanks go to Tom Perry and Michael Lucas at Toppan Printing for their assistance. I am especially appreciative to Joe D'Alto. He was instrumental in giving me the extra push to make this dream a reality. My heartfelt thanks go to B+W Creative Group, especially Larry Brill, for his imaginative designs, countless hours of hard work and great patience while working with Nancy and myself on the book. Most importantly, I offer my most sincere gratitude to Nancy Perelli DePalma for her collaboration. This book would not have been the same without her keen editorial sense, invaluable insight, tireless energy and commitment to excellence. Together, she and I crafted a lyrical writing style which indeed brings the pages alive.

The pictures highlighting favorites places around the world on the jacket cover and on the four photo collage pages at the beginning and end of the book are personal photographs taken by my daughter, Kimberly Wilson Wetty, and me. I thought you would like to know their identities. I'm sure you have traveled to many of the following places.

All photographs are described clockwise from the top right:

Jacket cover: *Sunset on Lake Como • Grand Canal, Venice • Pyramids of Giza, Cairo • Inlet in Indonesia*

Jacket back: *Paris by Night • Balinese Temple Entrance • Caribbean Beach •
New York Skyline by Night • Indian Temple in Delhi • Big Ben, London • African Elephants*

Page 1: *New York Harbor in Winter • French Riviera Coastline • Spanish Steps, Rome •
Golden Gate Bridge, San Francisco • Ancient Egyptian Statue*

Page 2: *Giraffe in Kenya • Beach Sunset • Hill town of Eze, France •
Grand Cascade, Peterhof, St. Petersburg • Jaipur Palace, India*

Page 323: *Caribbean Beach • Tower Bridge, London • Monet's Garden, Giverny, France •
Arno River Bridge Reflection, Florence • Japanese Temple*

Page 324: *Beach at Sunset • Canal in Venice • Arizona Desert Landscape •
The Forbidden City - Imperial Palace, Beijing • Haghia Sophia, Istanbul*

In addition, I would like to thank Concorde Hotels for providing the *Paris by Night* photo
and The Waldorf Towers for the photograph of *New York Skyline by Night*.

The hotels have generously provided the photography of their specific properties.

First published in the United States in 2001

Published by Valerie Wilson Publications
475 Park Avenue South, New York, New York 10016

ISBN 0-9713146-0-8
Printed in Japan by Toppan

# CONTENTS

# CONTENTS

# CONTENTS

# CONTENTS

# CONTENTS

# C O N T E N T S

# CONTENTS

# CONTENTS

# INTRODUCTION

No cinnamon French toast has ever lived up to the memory of the breakfast I had on a train pulling into Harper's Ferry while traveling from Iowa to Washington, D.C. Though I was only 16 and traveling for more than 24 hours halfway across the United States, my passion for travel was just beginning. Over forty years later, having traveled to countless destinations, I still find each trip an exhilarating experience, whether for a two day business trip, a long weekend getaway or a ten day vacation. For me, nothing matches the sensation of boarding a plane and arriving at a luxurious hotel or resort. Experiencing first hand an unknown location enlightens, educates and enthralls more than any textbook or lecture can possibly do.

Ernest Hemingway once quipped, "When I dream of the afterlife in heaven, the action always takes place at the Hotel Ritz." Though he was certainly joking, I could not agree more. After all, the very best hotels are rather like heaven, as these temples of luxury are blessedly free of quotidian concerns. They are places where you can rest your head on pillows fluffed to your specifications, relax poolside with frozen chocolate sorbet while being spritzed by Evian water, appreciate fine art from your own bed, or even watch wild game gather outside your window. Indeed, while ensconced in one of the world's top hotels and resorts, enjoying the finer points in life is de rigueur.

Whether you gaze upon the turquoise waters or green expanses from your suite's terrace, look across to ancient monuments or overlook legendary landmarks, truly great hotels and resorts bring you the world unlike anywhere else. Some have long, fascinating histories, filled with stories of glittering balls, scandals and illustrious characters, and many have been captured by the world's leading authors and artists. Others, long on style, invite you to contribute to their history in the making.

Within these pages, you will get a glimpse of my personal favorite hotels and resorts throughout the world. From grande dames to contemporary towers I have selected the following places for their superb ambience, impeccable service and dazzling panache. As a world traveler, I love absorbing the local culture, art and history while visiting museums, galleries and historical monuments. Admittedly, I am a frustrated hotelier as well, and I thoroughly enjoy sharing the joys of a hotel with you. I encourage you to sit back, relax and enjoy the trip.

Welcome to my world.

*Valerie*

Dedicated to my daughters, Jennifer and Kimberly,
who share my passion for travel and my commitment to excellence.

## About Valerie Wilson Travel

Founded twenty years ago this fall, Valerie Wilson Travel, Inc. is one of the largest privately owned travel consulting firms in the United States. Continually recognized for its impeccable knowledge and dedication to service, the agency has been counted among *Travel Weekly's* "Top 50 Travel Agencies" every year since 1998, has been rated among the top 40 corporate travel agencies in the country annually since 1999 by *Business Travel News*, was listed by *Crain's* as the second largest woman-owned firm in the New York area, and was most recently included in *Condé Nast Traveler's* "Book of Indispensable Travel Agents" in their August 2001 issue. Far from the initial staff of just three, today Valerie Wilson Travel employs nearly 300 people in the New York headquarters and branch offices in Purchase, New York; Hilton Head, South Carolina; Boothbay Harbor, Maine; New Canaan, Connecticut and affiliate offices in Greenwich, Connecticut and Hartsdale, New York. Together with her daughters, Jennifer Wilson-Buttigieg and Kimberly Wilson Wetty, Valerie Ann Wilson continues to live out her dream of providing quality travel experiences.

If you have any personal experiences or comments you would like to share, we look forward to hearing from you.

### Valerie Wilson Travel, Inc.

475 Park Avenue South
New York, New York 10016
Telephone: 212-532-3400
Fax: 212-779-7073

# Europe

| | | |
|---|---|---|
| AUSTRIA | GERMANY | PORTUGAL |
| BELGIUM | GREECE | RUSSIA |
| CYPRUS | HUNGARY | SCOTLAND |
| CZECH REPUBLIC | IRELAND | SPAIN |
| ENGLAND | ITALY | SWITZERLAND |
| FINLAND | MONACO | TURKEY |
| FRANCE | THE NETHERLANDS | WALES |

# Hotel Goldener Hirsch

From its country furnishings and décor to its warm welcome, Hotel Goldener Hirsch shares Salzburg's unique flavor with its guests.

The hotel has welcomed visitors since 1407 and this fifteenth century country ambience extends throughout the public rooms, restaurants and 64 guest rooms and 5 suites. The rooms invite you to beat the Austrian chill by settling into a cozy nook or comfortable chair.

The hotel's bar is a favorite of both locals

hotel and its staff, making sure all guests receive great care. His family is responsible for reviving the hotel in the late 1940's and their passion for antique treasures is evident today - even the bar was made from an antique trunk! Count Walderdorff's Salzburg walking tours are thorough, informative, and best of all, personalized. You haven't quite experienced Salzburg if you haven't walked its streets with him.

You know you are in Austria when you stay at the charming Hotel Goldener Hirsch.

and guests. The hotel offers two restaurants, Restaurant Goldener Hirsch and The Herzl. The Herzl serves traditional hearty Austrian cuisine in a folkloric setting, complete with staff in dirndls, while Restaurant Goldener Hirsch serves superb cuisine in a slightly more formal setting. Its delicious food is sought after in Salzburg and the restaurant is often called upon to cater the area's most exclusive events.

The incomparable Count Johannes Walderdorff oversees the

HOTEL GOLDENER HIRSCH
Getreidegasse 37
5020 Salzburg, Austria

# Hotel Sacher Salzburg Österreichischer Hof

Birthplace of Mozart and host of the annual music festival, Salzburg is a city filled with music. Its beautiful natural setting, on the banks of the Salzach River and surrounded by snowcapped Alpine peaks, contributes to the harmony of this charming Austrian city.

A 135 year tradition has established the Hotel Sacher Salzburg Österreichischer Hof as one of Europe's finest hotels. Enjoying a prime location on the banks of the river, the Hotel Sacher Salzburg faces the charming Old City, its hundreds of spires and the convent made famous by "The Sound of Music." Its sterling reputation makes it the official hotel for all state visits. Owned by the Gürtler family since 1988, the hotel is the sister property to the Hotel Sacher in Vienna. Both hotels share a dedication to excellence, along with an inviting and personalized manner.

The 115 rooms and 5 suites are traditional, yet stylish. Each room has its own character, with beautiful antiques and unique furnishings. The views of the old town and the Fortress Hohensalzburg are unforgettable.

The Hotel Sacher Salzburg is home to an array of dining and entertainment choices. The Roter Salon faces the river and offers international cuisine. The wood paneled Zirbelzimmer specializes in typical Austrian dishes, while the Salzach Grill spans the world for its offerings. A visit to the Café Sacher Salzburg is a must — especially for a taste of the original Sacher torte.

The Hotel Sacher Salzburg Österreichischer Hof encourages you to sing a happy tune.

**HOTEL SACHER SALZBURG ÖSTERREICHISCHER HOF**
Schwarzstrasse 5-7
5020 Salzburg, Austria

# Hotel Schloss Fuschl

The unique Hotel Schloss Fuschl is located in an 85 acre wooded park on Lake Fuschl. The castle dates from the 15th century and was built as a hunting lodge and summer residence for Salzburg Archbishops. It was transformed into a hotel in the late 1970's and recently underwent renovations to

include modern amenities like a health and beauty spa and advanced technology in the facilities.

The 84 rooms and suites in the castle maintain their 15th century country charm while incorporating all modern conveniences. Rooms offer views of the

spectacular lake or the beautiful grounds. You will most likely want to indulge in one of the many activities offered here, from cross-country skiing and sleigh rides in winter to golf, tennis and boat rides in summer months. The lake provides countless recreation and sporting opportunities, including fishing. Fish caught in the lake appear on the dinner menu and if you are lucky enough to catch one yourself, the chef will be happy to prepare it for you.

The public rooms maintain the castle's history with vaulted ceilings, massive fireplaces, antiques, plus fine accessories and tapestries. The restaurant offers three different dining areas under

the guidance of the same talented chef. Dine on haute cuisine and enjoy the beautiful lake view, whether sitting inside looking out, or outside on the sheltered terrace.

Schloss Fuschl embraces modern times with its innovative health spa and holistic therapy practice. Lakeside tai chi and meditation are just two of the offerings.

Schloss Fuschl is a historic castle with a unique atmosphere.

### HOTEL SCHLOSS FUSCHL
Fuschl,
5322 Hof bei Salzburg, Austria

# Hotel Imperial

Vienna is an exquisite city. Widely known for its virtuosos and delightful confections, it retains a link to its stately and imperial past.

The regal Hotel Imperial is built on the site of Vienna's old city walls. Originally constructed as a private palace for the Duke of Württemberg, the palace was inaugurated as the Hotel Imperial in 1873. It quickly gained a reputation as the official hotel for state visits. It is hotel tradition for all "official" guests to be accompanied by their Austrian counterparts and escorted to the first floor staterooms, where they wave to the crowd below. In some

cases, it is discreetly waived - Mussolini was secretly escorted through a back door after his escape from prison!

The hotel's entrance, originally designed to allow carriages, was lined with horses and feedbags for years. Today, this magnificent lobby leads to the resplendent foyer, known as the Yellow Room because of its yellow Giallo di Siena marble. The grand staircase, with gleaming marble, glittering chandelier and ornate ceiling, begs you to avoid the elevator.

The 76 glorious guest rooms and 62 sumptuous suites are all beautifully decorated in an elegant style with many antique furnishings and paintings. The proficient staff, including butler service, pampers the guests.

A visit to the Hotel Imperial instills reverence; even Russian troops occupying after World War II covered the precious wood floors to protect them from harm!

Savor Viennese tradition at the stately Hotel Imperial.

**HOTEL IMPERIAL**
Kärntner Ring 16
1015 Vienna, Austria

# Hotel Sacher

Hotel Sacher is a Viennese institution with a sweet history.

One evening in 1832, Prince Metternich demanded a special dessert for his discerning guests, proclaiming, "Tonight, I don't want any complaints about the sweet course!" Since the chef de cuisine was ill, the order was handed to a young apprentice, Franz Sacher. Sacher created a delectable chocolate cake with apricot jam and chocolate icing that set gourmets abuzz. This delightful sweet, known as the Sacher torte, became the most desired dessert in Austria and today has an extensive art collection of more than 1,000 original oil paintings and engravings, rare antique furniture and tapestries that can be enjoyed in every room and all public spaces.

The dining options are plentiful and delightful. Among other choices, you can relive the turn of the century at the traditional Viennese restaurant or linger over coffee at the typical, lively Austrian Café.

While the recipe for the Sacher torte is a well-guarded secret, it is no secret that Hotel Sacher is a delicious way to experience Vienna.

it is shipped worldwide in its famous wooden boxes.

Franz Sacher's son opened Hotel Sacher in 1876. Located across from the Vienna State Opera, it is closely linked to the arts. Beethoven's *Ninth Symphony* was played here for the first time and Graham Greene wrote part of *The Third Man* at the hotel.

The 66 rooms and 39 suites are distinguished and filled with history, yet all offer modern amenities. The hotel

HOTEL SACHER
Philharmonikerstrasse 4
1010 Vienna, Austria

# Hotel Metropole

**K**nown as the "capital of Europe," Brussels is a place with international dash and historical significance. Both NATO and European Union headquarters are here and though it is a modern city with flourishing businesses, the cobblestone streets, cafés and Art Nouveau of Belgium's past are duly honored.

Hotel Metropole, the only remaining 19th century hotel in Brussels, is an ideal home for visitors. Built in 1895, the owners and architect spared no expense, using rich materials and contracting the most highly skilled artisans and craftsmen of the time. The hotel's elevator was designed by Edoux, the French company that made its name by

to Internet access.

Since the Metropole is located in the heart of Brussels, exploration of the sights is a pleasure. Museums, theaters, galleries and restaurants, plus the city's best shopping are all within a short walk from the hotel.

Of course, befitting the premier hotel in the city of diplomacy, the spacious meeting rooms with excellent audiovisual facilities and natural daylight are perfect for hosting conferences and functions.

The world comes to Brussels, and when they do, they should stay at the Hotel Metropole.

providing the Eiffel Tower with elevator service. The Metropole was soon established as a grand palace.

Though rather large with 400 rooms and 10 suites, Hotel Metropole maintains a personalized charm. Rooms are individually appointed and in keeping with the times, all guests are treated

HOTEL METROPOLE
31, place de Brouckère
1000 Brussels, Belgium

# Anassa

The white-washed villas, terracotta tiled roofs and gently rolling hills make it easy to understand why Greece and Turkey fought over this magical place for so many years. Cyprus warms the spirit while giving the impression that time stands still. According to legend, Aphrodite, the goddess of love, sprang to life from these waters and first saw Adonis while bathing in the brilliant blue sea.

The alluring Anassa resort is in the unspoiled and largely undiscovered northwestern coast of Cyprus. Anassa, which means "queen" in classical Greek, is a recreated traditional Mediterranean village, complete with three pools, a state-of-the-art spa, four restaurants, organic farm and even a Byzantine chapel. A winding path shaded by olive and eucalyptus trees leads down to the beach, but you may also choose to unwind in the two spectacular outdoor pools with cascading waterfalls.

The 184 suites are serene, with neutral tones, cool marble and an understated luxury. All rooms have balconies with dazzling views of the sea, and some suites have private plunge pools or whirlpools. In addition to the main building, some suites are located within groups of individual residences set within the lush gardens.

Anassa blends harmoniously with the landscape, and local flavor abounds. The fresh fish served in all four restaurants is caught daily in the nearby village of Latchi.

Children are welcomed with open arms at Anassa. The "Smiling Dolphin Kiddies Club" provides year-round programs and activities and keeps both children and parents smiling.

Like a siren's song, Anassa beckons to you.

ANASSA
8830 Polis, Cyprus

# Four Seasons Hotel Prague

Prague welcomes its guests with open arms. It invites you to explore its architectural treasures, cobbled streets, sidewalk cafes and museums. In early 2001, Prague also welcomed the arrival of the new Four Seasons Hotel.

Set on the banks of the Vltava River in the Staré Mesto (Old Town), the Four Seasons Hotel Prague looks across to Prague Castle, one of the city's leading landmarks. Prague's famous Charles Bridge, with more than 600 years of history, is just steps away. Wenceslas Square, known for its shopping and fine Bohemian crystal, is nearby.

The Four Seasons Hotel blends past and present, with four interconnected buildings comprising the hotel. Three architecturally significant buildings in the Baroque and neo-Renaissance styles rest harmoniously with the newly constructed contemporary building. The 142 rooms and 20 suites, all with commanding views of the city, are the most spacious in Prague with clearly defined sitting, working or sleeping areas. For those who need more room, bi-level executive suites are the perfect answer. Three specialty suites, including one in a restored 17th century Italian Baroque villa, are exceptional. The sophisticated décor, modern amenities, latest technology and highly personal service are evident throughout this new Four Seasons Hotel.

The elegant restaurant offering regional specialties and international favorites has quickly become one of Prague's most sought after reservations. In summertime, enjoy al fresco dining on the terrace. Of course, a health club, saunas and spa services are available.

In the so-called "city of a hundred spires," Prague can be proud that one of its newest is the Four Seasons Hotel.

**FOUR SEASONS HOTEL PRAGUE**
Veleslavínova 2a
110 00 Prague, Czech Republic

# The Lygon Arms

The Lygon Arms, in the quaint village of Broadway, is the perfect place for a weekend getaway from London or to explore the Cotswolds.

A peek inside a hotel's guest book is normally a treat, but at The Lygon Arms, it is a step back in time and a history lesson as well. The first recorded date of the hotel is 1532, but there are indications that it is even older. A fireplace in one of the bedrooms is believed to date back to the 14th century! The Lygon Arms has lived through King Henry VIII's rule, the Gunpowder Plot, the Civil War and the Restoration. On the eve of the great Battle of Worcester, Oliver Cromwell rested his head here.

Over the years, The Lygon Arms has established a fine reputation for traditional country hospitality and excellent service. It has been honored twice with the prestigious Queen's Award for its appeal to foreign visitors. The 58 rooms and 7 suites are decorated in English country style, and a few feature fireplaces. One of the charms of The Lygon Arms is its respect for its heritage. Original staircases (complete with creaky stairs) and paneling have been carefully preserved. For centuries, the "great hall" has been the place to dine. Imagine the stories if these walls could talk.

With their idyllic meadows, stone cottages and grazing sheep, the Cotswolds are a perfect postcard of the English countryside. Nearby towns of Oxford and Stratford-upon-Avon also delight visitors and the antique stores of Broadway are just a short stroll from the hotel.

For a truly memorable English country experience, The Lygon Arms is an excellent choice.

**THE LYGON ARMS**
Broadway
Worcestershire WR12 7DU,
England

# The Chester Grosvenor

The Chester Grosvenor originates from 1865 and is located in one of Great Britain's oldest towns. This Tudor mansion is owned and named after the family of the Duke of Westminster, Gerald Grosvenor. Charming and inviting, Chester Grosvenor has the ambience of a country house with the services of a luxury hotel.

The town of Chester was established by the Romans in 70 AD. Though they relinquished their hold over the city in the fifth century, their presence is still strongly felt. The old Roman walls and the Roman street grid pattern are still visible today.

Chester's shopping is both terrific and intriguing. Two street levels are lined with stores, most likely due to medieval shopkeepers who built their stores on top and below the old Roman walls. Chester is also a perfect base for exploring northwestern England. It has been on the tourist's map for many years – its first guidebook was published in 1781!

The Chester Grosvenor has 73 rooms and 12 suites, all with a pleasant, country feel. All of the spacious suites are named and feature special room service menus. This exclusive feature also extends to the sommelier, who will personally visit your suite to assist with your wine selection. And what a bottle it may be! The Arkle Restaurant's wine cellar is one of the most extensive cellars in England. The Arkle offers contemporary dining and has held a Michelin star for the last ten years. La Brasserie is a less formal, airy dining option.

While the hotel has fitness facilities on the first floor, it also maintains a strong relationship with the nearby Old Hall Country Club for sporting activities.

Experience England's countryside at The Chester Grosvenor.

**THE CHESTER GROSVENOR**
Eastgate
Chester CH1 1LT, England

# Athenaeum Hotel & Apartments

The Athenaeum Hotel & Apartments' sunny disposition and ideal location make it a perfect "home away from home" in London.

On Piccadilly with views of Green Park, the Athenaeum is near many major attractions, including Trafalgar Square, Buckingham Palace and the Royal Academy of the Arts. The Athenaeum was originally built as a luxury apartment block and was furnished by Trollope & Co. of Belgravia, best known for fitting the Queen Mary on its maiden transatlantic voyage. The Athenaeum was transformed into a hotel in 1971, and it has been a favorite of visitors seeking a residential ambience with the conveniences of a large hotel.

The 111 guest rooms and 12 suites invite guests to relax and take comfort in their stylish surroundings. The 34 one and two bedroom apartments are ideal for longer visits or families traveling together. Apartment guests experience the ultimate in privacy, with a separate entrance, plus dining areas and kitchens. All accommodations reflect the Athenaeum's commitment to tradition while incorporating a contemporary flair.

Bullochs Restaurant is influenced by the Mediterranean in both cuisine and décor with antique mosaics and Jerusalem stone. The Windsor Lounge is a casual alternative for light meals and snacks. The Malt Whiskey Bar bears the distinction of having 76 different varieties of whisky.

Keep in shape at the well-equipped fitness center, or go for a jog in Green Park across from the hotel. No matter how you decide to fill your days while staying at the Athenaeum Hotel & Apartments, it is certain that you will feel right at home.

THE ATHENAEUM
HOTEL & APARTMENTS
116 Piccadilly
London W1V 0BJ,
England

# The Berkeley

Enjoy the civilized lifestyle of The Berkeley. The hotel is ideally situated in the exclusive residential Belgravia neighborhood, known for its tree-lined streets, impeccable townhouses and private gardens. The Berkeley has been in existence as a hotel since 1736. In the early 1970's, it moved to its current location in an enticing modern building just opposite Hyde Park. It enjoys a rich history filled with legend and romance; it was here that the Duke of Windsor courted Wallis Simpson.

The Berkeley's 112 rooms and 56 suites are graciously styled in classic English tradition. The rooms are incredibly spacious and inviting, and the bathrooms are done entirely in Italian marble. Three suites have private conservatories, lending an air of the countryside to this city hotel.

The Berkeley's rooftop heath club and spa allows you to escape without ever leaving the hotel. The swimming pool is a monument to tranquility with its soothing ambience and stunning views of Hyde Park and central London. It is one of only two rooftop swimming pools in London, and its glass roof retracts on nice days to let the golden sunshine blanket you with its warmth. The Christian Dior Beauty Salon has a full range of innovative beauty and relaxation treatments.

The Berkeley is well recognized for its fine dining establishments. Fusing the flavors of Thai cuisine with classic French cooking, Vong is the sensational creation of master chef Jean Georges Vongerichten. The masterful concoctions are complemented by the restaurant's inventive interior design comprised of rich Indonesian colors and unusual furnishings. Pierre Koffmann has earned two Michelin stars for his superb Gascon cuisine at Le Tante Claire, one of London's best French restaurants. The elegant decor in the dining room is inspired by the camellia flower.

Retreat to The Berkeley for a superb London visit.

**THE BERKELEY**
Wilton Place
London SW1X 7RL, England

# Claridge's

Claridge's masterfully blends British tradition with the drama of Art Deco design. Recently restored and redecorated by acclaimed architect and interior designer Thierry Despont, Claridge's sports a stylish décor combined with Edwardian and French influences. The cool beige palette of the foyer is punctuated by dazzling geometric patterned fabrics, but it is the silver white light sculpture that is the crowning glory. Created by renowned glass artist Dale Chihuly, the sculpture is comprised of over 800 individually hand-blown glass pieces. Its unique design captures your attention and imagination. The adjacent Reading Room is capped off by a roaring fireplace and sleek leather banquettes. It is

a stylish spot for Claridge's afternoon tea, served by liveried footmen.

Claridge's presents an elegant juxtaposition of Art Deco and Victorian design. Even the spacious hallways share a part of the legend; they were designed so that crinolined Victorian ladies could pass each other. The 141 guest rooms and 62 suites reflect Claridge's different design principles. The suites have been decorated by some of Britain's leading designers and several are themed, like the Tartan Suite. Two penthouse suites provide the ultimate

in privacy and luxury on the seventh floor, complete with large terraces overlooking the rooftops of London.

The Olympus Suite on the sixth floor provides a health and beauty oasis for guests of Claridge's. Fitness trainers will devise a new program for you or assist you with your current program. Beauty treatments feature the natural products of French therapist Anne Semonin.

The bronze and gilt metal doors of the Restaurant, designed by Basil Ionides in 1926, pay homage to Claridge's strong Art Deco heritage. Superb French and English cuisine is highlighted at this fine dining establishment.

Delight in the legend at Claridge's.

**CLARIDGE'S**
Brook Street
London W1A 2JQ, England

# The Connaught

The Connaught is one of London's most distinguished addresses. The hotel is delightfully located in the heart of Mayfair, with its charming shops, churches and public gardens. It was originally created as a place for England's landed gentry during their visits to London. Built in 1897, the hotel's name was changed to honor Queen Victoria's son, the Duke of Connaught.

Bearing a resemblance to an English club with French-polished mahogany paneling, doors and elaborate staircase, The Connaught is a British institution. Travelers from around the world choose the highly regarded Connaught and

whim is catered to at The Connaught, where each floor offers personalized butler service.

English favorites and French classics are served in The Connaught's two acclaimed Michelin-starred restaurants. The Restaurant's beautiful wood paneling and etched glass establish a clubby ambience, while the tables with corner sofas add a comforting touch. Intimate with just 11 tables, the Georgian style Grill Room is a wonderful alternative to the main dining room. The refinement of the Drawing Room is just perfect for a cozy cup of tea or a cocktail enjoyed fireside.

For a true London experience, stay at The Connaught.

its prestigious address; French General De Gaulle resided in a suite here during World War II.

The 90 rooms and 24 suites are traditionally decorated with lovely colors, beautiful chintzes and hand-tufted carpets, giving the effect of an English country home. Several suites have working fireplaces, and all rooms are enhanced by fine antiques and oil paintings. Renowned British interior designer Nina Campbell has added her personal touch throughout the hotel. Your every

## THE CONNAUGHT
Carlos Place, Mayfair
London WIY 6AL, England

# The Dorchester

The Dorchester is a proper English hotel.

Built on a site where nobles lived during the 18th and 19th centuries, The Dorchester has been a favorite of England's royalty since its opening in 1931. Prince Philip celebrated his bachelor party in the Park Suite, while the royal guests attending the wedding of HRH Queen Elizabeth primped at The Dorchester before proceeding to Westminster Abbey.

Overlooking Hyde Park in the center of Mayfair, The Dorchester brings a bit of the English countryside to the heart of London. The 195 rooms and 53 suites are influenced by Georgian country manors, and no two rooms

in 1953 was the talk of the town.

The Dorchester boasts several delightful restaurants. Resembling a Spanish palace in its gilded glory, the Grill Room is an alluring setting for traditional British food. The Oriental features fresh and delicious Cantonese cuisine in an exotic spot, while the Bar specializes in Italian favorites. The Delft-style tiled panels that line the walls of the Bar were handmade at the rate of only two per month - just another example of The Dorchester's amazing attention to detail.

The Dorchester Spa provides the perfect antidote for tired souls with its full range of beauty and health treatments.

Experience the tradition of The Dorchester.

are alike. Exclusive fabrics from Gainsborough and Percheron and silks hand-woven in India add a lavish touch to the rooms. Completed in 1953, the Oliver Messel Suite bears the inimitable mark of this famous theater designer. This luxurious suite shares a bit of whimsy with its unique designs like the drinks cabinet hidden behind a bookcase and the television housed in a miniature stage set. Messel's glorious decoration of The Dorchester's façade for the Queen's Coronation

**THE DORCHESTER**
Park Lane
London W1A 2HJ, England

# 47 Park Street

Don't let the discreet facade of this Edwardian townhouse fool you - you are about to enter one of London's best-kept secrets, 47 Park Street.

Situated in Mayfair, within walking distance to Hyde Park and London's best galleries and shops, 47 Park Street is a charming all-suite hotel. The townhouse was first built in 1926 by the first Baron Milford for landed gentry visiting London. Despite its acquisition of the neighboring townhouses in the 1960's, 47 Park retains much of its original splendor, including a magnificent

and shares paintings and decorative objects that she has discovered throughout the years in all rooms.

Perhaps one of Britain's best known chefs, Albert Roux is responsible for the exceptional cuisine at 47 Park Street's restaurant, Le Gavroche. For many years, the restaurant has earned coveted Michelin stars for its fantastic creations and Roux is widely recognized for his extraordinary talents. Designed like a typical British club, Le Gavroche's setting is as inviting as its menu.

47 Park Street is an English gem.

curved staircase and a series of appealing Art Nouveau windows.

Just 52 suites define the guest accommodations here, adding to the notion that you are visiting a genteel private residence. Expertly blending French panache with English aristocratic sensibility, 47 Park Street will quickly earn a place in your heart. Influenced by her travels, Monique Roux, who owns the hotel with her husband Albert, designs all the rooms with a personal flair

**47 PARK STREET**
47 Park Street
London W1Y 4EB, England

# Four Seasons Hotel Canary Wharf

Occupying a riverfront location, the Four Seasons Hotel Canary Wharf is a convenient base for travelers doing business in this area and the "City" of London.

Though only 9 square miles, Canary Wharf was historically the center of the world's shipping industry. Hundreds of years ago, Canary Wharf welcomed ships that had spanned the world collecting spices, tea and silks for England. Developed in the 1980's, Canary Wharf is now home to booming businesses of a different nature and is one of London's most energetic neighborhoods.

The Four Seasons Hotel Canary Wharf offers you a front row seat to the action of London's business center. A chic simplicity dominates all 142 rooms and suites. Clean, simple lines and sleek decorative objects create an uncluttered appearance and set a contemporary mood. An unobtrusive palette of beige and black is used in the rooms, hinting of modern Asian design philosophy.

The Four Seasons' Quadrato Restaurant celebrates the flavors of northern Italy in a relaxed setting. A pianist entertains in the evenings, and during the summer months, the restaurant has outdoor seating overlooking the gardens on the Thames.

After partaking in one of Quadrato's luscious desserts, head for the adjacent Holmes Place Health Club and Spa at Canary Riverside. This large complex is one of the leading facilities in London. Reward yourself for a job well done with a dip in the swimming pool or with one of the spa's rejuvenating and deep-cleansing treatments.

Rule your world from the Four Seasons Hotel Canary Wharf.

**FOUR SEASONS HOTEL CANARY WHARF**
46 Westferry Circus,
Canary Wharf
London E14 8RS, England

# Four Seasons Hotel London

London's fashionable Mayfair is home to the distinctive Four Seasons Hotel London. Set back from Park Lane, the Four Seasons Hotel overlooks tranquil Hyde Park.

Thirty years ago, Isadore Sharp, Canadian Founder and Chairman of Four Seasons Hotels, built The Inn on the Park, today known as the Four Seasons London, as his first hotel based on the concept of a mid-sized modern structure that provides exceptional quality, luxury and service. This property set the founding standards for all future Four Seasons hotels and resorts.

The interiors capture the essence of English charm while adding international influences throughout. The Four Seasons' 183 rooms, 11 conservatory rooms and 26 suites exude warmth and comfort. The spacious rooms appeal to all travelers while guests on business are accommodated with extensive professional services. The airy ambience in the Conservatory Rooms is unforgettable. The glass-enclosed conservatories are separated from the bedrooms and look out over balconied terraces. Many rooms overlook Hyde Park, and special suites have panoramic views of London.

The striking décor of Lanes Restaurant makes it a favorite of residents and guests alike. Set off by midnight blue marble and deep rich colors, the restaurant showcases an extensive collection of handmade glass artwork. The collection represents the work of 25 different Canadian artists. The enticing Continental menu also features many British favorites, including roast beef with Yorkshire pudding. Lanes Bar provides a cozy spot for an aperitif or cordial.

The Four Seasons Hotel London brings you the world in the center of London.

**FOUR SEASONS HOTEL LONDON**
Hamilton Place, Park Lane
London W1A 1AZ, England

# The Lanesborough

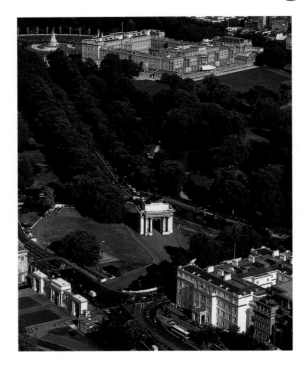

Just a stone's throw from Buckingham Palace on Hyde Park Corner, The Lanesborough introduces you to a regal style of its own.

The Lanesborough's location, facing Hyde Park and adjacent to the palace grounds, is one of London's most coveted and cherished spots. This special place was first developed by James Lane, Viscount Lanesborough, and was later home to the beloved St. George's Hospital. Occupying the former hospital's landmark Regency period building, The Lanesborough opened on New Year's Eve 1991.

The sophisticated, richly decorated style of The Lanesborough is reminiscent of England's finest

private clubs. Indeed, with just 49 guest rooms and 46 suites, The Lanesborough exudes privacy and intimacy. The accommodations are sumptuously defined by Greek-revival furnishings and jewel tones, while modern advances are tastefully concealed within antique furniture. Personal butler service, from the country that perfected the art of service, pampers you in style. The five room Royal Suite, with its floor-to-ceiling views of Constitution Arch and Buckingham Palace, just might convince you that you are a member of the Royal Family.

The Conservatory is one of The Lanesborough's many treasures. Inspired by the Brighton Pavilion, this glass-roofed room is gloriously decorated with exotic palms, Chinese lanterns and Oriental statues. The eclectic menu, which incorporates Mediterranean and Pacific Rim influences, is the creation of chef Paul Gayler. Salvatore Calabrese is another Lanesborough institution. Responsible for overseeing the Library Bar, Calabrese pours some of the world's rarest and oldest vintage cognacs, armagnacs and whiskies. The cigar collection also features some of the world's finest, including Diplomatic Trinidads, which are traditionally only given out by Castro and his government.

The Lanesborough entices you with its world-class style.

**THE LANESBOROUGH**
No. 1 Lanesborough Place
Hyde Park Corner
London SW1X 7TA, England

# Mandarin Oriental Hyde Park

Commanding a premier address in London for almost a century, the Mandarin Oriental Hyde Park is once again one of the city's most distinguished hotels.

The Mandarin Oriental Hyde Park, London has always welcomed prominent members of society, including many members of the Royal Family. Here, Princess Elizabeth and Princess Margaret learned to dance, and Prince Philip often held his cocktail and polo parties. While tradition holds that no entrances open out to Hyde Park, this hotel is the one exception. The royal entrance was added in 1926 and it was used during George VI's coronation in 1937.

The Mandarin Oriental

head to Buckingham Palace.

The spa's sleek design and contemporary approach make it one of the hippest places to unwind. Rather than choosing from a menu, clients reserve time with therapists who determine individualized needs. Calming music, soothing interiors and aromatherapy will guarantee a state of Zen.

The clever designs of Adam Tihany redefine the two dining rooms and bar. Award-winning chef David Nicholls has won acclaimed reviews for the new signature restaurant, Foliage.

The Mandarin Oriental Hyde Park, London is an exquisite hotel with a storied past and a bright future.

Hyde Park reopened its doors in May 2000 after a complete two year renovation. Lovingly restored, the 177 guest rooms and 23 suites are characterized by handcrafted finishes and luxurious fabrics. Thai silks with delicately embroidered details, exquisite art objects, English antiques and fine reproductions define the elegant accommodations. What a pleasure it is to occupy a suite looking out over the park and watch the Royal Horse Guards in parade formation

**MANDARIN ORIENTAL HYDE PARK, LONDON**
66 Knightsbridge
London SW1X 7LA, England

# The Ritz Hotel

Regal style and exceptional pedigree place The Ritz Hotel in a special class to which only a few hotels belong.

Shortly after opening the palatial Hotel Ritz in Paris, legendary hotelier Cesar Ritz set his sights on London. Mr. Ritz's determination to create a magical world within a hotel, where the upper crust of society could live and entertain in the style they were used to at home, revolutionized an industry. Sharing the formal style and gracious manner of its sister property in Paris, the Ritz Hotel opened in London in 1906.

The privately owned Ritz Hotel exudes the elegance of a

The venerable Ritz Hotel has long been a darling of the social set and it is here that King Edward VII, Sir Winston Churchill and Evelyn Waugh came to tea. Afternoon tea in the Palm Court remains delightfully traditional while echoing the graciousness of the hotel. The glass roof is perpetually lit to ensure soft mood lighting. The Ritz's restaurant is perhaps one of the most beautiful dining rooms in the world with its trompe l'oeil ceiling encircled by a series of bronze chandeliers and overlooking Green Park. The sumptuous setting and cuisine is renowned; the Queen Mother keeps a corner table here.

The Ritz Hotel is "puttin' on the ritz" for you.

French chateau from its expertly crafted exterior to its resplendent Louis XVI interiors. The 115 rooms and 18 suites are lavishly decorated with 24-karat golf leaf details, glittering chandeliers, gleaming bronze sconces and luxuriant fabrics of jacquard and damask. All rooms, though individually decorated, reflect a blue, peach, pink or yellow color scheme. Many of the refined accommodations even feature original marble fireplaces.

**THE RITZ HOTEL**
150 Piccadilly
London W1V 9DG, England

# The Savoy

The Savoy shares a dramatic history in the heart of the theater district, situated between the City of London and Houses of Parliament.

Founded in 1889 by Richard D'Oyly Carte, the producer of Gilbert & Sullivan operas, The Savoy has more than just a passing interest in the arts. It has been privy to early and private performances by some of the world's biggest stars. Prima ballerina Anna Pavlova first danced in a cabaret at The Savoy, while Caruso sang and Strauss conducted in the hotel's Thames Foyer. One of the hotel's most talented guests was certainly Claude Monet, who painted scenes of the Thames River from his fifth floor window at The Savoy.

industry, and many business deals are transacted over meals here. Sir Winston Churchill was a regular at the Grill and his table remained unoccupied in his memory for one year following his death. The formal River Restaurant enjoys a beautiful riverside setting, excellent English fare and dinner dancing on the weekend. The Thames Foyer is open throughout the day for breakfast, "high tea" and cocktails. Cecil Beaton, society designer and photographer, designed this ceiling for the Savoy Coronation Ball, held the night of Queen Elizabeth II's coronation in 1953.

All the world's a stage at The Savoy.

The Savoy's special flair is evident in its 180 guest rooms and 48 suites, many of which overlook the Thames. The traditional English or Art Deco décor delights all guests and the spacious marble bathrooms are notable for their large chrome shower fittings.

All of London meets at The Savoy. The brasserie-style Grill Room is the preferred meeting place for leaders of

**THE SAVOY**
Strand
London WC2R OEU, England

# The Stafford

Nestled on a quiet cul-de-sac in St. James's Place, The Stafford is neatly tucked away from the hustle and bustle of London.

The Stafford's aristocratic bearing stems from its origins as three private townhouses dating to the mid 1800's. St. James's Place has always been an exclusive residential area and many interesting historical figures have resided here through the years. The Stafford opened as a hotel in 1912 and was used as a club for Canadian and American soldiers during World War II. The adjacent 18th century stables were acquired by The Stafford in the late 1980's. The Carriage House is built in the middle of Blue Ball Yard, an

fireplaces. The public rooms revive the intimate style of an English country manor house.

Modern dishes and traditional English fare are served in the restaurant, while private dining in the wine cellar always proves to be an unforgettable experience.

The Stafford's stone wine cellars are of historical and architectural importance. Originally the site of the private home of Sir Christopher Wren, the architect who rebuilt London after the Great Fire in 1666, the cellars were built more than 350 years ago. The American Bar is a popular watering hole for Londoners and guests.

You will cherish your stay at the quintessentially English Stafford.

18th century stable yard that was once part of the Royal Mews. Originally used to house the thoroughbreds of the nobility, today the Carriage House has been transformed into 12 luxurious guest suites. The one-of-a-kind Guv'nors Suite, a split-level suite resembling a country cottage with beamed ceilings, is one of my favorites.

The 68 rooms in the main hotel maintain English tradition with charming antique period pieces, chintz patterns and cozy

**THE STAFFORD**
St. James's Place
London SW1A 1NJ, England

# Stapleford Park

Just two hours north of London, Stapleford Park Country House Hotel & Sporting Estate is set in the lush English countryside.

Stapleford Park was built as a private residence during the Edwardian era and the romance and elegance of that time is preserved today. Public rooms range from a lodge atmosphere in the Saloon Room to the Grand Hall where magnificent murals of Vienna's Spanish Riding School brighten the walls. Guests may choose from one of the 51 elegant, creative and often whimsical rooms. The Lady Gretton Room, designed to reflect the historical style of the estate, is the only guest room that recognizes the estate's history. Well-known interior

you an idea of the long tradition of hunting and field sports at Stapleford Park.

The dizzying array of country pursuits will keep you occupied during your entire stay. The Donald Steel golf course, falconry school, off-road driving program and archery are just some of the activities. Stapleford Park's stables, widely recognized as the finest example of Victorian stables, provide excellent instruction for riders of all abilities. Country picnics and relaxation treatments at the Clarins Spa can also be arranged.

For country elegance, Stapleford Park is an excellent choice.

designers like David Hicks and Nina Campbell have designed rooms reflecting their signature style and highly regarded companies like Tiffany, Turnbull & Asser and Mulberry have themed rooms. The Wedgwood room even has a specially designed Wedgwood Jasper phone!

A quick glance at the Saloon Room, with various hunting trophies, will give

**STAPLEFORD PARK**
Near Melton Mowbray
Leicestershire LE14 2EF,
England

# Chewton Glen

Once you enter the magical world of Chewton Glen, you may never want to leave.

Southwest of London, Chewton Glen is set between the sea and the ancient New Forest. Its history is captivating. Smugglers traveling inland once used the path that runs along the house down to the sea. Today, though you may not be running from the law, it is an excellent path for jogging. It is here that Captain Frederick Marryat penned his famous book, *The Children of the New Forest*. Chewton Glen recognizes that

history by naming many of the 43 rooms and 19 suites after Marryat's titles and characters.

The bedrooms, located in the main building and coach house, are delightfully English and all are individually decorated. It is very clear that the owners, Martin and Brigitte Skan, pour their hearts and souls into this property and that warmth is felt all over the hotel. The cuisine is absolutely divine.

The activities are boundless at Chewton Glen. The property offers a 9-hole golf course, plus 12 of the most spectacular British courses are

within 20 miles. Tennis can be enjoyed both indoors and out and croquet can be played on the lawn. Horseback riding in the New Forest, known as William the Conqueror's hunting ground, is sure to be memorable. The Spa, with advanced exercise equipment, beauty treatments and beautiful indoor pool, is spectacular.

Chewton Glen, with its incredible style and gracious manners, will always be one of my favorites.

**CHEWTON GLEN**
Christchurch Road
New Milton
Hampshire BH25 6QS, England

# The Vineyard at Stockcross

With a strong commitment to providing the best – in food, wine and surroundings - The Vineyard at Stockcross in the Berkshire countryside is a wonderful hideaway.

It has been called "the restaurant with room to stay" for a good reason. Billy Reid presides over this creative kitchen that is considered one of England's best and promises of exceptional food are never broken. The incomparable wine lists are thanks in large part to founder Sir Peter Michael, whose own California vineyard supplies many of the cellar's wines. The cellar has approximately 600 California wines, many not available elsewhere in England. Of course, lists this size may appear daunting at first, but the excellent team of sommeliers will guide your every sip.

The Vineyard's commitment to excellence extends beyond the restaurant as well. The 33 sumptuous suites range from luxurious and contemporary to more traditional, cottage rooms. Taking tea in the Conservatory is a lovely way to spend your late afternoon and the hotel's unique chocolate room is well worth exploring.

The Vineyard's art and sculpture collection can be enjoyed throughout the property, from hand-painted murals in the spa's treatment rooms to William Pye's "Fire and Water" piece located near the restaurant within the diner's view. Known for its patronage of the arts, The Vineyard is also often home to artists-in-residence.

With 19th century roots and 21st century ideals, The Vineyard at Stockcross is perfection.

**THE VINEYARD AT STOCKCROSS**
Newbury, Berkshire
RG20 8JU, England

# Stoke Park Club

Minutes from the royal town of Windsor, Stoke Park Club is a gracious mansion where you can unwind after playing on one of the world's best parkland golf courses or contemplate tomorrow's activities.

Stoke Park Estate, more than 900 years old, is rich in English history, from ownership by Queen Elizabeth I to imprisonment of King Charles I in 1647. John Penn, grandson of William Penn and founder of Pennsylvania, purchased Stoke Park in 1790 and spent a considerable amount of the family's fortune building much of what you will see today. He hired John Wyatt, King George III's architect, to design the

mansion that was completed in 1795. It remained a private estate until 1908 when it became the Stoke Poges Golf Club. Legendary golf course designer Harry Shapland Colt designed the course. Its superb mix of par-4's and its 7th hole, often considered the inspiration for Augusta's notorious 12th hole, make this course both challenging and exciting for all golfers. Probably the most famous game of golf in film history was played here in 1964 when Sean Connery as James Bond defeated

Goldfinger on the 18th green.

A hotel and club since 1998, the 18th century Stoke Park again sparkles with beautiful antique furniture, tapestries, paintings and chandeliers. Stay in one of the 20 sumptuous rooms or suites overlooking the estate's 350 acres, some with views of Windsor Castle.

Besides golf, there are all weather and grass tennis courts plus fishing on the estate's fresh water lakes. A sensational new Spa Pavilion complete with indoor tennis courts and swimming pool will open in the spring of 2002.

Create your own memories at the exceptional Stoke Park Club.

**STOKE PARK CLUB**
Park Road, Stoke Poges
Buckinghamshire SL2 4PG,
England

# Holbeck Ghyll Country House Hotel

England's magnificent Lake District is home to Holbeck Ghyll, a truly delightful, privately owned country house hotel.

With just 20 rooms, guests at Holbeck Ghyll instantly feel right at home. Holbeck Ghyll was built early in the 19th century and was purchased in 1888 by Lord Lonsdale as his hunting lodge. A crackling fire burns most of the year in the inglenook fireplace in the entrance hall while a scrumptious tea or cocktails are served fireside in the inviting and cozy lounge.

The charming rooms offer balconies or patios with fantastic views of beautiful Lake Windermere and Langdale Fells. Most rooms are

located in the main building, but six of the largest are located in the Lodge. These rooms are interconnecting and are perfect for families.

Though four of the suites are equipped with kitchens, the restaurant, recently awarded with a coveted Michelin star, is too tempting to resist. The delectable menu of French and English cuisine, extensive wine list and stunning lake or mountain views make for a memorable dining experience.

Holbeck Ghyll's serenity can be savored by a walk or jog in the seven acres of woodlands, by

playing croquet, or by pampering yourself at the spa where your feet can be soothed with pink mud and your tensions eased with luxurious massages. Breathe the pure Lake District air as you explore the area, whether energetically playing golf or walking through the countryside, or quietly cruising on the lake, or visiting Beatrix Potter's home and William Wordsworth's Dove Cottage.

David and Patricia Nicholson will make Holbeck Ghyll your country manor house in the Lake District.

**HOLBECK GHYLL COUNTRY HOUSE HOTEL**
Holbeck Lane
Windermere LA23 1LU, England

# Hotel Kämp

Nicknamed, "the land of a thousand lakes," Finland is a country defined by water. Characterized by its bays and peninsulas, Helsinki is the heartbeat of this beautiful country.

Appealing and eye-catching, Hotel Kämp is one of the city's most historic buildings. Developed by Carl Kämp, the hotel opened in 1887. It is situated across from Esplanade Park in an exclusive shopping area, and Helsinki's major cultural attractions are all within a short walk. Though the original building was taken down, it was meticulously rebuilt in 1969.

Reopened in May 1999, Hotel Kämp was faithfully restored respecting its original spirit and former glory. Today it is the center of attention in Helsinki. Its exuberant and dazzling décor made

technology suitable for the contemporary traveler. The innovative design is especially evident in the lobby, where a striking black and white floor resembling a compass competes with the mesmerizing chandelier and ceiling.

Restaurant Kämp is a legendary watering hole, patronized by the city's residents. The restaurant is the least altered section of the hotel, and the décor preserves the original character with copies of the original sconces, dining chairs, upholstery and even the crystal chandeliers. CK's Brasserie is a trendier, more casual alternative, while the Terrace is a perfect option for warmer days.

Hotel Kämp marries old and new Finland perfectly.

it a favorite of artists and intellectuals, as well as politicians and diplomats. Much of Finland's history transpired within these walls. During the Czarist oppression, Hotel Kämp was the meeting place of the secret underground movement. Many lively conversations regarding the direction of the nation took place here.

The 167 rooms and 12 suites are stylish. The interiors respect Finland's heritage while incorporating cutting-edge

**HOTEL KÄMP**
Pohjoisesplanadi 29
00100 Helsinki, Finland

# Oustau de Baumanière

The region of Provence has been delighting visitors for centuries. Its natural beauty and pleasant lifestyle have inspired countless artists, including Cezanne and Van Gogh who painted many of their masterpieces here.

Oustau de Baumanière echoes the essence of Provence, from its charming rooms to its fine cuisine enhanced by local specialties. Built in the hollow of Vallon de La Fontaine, Oustau de Baumanière is shaded by trees and surrounded by trickling streams; quite a contrast to the imposing rock formation of Les Baux in the distance. It was founded more than 50 years ago and its gentle manner and tranquil setting have become synonymous with the best of Provence.

Cuisine is an integral part of the Oustau de Baumanière experience. The food is delicately prepared with the finest and freshest ingredients available, and many are grown right on the property. The menus pay tribute to the seasons, incorporating seasonal fruit, vegetables and herbs. Dining is a casually elegant experience, with an outdoor terrace shaded by mulberry trees or a delightful, vaulted dining room in a soft and comforting palette.

The casual elegance of Oustau de Baumanière extends to the 15 rooms and 12 suites in several centuries old stone buildings. Decorated in Provencal colors in a French country style, the rooms are appealing and luxurious.

Family-owned, Oustau de Baumanière was founded by legendary Raymond Thuilier. The grand tradition of fine dining and warm hospitality he began is carried on today by his grandson, Jean-André Charial.

Without a doubt, you too will feel like part of the family at Oustau de Baumanière.

**OUSTAU DE BAUMANIÈRE**
Les-Baux-de-Provence
13520 France

# Hotel du Palais

The waters of France and Spain meet in the Basque village of Biarritz, home of the fairy tale Hotel du Palais.

The Hotel's romantic history is as enchanting as its clifftop views of the crashing sea. The palace was built by Napoleon III for his wife Eugenie, who spent her summers here as a child. Though its famously rough waters almost claimed her life, Eugenie was forever captivated by the stunning coastline.

The arrival of Eugenie and Napoleon III transformed Biarritz from a sleepy fishing village to the playground of royalty almost overnight. The cavalcade of nobility helped Biarritz earn its nickname as "the Queen of Resorts and the Resort of Kings." After the imperial villa became the Hotel du Palais in 1883, the grand fetes and balls continued, prompting Sacha Guitry to write in the hotel's guest book, "Whenever one hesitates between two resorts, one of them is always Biarritz."

The majestic Hotel du Palais is one of the world's grandest palace hotels where guests are made to feel like royalty. Opulent without being gaudy, the Hotel's 134 rooms, 22 suites and superb restaurant are lavishly decorated with fine French antiques and the views of the wild sea are incomparable. The manicured gardens also reflect the noble and romantic heritage, with a topiary of the initials "NE."

Embodying the love for a village and for a woman, the Hotel du Palais is a romantic seaside resort.

**HOTEL DU PALAIS**
1, Avenue de L'Imperatrice
64200 Biarritz, France

# Hotel Martinez

Film stars gather here only once a year, but they leave an indelible mark on chic Cannes and its most glamorous hotel, Hotel Martinez.

Hotel Martinez overlooks the sea and has an ideal location right on the famous palm tree-lined boulevard known as the Croisette. The Martinez opened in 1929 with an Art Deco flair. The spacious 369 rooms and 24 suites all reflect colors relating to the sun or the sea. The entire seventh floor is devoted to two gigantic suites with wraparound terraces.

Palme d'Or, the hotel's dignified gourmet restaurant pays homage to its movie star clientele with portraits of films' biggest stars. Marilyn Monroe, Alfred Hitchcock, Greta Garbo and Clark Gable are just a few of the stars that grace the walls.

More simple dining options are available at Le Relais Martinez, where service extends to the pool's edge and at the Amiral Bar, the poolside cocktail lounge.

Even if the paparazzi do not snap your photo, the Martinez is the place to be seen in Cannes.

The Martinez has a private beach with various water sports and activities. The heated, octagonal swimming pool is at the foot of the hotel and is surrounded by 100 year-old palm trees.

Of course, Cannes is best known for its annual International Film Festival with its snapping flashbulbs and glamorous movie stars who come here with dreams of winning the coveted Palme d'Or. It is during this time that Hotel Martinez really shines as the host for the most discerning members of the film industry.

**HOTEL MARTINEZ**
73, La Croisette
06406 Cannes, France

# Hôtel de la Cité

The unique Hôtel de la Cité rests in the heart of the medieval city of Carcassonne, in the foothills of the Pyrenees.

Equidistant from Bordeaux and Monte Carlo, Carcassonne is the largest medieval walled city in Europe. History abounds here, from the nearby valley where dinosaurs once roamed to the Cathar Castles that dot the countryside and serve as reminders of the violent 13th century Crusades. The largest hawks in the world fly freely throughout Carcassonne's town.

The hotel was built in 1909 on the site of a former Episcopal Bishop's Palace and rests between the two major attractions - the Basilica St. Nazaire and the Chateau Comtal. The 49 guest rooms and 12 suites are individually furnished yet all bear the same aristocratic ambience. The lobby, listed by the French National Trust, features four large Ourtal paintings. Mosaic floors, beamed ceilings, old oak wainscoting, solid stone walls and beautiful stained glass windows set the tone throughout. Hôtel de la Cité was recently purchased and totally renovated by renowned Orient-Express Hotels.

The heated outdoor swimming pool, the only one within the walls of the town, is set in the tranquil private gardens.

The gardens afford spectacular views of the Château Comtal and the breathtaking ramparts.

La Barbacane, with its neo-gothic décor of stained glass windows and cathedral chairs, is renowned for its French haute cuisine. Other dining options include Chez Saskia, which serves regional specialties and Le Jardin de l'Evêque, open during the summer months.

Nestled within the stone walls of the medieval city, Hotel de la Cité is a special hideaway.

**HÔTEL DE LA CITÉ**
Place de l'Église
11000 Carcassonne, France

# Royal Parc Evian - Hôtel Royal

Synonymous with health, beauty and youth, Evian has been known throughout the world for its purifying water. For over a century, many have traveled here in search of relaxation and serenity.

The Hôtel Royal epitomizes Evian's history and style. Located at the foot of the French Alps and on the southern bank of Lake Geneva, it is a truly magnificent place set within the 42 acre Royal Parc Evian estate.

cuisine served at the hotel is shared through the culinary classes that are offered throughout the year. Each year, the estate hosts the Evian Music Festival in their own music hall, which has been created entirely of pine and has successfully blended modern architecture with nature.

Hôtel Royal is fit for everyone, even a king.

Surrounded by verdant gardens and forests, the Hôtel Royal was originally created as a retreat for King Edward VII. It still retains its Belle Epoque elegance today.

In addition to the stunning landscape and the awe-inspiring mountain vistas, the Hôtel Royal is a veritable playground with an abundance of thrilling adventures and activities for all seasons with a spectacular golf course. The Hôtel's Better Living Institute, a world-renowned spa, offers innovative body treatments, relaxation techniques and exercise regimens.

The artful and delicious

**ROYAL PARC EVIAN - HÔTEL ROYAL**
South Bank of Lake Geneva
74500 Evian-Les-Bains,
France

# Château de la Chèvre d'Or

The enchanting Château de la Chèvre d'Or is tucked away in the tiny Côte d'Azur hamlet of Èze. Château de la Chèvre d'Or invites you to experience a different side of the French Riviera. The rooms are quaint, some with stone walls, arched entrances and roaring fireplaces that transport you to the Middle Ages. Its location perched on a cliff top affords sensational views and the ambience of the swimming pools and flowering gardens is tranquil. Though relatively small with only 22 rooms, 1 suite and 9 apartments, the intimacy

golden fleece, a peasant discovered the abandoned house and the secret. He was overjoyed that he was able to fulfill his dream of building a new, magnificent house at the top of the village, but he disappeared soon after and was never heard from again. Another owner acquired the chateau and while reading one summer evening, a golden goat appeared before him. When he went to touch it, the goat disappeared. This magical feeling remains at the Château de la Chèvre d'Or.

Perhaps you will catch a glimpse of "the golden goat" while staying at Château de la Chèvre d'Or!

at Château de la Chèvre d'Or is part of its charm. The hotel is consistently honored with awards for its hospitable service and fine dining.

The namesake of the hotel, "the golden goat," is a wonderful tale. Many years ago, an elderly woman carefully hid gold coins among the stones in her modest house. When she died, her secret remained with her. Years later, after he was led by a goat with a

### CHÂTEAU DE LA CHÈVRE D'OR
Rue du Barri
06360 Èze-Village, France

# Hotel Le Bristol

Le Bristol resides on the world-famous rue du Faubourg Saint Honoré, yet it gives the feeling of being tucked away in a special, private corner of Paris.

Elegant and airy, Le Bristol has a refined, sophisticated atmosphere and an old world charm, evident in unique touches like the grilled elevator nestled in the curve of the marble staircase. Crystal chandeliers, period furniture, antique engravings and Oriental carpets set a dignified tone throughout the hotel's public rooms, 134 rooms and 46 suites. Many of the suites have terraces that invite you to unwind and ponder your next Parisian sojourn.

The idyllic garden adds to the singular experience of

is now the hotel's oval-shaped winter garden restaurant, in use from November to April. Ornately decorated with hand-carved woodwork and a grand Lille tapestry, the winter garden delights both the eye and the palate. In warmer months, the summer restaurant extends tables to the inviting garden.

It is no mistake that the glass encased, teak framed rooftop pool makes visitors feel as if they are stepping onto a private yacht. It was built by Pineau, yacht architect to the rich and famous like Onassis.

Le Bristol is always elegant with superb service.

Le Bristol. It is simply magnificent, from its sweet honeysuckle, vibrant azalea and rhododendron to its peaceful fountain that gently trickles in the background. This French-style garden is the largest private garden in all of Paris.

In the 19th century, Le Bristol was a private residence belonging to Jules de Castellane, an eccentric patron of the arts. His private theater

**HOTEL LE BRISTOL**
112 rue du Faubourg
St. Honoré
75008 Paris, France

# Hôtel de Crillon

The glittering Hôtel de Crillon is one of the two majestic facades of the world's most famous square, the Place de la Concorde. It is here where much of the French Revolution was staged and where many, including Marie Antoinette, met the guillotine.

This 18th century palace was commissioned by King Louis XV and was later acquired by the Count of Crillon as his residence. It opened as the Hôtel de Crillon in 1909. The Hôtel de Crillon is the only privately owned and managed hotel in Paris. Perhaps best known for champagne, the Taittinger family has magnificently restored their

its large windows overlooking the Place de la Concorde, antique mirrors, high ceilings and candelabras at each table, has been called "fairytale" and is always considered one of the top restaurants in Paris. L'Obelisque is a more casual alternative with classic French cuisine.

The Crillon's function rooms are the most elegant in Paris and are perfect for weddings or private dinners.

With its aristocratic heritage, regal atmosphere and superb location, across from the American Embassy and steps away from Hermes and Lanvin, a visit to Hôtel de Crillon is quintessentially French.

hotel in the finest French tradition of taste and elegance.

Hôtel de Crillon's 95 guest rooms and 52 suites have recently been restored in Louis XV style by a joint effort with French fashion designer Sonia Rykiel and the French National Historic Landmark Commission.

Guests at the Crillon need not venture outside the hotel for superb cuisine, as two of the city's finest restaurants are located within. Les Ambassadeurs, with

**HÔTEL DE CRILLON**
10, Place de la Concorde
75008 Paris, France

# Four Seasons Hotel George V Paris

With its style and sophistication, Paris is one of Europe's most glorious cities, and my personal favorite. First-time visitors and Parisians alike never tire of its charms. From its tree-lined boulevards full of sidewalk cafes and couturier shops to its world-class museums, Paris is the meeting place for the worlds of fashion and culture.

The Four Seasons Hotel George V mirrors the city's harmonious relationship with the past and present. The George V originally opened its doors in the late 1920's and quickly became one of the legendary hotels of Paris. After an extensive two-year renovation, this legend reopened in the new millennium as the Four Seasons Hotel George V. This landmark's soul was maintained while it was modernized for the contemporary traveler. In inimitable Four Seasons style, large marble bathrooms, multi-line telephones and modems are at home with 17th century Flemish tapestries and the magnificent 500 square foot Savonnerie carpet.

The Four Seasons Hotel George V's location between the Champs Elysées and the Seine is superb. Its 184 guest rooms and 61 suites are decorated in a contemporary French style and 30 rooms have exceptional private terraces that showcase all of Paris' sights and sounds. Epicureans will adore the new Le Cinq, the hotel's restaurant, which was awarded a Michelin star shortly after opening.

With a 350 square foot swimming pool, sophisticated spa and modern exercise equipment, the hotel's Health Club is the perfect retreat - especially after indulging at Le Cinq!

With its nod to tradition and its foot in the future, The Four Seasons Hotel George V is a perfect way to experience Paris.

**FOUR SEASONS HOTEL GEORGE V PARIS**
31, avenue George V
75008 Paris, France

# The Lancaster

Guests at The Lancaster are only steps away from the famed Champs-Elysées, yet inside, worlds apart from the hectic pace surrounding it.

The Lancaster is a 19th century townhouse that was the private home of Monsieur Santiago Drake del Castillo until the 1920's when it was transformed into a hotel. A stay at the Lancaster is like a visit to a wealthy relative with impeccable taste and style. The comfort and charm of owner Grace Leo-Andrieu's style is evident in each of the uniquely decorated 50 rooms and 10 suites…even in the hallways with her personal touches.

In contrast to other Parisian hotels, the style of the

serenity, reflection and relaxation.

While the Lancaster has been in the black books of celebrities for many years, the hotel's discretion is perhaps more famous than its guest book. This discretion extends to the restaurant, which is closed to the public to maintain guests' privacy. Not prone to name-dropping, the Lancaster has allowed one famous guest to be immortalized. Marlene Dietrich lived in the hotel from 1937-1940. Today, one of the suites is dedicated to her and is decorated in her favorite shade of lilac.

The Lancaster is an intimate jewel to be savored.

Lancaster is informally elegant. It is a harmony of French antiques, Chinese and Japanese decorative arts and contemporary pieces by designers such as Christian Liaigre. Celebrating its eastern influences, a feng shui expert was brought in to help balance the rooms and encourage energy and well-being. The Lancaster's Asian-inspired courtyard garden, once the townhouse's private stables, is a haven for

**THE LANCASTER**
7, rue de Berri
Champs-Elysées
75008 Paris, France

# Hôtel du Louvre

The moment you step through the revolving doors at the Hôtel du Louvre, you know you are in a special place. The friendly smile on the porter's face is not only welcoming, but also a sign of things to come.

Hôtel du Louvre is full of character and charm, yet has a modern, fresh style. Jewel tones are used throughout the hotel from the entrance foyer to public spaces to accommodations. Intriguing touches, such as a chandelier made of braid and trimmings or tapestries of velvet add a richness to the Hôtel du Louvre.

The 190 rooms, 9 suites and 1 apartment are decorated in one of four color schemes, whether it is soft blue with beige, dark green with mahogany, bright yellow, or blue and red. The views of the Opera House, square of the Royal Palace and the Louvre Museum are splendid, plus the hotel is within a ten-minute walk from the major sights of Paris.

The vivid colors and cozy atmosphere extend to the intimate bar, a perfect place to take tea or enjoy a cigar. A touch of whimsy can be found in the two locomotives that line the sides of the entrance and the card game that helps players choose their drinks. The Brasserie echoes the exuberance of the hotel and serves traditional French food in a lively atmosphere.

The Hôtel du Louvre has inspired greatness from some of its guests. Impressionist painter Camille Pissarro resided here for some time and painted several of his masterpieces from his window. Sir Arthur Conan Doyle was so enamored with the hotel he featured it in many of his Sherlock Holmes stories.

Hôtel du Louvre will tantalize and inspire you.

## HÔTEL DU LOUVRE
Place André Malraux
75001 Paris, France

# Hôtel Meurice

Two years seemed too long to wait for one of my favorite Paris hotels to reopen, but when the Hôtel Meurice again opened its doors on a warm sunny day in July 2000 with its restored grandeur, it was clear that it was worth the wait.

Known as the "Hotel of Kings" because of its long list of royal guests, the elegant Meurice has dazzled visitors for the better part of two centuries with its Rococo salons and unique touches, such as the replica of Marie Antoinette's sedan chair that once served as an elevator.

The staff at the Meurice is superb, attending to guests' every whim. Salvador Dali, a frequent guest at the hotel, was known to make peculiar requests. He once demanded

that a herd of sheep be brought to his room; another time he wanted flies caught in the Tuileries Gardens. Not surprisingly, the staff delivered, but please don't ask for this today!

While every corner of this grand hotel was touched during the total restoration, the newly constructed Belle Etoile Suite is quite literally, the height of luxury. This 3,700 square foot suite with a 2,960 square foot panoramic terrace offers breathtaking views of the Tuileries and central Paris. It was cleverly designed on top of the building to allow magnificent views while shielding the occupants from view.

The Meurice's 125 rooms and 34 suites are equally dazzling, with five major decorative styles used: Louis XVI, Empire, Academy, Trianon Gardens and Parisian apartments.

The spectacular glass Art Nouveau roof, painstakingly restored pane by pane, bathes the Jardin d'Hiver in glorious sunlight. The Winter Garden is an enchanting place for a light meal. A new addition that will be treasured is the Fontainebleau Bar, an intimate setting for cocktails or nightcaps.

Good things *do* come to those who wait, especially at the Hôtel Meurice.

HÔTEL MEURICE
228, rue de Rivoli
75001 Paris, France

# Le Parc

In the heart of the exclusive residential 16th arrondissement, Le Parc graciously welcomes guests with its English style and French savoir-faire.

Comprised of five town houses, Le Parc has a wonderful country home feeling that extends from the clubby lounge to the beautifully appointed rooms and suites. All 96 rooms and 20 suites integrate one of the ten decorating schemes created by renowned British interior designer Nina Campbell. Campbell also commissioned David Linley, Queen Elizabeth II's nephew, to design furniture for the rooms. The English manor feel can be seen in the fabrics, the four-poster and canopy beds, the furnishings and the lighting. Le Parc's comforting touches make it a peaceful place while visiting Paris.

The restaurant and bar reflect the hotel's philosophy of quality in a relaxed atmosphere. The Relais du Parc stands out for its inventive and delicious food as much as it does for its style — it is one of the only brasseries in Paris' deluxe hotels. In the summer months, the lovely restaurant opens its doors and extends to the private, secluded garden. The cozy bar is decorated by Nina Campbell in a jazz theme. The cocktail tables were designed by noted French sculptor Arman and are in the shape of musical instruments. Alain Ducasse keeps a watchful eye on the new 59 Poincaré restaurent.

Le Parc is an ideal choice for a little bit of England without leaving Paris.

LE PARC
55-59, avenue Raymond Poincaré
75116 Paris, France

# Hôtel Plaza Athénée

In a city where style reigns, the Hôtel Plaza Athénée stands out for its panache.

Its signature color red, best expressed in the geraniums, window awnings and garden parasols, is a calling card for a fashionable clientele that has made the Hôtel Plaza Athénée their home since 1911.

Recently modernized and renovated, the Hôtel's 106 rooms and 81 suites retain their grand style and charm while welcoming the most modern travelers. The first six floors are classically French, with Louis XV, Louis XVI and Regency period furnishings. The hotel's top two floors are dedicated to Art Deco, adding a unique element to the style and feel of the Hôtel Plaza Athénée. You will be enchanted by the views, whether you overlook the inviting courtyard with its colorful vines, gaze upon the chestnut trees of avenue Montaigne, or enjoy panoramic views of the Eiffel Tower and the rooftops of Paris.

The restaurants, like the Hôtel Plaza Athénée itself, combine impeccable service and incredible style, along with exquisite cuisine. During the late spring, summer and early fall months, La Cour Jardin is open in the courtyard; arguably the most famous in Paris for its red parasols and foliage. The celebrated chef Alain Ducasse oversees the restaurant that bears his name and it is not to be missed. Other restaurants include Le Relais Plaza, a Parisian institution for lunches or informal dinners.

In the heart of the business, fashion and tourist district, the Hôtel Plaza Athénée is a refined bit of home.

**HÔTEL PLAZA ATHÉNÉE**
25 Avenue Montaigne
75008 Paris, France

# Prince de Galles

Built on the site of the Chaillot Quarry, where the stones were selected for the Arc de Triomphe, the Prince de Galles is an Art Deco hotel closely tied to the past, present and future of Paris.

Prince de Galles' distinguished address on the avenue George V places it in the heart of Paris. Built in 1928, the hotel's impeccable taste and intimate character transport guests to a special place.

The 138 rooms and 30 suites are decorated in soft tones of blue, white and yellow. Great care has been taken to make memorable visits and the warmth and comfort can be felt throughout the hotel. The luxurious accommodations tempt, but never intimidate, thanks to the first-class personalized service that is a trademark of the hotel.

The Jardin des Cygnes and its private extension, the Trianon, extend a gracious welcome and share the sunny flavors of Provence with diners. The cozy Regency Bar's natural oak wall paneling, beige stone and marble floor, dark green sofas and gold leaf chandelier mix 1930's French and English style.

The Prince de Galles is well suited to business travelers who seek an office away from home. The meeting rooms are spacious, pleasant and handle today's technological requirements.

Prince de Galles is a wonderful selection in Paris.

**PRINCE DE GALLES**
33, avenue George V
75008 Paris, France

# Ritz Paris

The Place Vendôme, Paris' most exquisite square, is home to the venerable Ritz Paris. Founded in 1898 by Cesar Ritz, Ritz not only gave his name to the hotel, but also left an indelible mark on the standard of accommodations, luxury, service and attention to detail that have continued through the years.

The Ritz Paris has been more than a destination for many throughout history. A former 18th century private residence, Ritz's desire for it to be a home attracted the likes of Coco Chanel and Marcel Proust who resided in suites here. The history that has unfolded within is incomparable. It has seen the opulence of the Belle Epoque, the "fireworks" of World War I (witnessed by Proust from the balconies), the free-spirited 1920's, the destruction of World War II (when it was occupied by German soldiers), and in most recent years, has undergone a $250 million restoration that is a history in itself. Like a grand dame, it has seen it all and not aged a bit.

From the hand-carved iron staircases in the grand hall to the gilded swan faucets in the marble bathrooms to the famous hallway known as "temptation walk" where you gambol among the finest gifts, The Ritz Paris satisfies both the eye and the soul. The 133 rooms and 42 suites dazzle you with their glorious French design. Whether you are a gastronome tasting the culinary style of Auguste Escoffier, a Francophile or a history buff, there is something around every corner for you.

Ernest Hemingway once said, "When I dream of the afterlife in heaven, the action always takes place at the Paris Ritz." I couldn't agree more.

**RITZ PARIS**
15 Place Vendôme
75001 Paris, France

# Grand-Hotel du Cap-Ferrat

Since the turn of the century, the French Riviera has dazzled debonair gentlemen and stunning beauties with its azure sea and balmy climate. While other resort destinations have been in and out of favor, the Riviera has remained as the ultimate escape from quotidian life. Though only a small stretch of coastline from St. Tropez to Monte Carlo, the Riviera has a variety of posh beach resorts and medieval villages with panoramic views.

Just 20 minutes from Nice, the Grand Hotel du Cap-Ferrat rests at

with the natural beauty of the sea. The Grand-Hotel du Cap-Ferrat is always inviting. With 44 rooms and 9 suites, it is an intimate setting. Dining varies from inside at Le Cap, to outdoors on the terrace, to sitting at the edge of the sea by the pool. The discreet and superb service earns accolades from guests and the hotel is consistently listed among the top ten in Europe for service.

The heated saltwater pool stretches infinitely into the Mediterranean horizon, just as your imagination will at Grand-Hotel du Cap-Ferrat.

the tip of the Cap-Ferrat peninsula. Rising above the Mediterranean and set within a 14 acre private park, the hotel boasts some of the most magnificent views in the region. The air is filled with the heady aromas of rosemary, myrtle and thyme, all of which grow abundantly in this region. Indeed, it seems that the sun shines brighter and longer here; perhaps it too enjoys the repose of the Riviera.

The Grand Hotel du Cap-Ferrat's emblem, two dolphins with a crown, symbolizes the marriage of a luxurious palace

**GRAND-HOTEL DU CAP-FERRAT**
06230 Saint-Jean Cap-Ferrat France

# Hotel Byblos

Saint-Tropez's sexy and sun-drenched Hotel Byblos has attracted the jet set for almost thirty years with its élan.

Hotel Byblos resembles a tiny Provencal hamlet with its brightly colored fishing cottages, tiled roofs and cobbled courtyards. Though decidedly French, the Byblos honors various Mediterranean cultures in its use of Greek, Roman and Iranian mosaics. The scents are indicative of the region; an intoxicating blend of plentiful jasmine and lavender perfumes the air.

Each of the 52 rooms and 43 suites is unique, yet all incorporate Provencal images and colors. Boldly patterned fabrics and distinctive artwork enhance each room.

a depiction of the abduction of Europa by Zeus, is represented in mosaic form at the pool.

The restaurant serves sophisticated Mediterranean cuisine both inside and outdoors on the delightful terrace. The delicious food can also be delivered to the foot of your chaise should you so desire.

All is not over when the sun sets, however. Les Caves du Roy, the Riviera's hottest discotheque, is located in the hotel. Bejeweled and plush, Les Caves du Roy entertains you and international celebrities in the finest style.

Hotel Byblos is the seductive Riviera at its best.

Hotel Byblos' elevation allows for fantastic panoramic views of the Mediterranean, but it is only ten minutes from the beaches. Saint-Tropez's beaches are not only the largest in the Riviera, but are perhaps the most famous and stylish, thanks in part to Brigitte Bardot's beachside exploits.

The swimming pool anchors the Byblos' village and the waterfall and lush landscaping soothe guests. The hotel's omnipresent logo,

**HOTEL BYBLOS**
Avenue Paul Signac
83990 Saint-Tropez, France

# Château du Domaine St. Martin

Standing amid centuries-old olive trees within the Domaine's flourishing 32 acres, Le Château du Domaine St. Martin, in the heart of the French Riviera, overlooks the charming town of Vence and the glittering Mediterranean coastline.

Château St. Martin was built on the ruins of an ancient Knights Templar castle from the 12th century. It is comprised of 32 wonderful junior suites and 6 cottages decorated in gentle floral fabrics and soothing colors. The spacious suites are exquisitely furnished in Louis XV or Louis XVI style and

most have balconies or terraces facing the blue sea with relaxing chaise lounges. The individual cottages, located on a hill across from the hotel, offer the unique experience of French château life with complete privacy and the comfort, convenience and efficiency of all hotel services.

Life at Château St. Martin is relaxing or stimulating, depending upon your mood. From the sporting activities of the clay tennis courts, infinity swimming pool, biking in the area and nearby golf courses, to the intellectual pursuits of the nearby Matisse chapel, museums dedicated to Picasso and Chagall, or exploration of the delightful neighboring ancient towns.

The resort's charm and elegance, combined with the sights, sounds and senses of the Côte d'Azur countryside open the gates to the "waiting room to Paradise," as Château St. Martin was called by a famous head of state.

Every detail at Château St. Martin is perfection.

**LE CHÂTEAU DU DOMAINE ST. MARTIN**
Avenue des Templiers
06140 Vence, France

# Brenner's Park-Hotel & Spa

On the edge of Germany's famed Black Forest, Baden-Baden has attracted visitors in search of the relaxation and detoxification benefits from its thermal springs for centuries. Brenner's Park-Hotel & Spa, in a private park with beautiful grounds, is the perfect hotel to enjoy this rejuvenating atmosphere.

Brenner's commitment to personal well-being is evident in its beauty spa, which is constantly adapting to incorporate modern advances and treatments. Virtually everything you can imagine is here. Asian influences abound, from the Japanese

gentlemen wear jackets and ties to dinner. Dinner is served in the formal Park Restaurant or in the cozy Black Forest Grill. While regional specialties are the focus of both menus, the spa's delicious gourmet diet may be substituted at any meal. After dinner you might want to try your luck at the Baden-Baden Casino or attend a performance in the new concert hall.

With white glove service, Brenner's Park-Hotel & Spa soothes and rejuvenates.

garden for meditation to the new Japanese flower blossom steam room and Finnish, Turkish or Bio saunas are offered. Brenner's recently added the Spa Suite, a special private place for parties of up to four. In addition to whirlpool, vitalizing shower, steam room and sauna, the suite features green quartzite benches charged with radiant heat. In case you are not feeling properly pampered, a Spa Butler is at your service for the duration of your stay.

The public rooms and 100 guest rooms are refined and elegant. In grand European style,

**BRENNER'S PARK-HOTEL & SPA**
Schillerstrasse 4-6
76530 Baden-Baden, Germany

# Hotel Adlon

It is fitting that Hotel Adlon rests across from the Brandenburg Gate, for two great landmarks belong near each other.

Hotel Adlon opened its doors in 1907 as the realization of Lorenz Adlon's dream. The luxurious interiors and sophisticated systems that included advanced refrigeration and cooling systems and a special power plant immediately placed Hotel Adlon at the forefront of leading hotels.

The Adlon's urbane atmosphere attracted

foreigners and Berliners. Many noble families sold their winter residences to reside in suites at the hotel. Though its most loyal guest was certainly Kaiser Wilhelm II, who demanded that no one step foot inside the new hotel before him, the Adlon has hosted many celebrities. It is here that Marlene Dietrich was discovered, Greta Garbo spoke her famous words, "I want to be alone," and Charlie Chaplin nearly lost his pants here due to zealous fans tugging at his trousers.

Though the original Adlon suffered a devastating fire and was eventually torn down, today's reconstructed Hotel Adlon opened in 1997 and respects its grand

heritage while delighting modernists. The 256 rooms and 81 suites are classically styled, spacious and ideal for both business and leisure travelers. The shopping arcade carries the finest in art, antiques, clothing and jewelry. The Adlon offers a spa and swimming pool and each floor has a special elevator designed to carry guests downstairs. There are numerous dining options, from gourmet French cuisine to German specialties.

Like Berlin itself, Hotel Adlon shines once again.

HOTEL ADLON
Unter den Linden 77
10117 Berlin, Germany

# Four Seasons Hotel Berlin

Four Seasons Hotel Berlin, located in what was once called East Berlin, opened in 1996 as the first Four Seasons property in Germany.

It has an ideal location in the historic district of Friedrichstadt, adjacent to the famous Gendarmenmarkt Square and around the corner from Friedrichstrasse's world-class shopping. The State Opera and Museum Island and the charming Nicolai Quarter are just a short walk from the hotel.

The Four Seasons was designed by well-regarded Berlin architect Professor Josef Kleihues. It is part of the Hofgarten complex, an eye-catching and appealing city block with an interesting combination of historic and modern buildings. The hotel's site was the former location of a famous restaurant and wine company whose wine cellar inspired the *Tales of Hoffman*. The site also includes the former residence of the architect of the Brandenburg Gate.

The 162 rooms and 42 suites are located on the hotel's eight floors. Warm and soft colors are used and the glorious windows open onto either the bustling street or the Hofgarten's serene courtyard. Naturally, advanced technology is offered in all rooms and business travelers are well accommodated with three phone lines for fax and computer designation and a professional business center.

Seasons, the hotel's restaurant, serves all three meals daily and offers something for everyone with international cuisine, regional specialties and a healthy gourmet menu.

The Four Seasons Hotel Berlin knows the way to your heart – even smaller guests are treated to a welcome milk and cookies!

**FOUR SEASONS
HOTEL BERLIN**
Charlottenstrasse 49
10117 Berlin, Germany

# The Ritz-Carlton Schlosshotel, Berlin

The intimate atmosphere of an elegant mansion and the impeccable Ritz-Carlton standards join together at The Ritz-Carlton Schlosshotel.

This magnificent building is located in the affluent residential section of Grunewald. Though it is only five minutes from Berlin's famous Kurfuerstendamm Boulevard, the wooded hills and ancient trees make you easily forget the frenetic pace of city life. The palace, completed in 1914, incorporates the original owner's travel experiences and dedication to the arts. The small spiral staircase is based on the one in Chartres Cathedral, the main stairway

takes its inspiration from Palazzo Gondi in Florence and the beautiful lion on the staircase is from an old gothic house near Berlin.

Deep, rich tones are used in the public rooms and the 42 rooms and 12 suites. The most recent renovation involved the flair of legendary designer Karl Lagerfeld, who was responsible for the creative redecoration of the rooms. His personal suite, which he accepted in lieu of payment for his services, is available when he is out of town.

Of course, The Ritz-Carlton Schlosshotel takes the ordinary and makes it extraordinary. The hotel offers unique services like bath butlers, who draw the most divine baths complete with rose petals and essential oils, and technology butlers, who are on call for technical support. Also provided is a special edition Audi limousine equipped with a mobile office for harried executives on the go.

Berlin is an exciting city again and The Ritz-Carlton Schlosshotel is the jewel in the crown.

**THE RITZ-CARLTON SCHLOSSHOTEL, BERLIN**
Brahmsstrasse 10
14193 Berlin, Germany

# Kempinski Hotel Taschenbergpalais

Completely destroyed during World War II, Dresden has been rebuilt to reveal its former glory and is now one of Germany's most exciting places to visit.

Dresden is often considered "Florence on the Elbe," because of its art and culture. The impressive castles, luxurious palaces and gardens are ideal for exploring while modern touches include terrific shopping in the new arcades.

Kempinski Hotel Taschenbergpalais has a prime location, right in the heart of the old city of Dresden and next to the baroque Zwinger and Semper Opera House. The grand Taschenbergpalais was built in the early 18th century for Augustus the Strong, the

fabrics, whimsical touches and black granite bathrooms.

Various dining options are offered, from the brasserie to the Mediterranean influenced light cuisine of Intermezzo to the traditional, old-style restaurant located in the original Cellar Vaults. Dining in the courtyard is available during the summer and it is truly an experience. Whether you gaze up at the hotel's grand façade or look across to the baroque masterpieces, you will feel a sense of triumph.

Relive Dresden's glorious past at Kempinski Hotel Taschenbergpalais.

Elector of Saxony and King of Poland. Its regal bearing attracted visitors for almost 250 years until February 13, 1945 when the Bombennacht (night of the bombs) struck Dresden. Completely destroyed, the palace lay in ruins until its meticulous restoration in the early 1990's.

Though the hotel's exterior is baroque, the 188 rooms and 25 suites are done in a contemporary style with red elm wood, vibrant

**KEMPINSKI HOTEL TASCHENBERGPALAIS**
Taschenberg 3
01067 Dresden, Germany

# Steigenberger Frankfurter Hof

Germany's economic and banking center is home to the well-respected Steigenberger Frankfurter Hof.

Situated on the fashionable Kaiserplatz, or Emperor's Square, the Frankfurter Hof has a prime location in the heart of the commercial and historic center of Frankfurt. Opened in 1876, the Frankfurter Hof has been run by some of the most influential leaders in the hotel industry, including Cesar Ritz.

Celebrating its 125th anniversary this year, the Frankfurter Hof has just completed a $35 million dollar renovation. Its 332

rooms and suites are elegantly appointed in a contemporary design with unusual fabrics and polished woods. Though each room is furnished in a different style, all rooms are equipped with state-of-the-art technology.

Three restaurants offer unique and delightful dining experiences. Francais is gloriously decorated with rich green and gold tones. This restaurant has earned a Michelin star for its light, French-inspired dishes. Innovative cuisine is served at the bistro-style Oscar's, and a Japanese restaurant rounds out the selections. Autorenbar is a pleasant spot for drinks or snacks. The special Frankfurter Hof Torte, made without flour, is served exclusively here.

The Frankfurter Hof is ideal for business travelers. The business center helps you keep in touch while away, and secretaries are provided for clerical assistance or translation. The sixth floor health club responds to guests' fitness requirements with excellent equipment and attentive service.

The service is superb here; a staff of 280 employees speaks a combined total of 17 different languages.

Experience the hospitality of Europe and Germany at the Steigenberger Frankfurter Hof.

**STEIGENBERGER FRANKFURTER HOF**
Am Kaiserplatz 17
60311 Frankfurt, Germany

# Hotel Bayerischer Hof

Hotel Bayerischer Hof is a Munich institution and a must for visitors to this vibrant city.

The hotel has been in the center of the historical and cultural center of Munich for 159 years. It has been owned and operated by the Volkhardt family for four generations and this unique position allows for a very personal touch that guests recognize and appreciate. The diligent staff of 700 carefully preserves the friendly touch and is at your disposal during your stay.

Hotel Bayerischer Hof celebrates its Bavarian heritage while encouraging diversity in

317 rooms and 47 suites all guarantee comfort and service but retain their individuality. The Laura Ashley suite, Tyrol suite and Paris suite take inspiration from their names and provide an intriguing alternative to a traditional room. The adjacent Palais Montgelas, a historic building owned by the hotel, houses most of the outstanding conference and meeting facilities.

A stay at the Hotel Bayerischer Hof is not complete without a swim in the rooftop pool. The exercise will invigorate, but the views will inspire you.

its restaurants. You will enjoy the draught beer, homemade pretzels and traditional setting at Palais Keller, known for its Bavarian specialties. Trader Vic's will transport you to the Far East, where you can enjoy Polynesian cuisine. For more contemporary and light dining, the Garden Restaurant is the right choice. Munich's upbeat spirit can be enjoyed in all of the hotel's bars and the Night Club has some of Germany's best jazz.

Hotel Bayerischer Hof's

**HOTEL BAYERISCHER HOF**
Promenadeplatz 2-6
80333 Munich, Germany

# Mandarin Oriental, Munich

The Mandarin Oriental, Munich is a haven from the pace of urban life. Formerly known as the Hotel Rafael, its sterling reputation was further enhanced after its recent acquisition by the Mandarin Oriental Hotel Group.

The hotel enjoys a prime location in the center of the city. The legendary Hofbrauhaus and Maximilianstrasse, known for Munich's best art galleries, boutiques and restaurants are in one direction. Viktualienmarkt, a cobblestone market that sells regional wares and gourmet food, is in the other. Though it is within walking distance of the major sights

appreciated.

Mark's Restaurant entertains you in the finest style. Tables are set with crisp linens, fine crystal and delicate bone china and the menu always offers a variety of delicious selections. Mark's Corner, located in the bay window of the lobby, is a city favorite for lunch.

If wandering around the city's sights does not satisfy your fitness quotient, the hotel offers excellent exercise facilities and a rooftop swimming pool.

Mandarin Oriental, Munich is your intimate home away from home.

of Munich, its location on a quiet side street helps it maintain the feeling of a private residence.

The well-appointed Neo-Renaissance 54 rooms and 19 suites also contribute to the exclusivity with special antiques and beautiful fabrics. The private and public rooms are bathed in soft, golden light. Little luxuries, like heated bathroom floors and fresh flowers, are much

**MANDARIN ORIENTAL, MUNICH**

Neuturmstrasse 1
80331 Munich,
Germany

# Hotel Nassauer Hof

Sometimes called the "Nice of the North," because of its temperate climate and jovial residents, Wiesbaden has it all. It is just 30 minutes from Frankfurt and it rests between the southern foothills of the Taunus Mountains and the Rhein. The nearby Rheingau region is worthy of exploration for its Riesling producing vineyards and picturesque castles.

Indeed, the most alluring attribute of Wiesbaden is its abundant therapeutic and mineral-rich hot springs. The

mind for some, rejuvenation is certainly the mood here. The advantageous position of the hotel allows the hot springs to run off directly into the fifth floor swimming pool. A soak in the mineral-rich water will cure whatever ails you. The Estee Lauder Beauty Center provides a variety of beauty and relaxation treatments.

After feeling sufficiently rejuvenated, perhaps try your hand at the casino across from the Hotel Nassauer Hof. It inspired Dostoyevsky to write his novel, *The Gambler*.

springs prompted the Romans to build a fortress here and they opted to build directly upon one of the town's best springs. The Hotel Nassauer Hof occupies that identical spot today.

The Hotel has a contemporary style due to its total reconstruction after World War II. Recent renovations have updated the lobby and the 178 rooms and 20 suites. Since many of the visitors are business travelers who prefer the peaceful atmosphere of Wiesbaden to nearby Frankfurt, rooms are easily transformed into offices thanks to advanced technology.

While business may be on the

**HOTEL NASSAUER HOF**
Kaiser-Friedrich-Platz 3-4
65183 Wiesbaden, Germany

# Elounda Beach Hotel & Villas

As far as I am concerned, no other resort captures the magic of the Greek Isles like Elounda Beach Hotel.

Set on the northeast coast of Crete, Elounda Beach is the only hotel in Greece that has rooms right on the water's edge. The hotel's 215 suites and villas, including two Royal Suites and the Imperial Suite, are located within 40 acres of gardens and laid out to resemble a traditional Greek village. The rooms highlight simple, yet elegant style with wooden furniture and deep, Mediterranean blue fabrics that complement the beauty of the sunshine and the sparkling sea just outside. Romantic and spacious, the bungalows offer intriguing amenities like private

swimming pools that are filled with your choice of fresh or salt water.

Offering a world of unparalleled luxury, the Royal and Imperial Suites are fully staffed with a personal trainer to assist you in your private gym, a personal chef to cater to your every whim, a personal pianist and an English-style butler.

Leisure facilities abound, including two private, secluded beaches, water sports center, health and beauty club, flood-lit tennis courts, shopping center, museum of Cretan art, and yacht charter for excursions to nearby islands. Seven restaurants delight your senses and include Polynesian, Italian, Sushi and Teppan-yaki. At night, four bars and a nightclub are guaranteed to entertain.

Even arrival at Elounda Beach is beyond compare. A choice of chauffeured limousine, helicopter or Lear jet service is available.

Discover the exclusive retreat of Elounda Beach Hotel & Villas while rediscovering yourself.

ELOUNDA BEACH
HOTEL & VILLAS
720 53 Elounda,
Crete, Greece

# Kempinski Hotel Corvinus

Budapest has reemerged as Eastern Europe's culture and business capital.

On Elizabeth Square, a small park on the Pest Bank of the Danube River, is Kempinski Hotel Corvinus. The hotel was built in 1992 and named for Corvinus, a famous Hungarian king. Though located in the business area, it caters to both business and leisure guests.

Kempinski Hotel Corvinus has set new standards in Budapest with its efficient service, fine food, and classical modern design. The hotel has two Audi A-6

The 340 rooms and 29 suites are modern without being stark and please the most well traveled. The Presidential suites, known as the Corvinus Suite and Deák Suite, are divine.

The Kempinski Art Gallery houses a fine collection of art with changing exhibitions of Hungarian artists. Spectacular golf is just a thirty-minute chauffeured drive away.

Explore the old and the new of Budapest, but stay at the worldly Kempinski Hotel Corvinus.

limousines, the only two in all of Hungary, available for short sightseeing excursions or special events.

Due in large part to its clientele, the hotel has a distinctly international flavor. Its restaurants and bars honor cuisines from all over the world, including American and Italian. A jazz brunch is offered on Sundays and a Hungarian buffet is served once a week to enable you to sample local delicacies.

**KEMPINSKI HOTEL CORVINUS**
Erzsébet tér 7-8
1051 Budapest, Hungary

# Ashford Castle

A visit to Ashford Castle is an experience to cherish. Not far from Galway, Ashford Castle is on the shores of Lough Corrib in western Ireland. Dating back to 1228, the castle is full of folklore and tradition and both are best experienced in the Dungeon Bar, where the resident storyteller will bring you up to speed.

Equestrian activities are popular at Ashford Castle, where advanced riders and beginners are equally accommodated. Three thousand acres of coastline make for scenic rides - and the indoor school and outdoor jumps, both man-made and natural, are perfect for more experienced riders. Those interested in the thrill of the hunt may enroll in Mark Phillip's Pre-Hunting Course.

Nearby Lough Comb provides some of Europe's best salmon and brown trout fishing and local ghillies, or fishing guides, can be hired for half or full day charters. Spontaneity is encouraged at the castle's riverbank, where great fishing requires no advance reservations. Complimentary for residents, the Eddie Hackett designed golf course is a terrific way to round out your day.

Ashford Castle boasts that all 77 rooms and 6 suites are individually designed by different decorators. The staterooms feature four poster beds and old-fashioned claw-foot bathtubs.

The Castle offers two restaurants, the George V and the Connaught Room. The Connaught Room, with seating for 40 people, has a gorgeous inglenook that reaches twenty feet up to the oak ceiling.

Though you certainly cannot take the Castle with you, your memories will linger forever.

**ASHFORD CASTLE**
Cong
County Mayo, Ireland

# Four Seasons Hotel Dublin

While Dublin has always been associated with a great literary tradition, cozy pubs and friendly residents, it can now be associated with the Four Seasons.

Four Seasons Hotel Dublin opened in early 2001 in Ballsbridge, an exclusive and historic neighborhood just outside of the city center. The Four Seasons occupies seeveral acres of the Royal Dublin Society's 42 acre showgrounds, host of the annual Dublin Horse Show. The six level Georgian inspired building with a red brick exterior, slate roof and landscaped interior courtyard, puts it right at home in this tranquil area.

The Four Seasons Hotel has 192 rooms and 67 suites that are the most spacious guest rooms in Dublin. The rooms have views of the hotel gardens, Ballsbridge, Dublin Bay or the Wicklow Mountains. The décor is decidedly Four Seasons; open, spacious and contemporary, with Irish touches. Bathrooms are fitted with Calacatta marble and Tibetan granite.

The public rooms are grand, with Brazilian granite, polished Italian marble, inlaid maple and cherry woods and handwoven carpeting from Ireland covering the floors. In the lobby, a glorious green and gold crystal chandelier hangs from the ceiling.

The majestic setting can also be enjoyed from the restaurant that serves Continental cuisine with seasonal Irish specialties. Afternoon tea is served fireside in the living room. The indoor lap pool and Jacuzzi also benefit from the natural setting; they overlook the outdoor sunken garden just outside the windows.

Four Seasons Hotel Dublin makes Irish eyes smile.

**FOUR SEASONS HOTEL DUBLIN**
Simmonscourt Road
Ballsbridge
Dublin 4, Ireland

# The Merrion

Meticulously converted from four Georgian townhouses, The Merrion feels like traditional Dublin, because it is.

The spirit of the previous owners of the buildings, Lord Monck, Lord Mornington and the Duke of Wellington, lives on at this gracious hotel with impeccable standards. The Merrion is located in the center of Dublin, across from the Irish Parliament and Government Buildings. Dublin's esteemed Trinity College is a few blocks away and the best museums are just down the street.

There are 125 rooms

formal style, and an important collection of art, including a 16th century Gobelins tapestry and works by 20th century Irish artists.

The Tethra Spa draws on Irish literary history for its name. Tethra, or "land of the young and living," comes from a collection of stories, and is an appropriate name for this revitalizing place. It is one of Dublin's best.

Lord Mornington, Lord Monck and the Duke of Wellington would feel right at home and would love the modern conveniences at The Merrion... so will you.

and 20 suites in the main hotel and the specially commissioned garden wing. The interiors were carefully selected after detailed research on the Georgian period and all colors, fabrics and furnishings, including many antiques, depict that era. Even the lamps, based on Delftware, were designed exclusively for The Merrion.

The Merrion has two glorious private gardens, designed in the 18th century

**THE MERRION**
Upper Merrion Street
Dublin 2, Ireland

# Park Hotel Kenmare

Tucked inside the Ring of Kerry, a dramatic and scenic coastal loop beside the Atlantic Ocean winding its way around the southwest of Ireland, Kenmare is fortunate to be surrounded by Ireland's highest range of mountains. Park Hotel Kenmare shares this great fortune with its guests with its magnificent views and tranquil gardens.

Park Hotel Kenmare is the sort of place where you go to escape the world. Its gracious manner welcomes you and encourages you to leave your distractions behind. The limestone manor house is just over

competitive 18-hole golf course is adjacent to the property and some of Ireland's best courses are within close proximity.

Irish and European antiques decorate the 41 rooms and 9 suites. The views of Kenmare Bay and the terraced gardens are lovely. Park Hotel Kenmare's restaurant is recognized for its innovative dining in a traditional setting. For moments of quiet reflection, retire to the lounge, where soothing piano music and an extensive selection of malts tempt your palette.

Park Hotel Kenmare shares the best of Ireland with you.

100 years old and was transformed into a hotel only twenty years ago. Today, Francis Brennan owns and operates the Park Hotel Kenmare with assistance from his brother, John, and a friendly, warm staff.

The hotel's peaceful and natural setting provides plenty of activities. The views of Kenmare Bay are worthy of the hike and crystal clear rivers and lakes are ideal for fishing. Biking and horseback riding are great ways to explore the blessed area. A

### PARK HOTEL KENMARE
County Kerry
Kenmare, Ireland

# Palazzo Arzaga

Though only two hours from Venice, just under half an hour from Verona and only minutes from Lake Garda, Palazzo Arzaga is a destination in itself. Once a 15th century monastery, Palazzo Arzaga is now an intriguing hotel in Italy's Lombardy region.

The incredibly romantic 79 rooms are delightful and several boast original frescoes in the style of Guido Reni. Four suites are available and some have hand-painted ceilings and marble fireplaces. All windows open to views of the majestic 1,000 acre estate.

While most rooms are located in the main building, 13 of the guest rooms are in the adjacent 15th century church.

Palazzo Arzaga offers a cooking school, though one can always skip the homework and relax in one of the many delicious restaurants. A 15th century conservatory, an antique gallery and an ancient cellar comprise the inventive locations in which Palazzo Arzaga houses its restaurants. Outdoor picnics in the rolling hills may also be enjoyed.

Golfers will rejoice at the fabulous facilities offered here. In addition to the 18 hole and 9 hole golf courses, designed by Jack Nicklaus II and Gary Player, Palazzo Arzaga is home to the PGA Golf Academy. These facilities will surely change your opinion about golf in Italy.

The Saturnia Spa has become a destination within a destination, with daily and weeklong packages. Its wellness program puts it at the top of Europe's best spas.

With its idyllic setting, romantic rooms and bountiful activities, this former monastery will have you counting your blessings.

**PALAZZO ARZAGA**
Carzago di Calvagese della Riviera
25080 Brescia, Italy

# Villa d'Este

Legendary and in a class of its own, Villa d'Este is the embodiment of la dolce vita.

Overlooking majestic Lake Como in northern Italy, Villa d'Este has been attracting visitors for nearly 500 years. Nuns first made their presence here, and today's gardens contain columns that are attributed to their convent. The palatial villa was constructed in 1568 and it has been home to many, including cardinals, aristocrats, an empress and an English queen.

Since opening as a luxury hotel in 1873, Villa d'Este has inspired passion in its guests. Giovanni Ricordi, the music publisher, was the hotel's first guest. Both Puccini and Verdi visited Ricordi here, and it is said that Verdi composed his *Traviata* at Villa d'Este. Four generations of the Ricordi family spent their summers here, and the floor they rented in the Queen's Pavilion is known as the Piano Ricordi today.

The precious world of Villa d'Este is shared in its 162 guest rooms and suites, with 131 in the Cardinal's villa and 31 in the Queen's Pavilion, dating from 1856. Rooms are regal. Fabulous silks, for which Como is famous, are used for upholstery and draperies.

Dining is an event at Villa d'Este, whether at the Grill, poolside café, Enoteca or Verandah. The glass-enclosed Verandah restaurant has sensational service, delectable cuisine and views of the lake and gardens. With the push of a button, the glass disappears into the ground for open-air dining.

A fantastic floating pool, supported by pontoons, uniquely caters to swimmers and sunbathers. If meandering in the stately gardens does not occupy your time, there are tennis courts, a health club, water sports and all of Lake Como to explore.

Villa d'Este compels you to rediscover romance.

**VILLA D'ESTE**
Via Regina 40, Lake Como
22012 Cernobbio, Italy

# Hotel Excelsior

Hotel Excelsior's grand style and perfect location make it one of the best in Florence.

The Excelsior sits on the Arno River and dominates Piazza Ognissanti, with its shops dating back to the Renaissance and today's modern luxury boutiques. The hotel opened in 1927, but the site has seen more than 700 years of Florentine history. In the 13th century, this area was marshland and was first settled by a religious order. Eventually, religion gave way to nobility and this area was home to glorious private residences. These houses passed through the hands of Florence's most important and powerful families. In the mid 1800's, Carolina Bonaparte, Napoleon's sister, lived here.

Terracotta tiles, marbles, precious woods and rich antiques set the scene in the Excelsior's public rooms. The classic Italian lobby dazzles the eye with its sophisticated furnishings and splendid attention to detail. The Excelsior's Renaissance atmosphere is echoed in the elegantly refined 152 rooms and 16 suites.

The elaborate wood ceiling and soft candlelight of Il Cestello provide a beautiful and warm setting for its delicious Florentine cuisine. Light meals, aperitifs and after dinner drinks are served in the Donatello Bar.

All of Florence's landmarks such as the Duomo, Pitti Palace, Uffizi and Santa Maria Novella are within blocks of the hotel. After a day of sightseeing, you will be delighted to arrive home at the Hotel Excelsior.

**HOTEL EXCELSIOR**
Piazza Ognissanti, 3
50123 Florence, Italy

# Grand Hotel

The Grand, on Piazza Ognissanti overlooking the Arno, truly lives up to its name.

Inextricably linked to Florence's history, the building was designed by Renaissance architect Brunelleschi, who also designed the city's recognizable cathedral dome. Originally a private palace, it became the Grand Hotel 400 years later, and has always hosted the most discerning world travelers. The Grand Hotel held the most important society events and royal marriages. Imagine what you would hear if the walls could only talk. Today, the resplendent ballroom is still ideal for the most special occasions.

same name serves delicious Tuscan cuisine.

The Grand's Empire-style 90 rooms and 17 suites are sumptuous. Marble inlays and handmade fabrics of the finest materials are in all rooms. The walls are decorated with frescoes of Renaissance life. The Masaccio Suite is notable for its striking ceiling with individually painted squares. Though the rooms and suites evoke Florence's history, modern conveniences are never overlooked and the comfort of all guests is ensured.

The Grand Hotel gloriously bridges Florence's past and present.

The Wintergarden is the architectural center and spiritual heart of the hotel. Its stained glass roof, terracotta tiles and rare antiques highlight the best of the Florentine decorative style. It is a fashionable meeting place for residents and visitors. Its welcoming ambience makes for a perfect location for Il Fiorino, the serene hotel bar. The restaurant by the

**GRAND HOTEL**
Piazza Ognissanti 1
50123 Florence, Italy

# Hotel Helvetia & Bristol

Hotel Helvetia & Bristol is a quaint establishment with just 52 rooms and suites that opened in the second half of the 19th century.

Founded by a Swiss family, the hotel is a blend of British and Italian styles. Antique collectors will adore this hotel with its important and whimsical pieces that decorate the public spaces and private rooms. The décor is a tribute to patience, as the period furnishings and important paintings of the original décor were tracked down. Its charming ambience has attracted many of the world's most influential figures in the

della Signoria, with the fabulous backdrop of Palazzo Vecchio, the Loggia della Signoria and wings of the Uffizi Gallery.

The Winter Garden, Stravinsky's favorite part of the Helvetia & Bristol, is a perfect spot for afternoon tea. For over one hundred years, the Winter Garden has been the meeting place for Florence's intellectuals. This ground-floor restaurant serves Tuscan cuisine based on tradition but with modern adaptations.

Staying at the Helvetia & Bristol is like being a native Florentine, as you are in the heart of Florence.

arts and music, including Igor Stravinsky and Giorgio De Chirico. Renowned for its interior design, the hotel was honored with an award several years ago for the world's finest hotel décor.

Hotel Helvetia & Bristol faces Palazzo Strozzi and Via Tornabuoni, having the good fortune to be centrally located. You are only steps away from Florence's political stage - past and present - the stunning Piazza

**HOTEL HELVETIA & BRISTOL**
Via dei Pescioni, 2
50123 Florence, Italy

# Hotel Savoy

Hotel Savoy, located on Piazza della Repubblica, offers a contemporary slant on historic Florence.

First-time visitors and seasoned travelers alike will delight in the convenience of the Hotel Savoy's prime location. Midway between the Duomo and the Palazzo Vecchio, Florence's sights are within a short walk and many can be viewed from the windows of the hotel.

Recently reopened, the hotel's total renovation breathes fresh air into the city with its chic design and clean, simple décor. White and cream provide the backdrop for the rooms with creative splashes of color and modern artwork interspersed. The large windows of the 98 rooms and 9 suites allow for undisturbed views of the Piazza and the Duomo. Hotel Savoy's contemporary design is sleek without being stark and chic without being impersonal. Service is always friendly and efficient.

Hotel Savoy's restaurant and bar, L'Incontro, opens onto the Piazza from spring through fall and affords the best vantage point for people watching while enjoying terrific dining. It has a simple, yet stylish design and the menu provides traditional Florentine dishes with an emphasis on local produce. The wine list has some of the best Tuscan wines that Italy has to offer.

Sleep in style at the Hotel Savoy; the Renaissance is a walk away and the contemporary is just inside your door.

**HOTEL SAVOY**
Piazza della Repubblica, 7
50123 Florence, Italy

# Villa La Massa

Only five miles from Florence, Villa La Massa's heart is in the Tuscan countryside.

The Landini family built the exquisite pale yellow Villa La Massa in the 16th century. Several Italian, English and Russian aristocratic families also resided here. In 1948, Villa La Massa was transformed into a luxury hotel. Winston Churchill, Barbara Hutton, Elizabeth Taylor and Richard Burton all paid visits throughout the years. Recently purchased and totally renovated by Villa d'Este Hotels, it has become one of Tuscany's jewels once again.

during the summer only, provides light meals, snacks and salads. The Mediceo Bar operates on the terrace and around the pool every night.

Tours of nearby Tuscan towns are informative and excursions along the Chianti region with visits to wineries and olive oil farms are a must. Of course, Florence is also just a short drive away, and the hotel provides daily shuttle service to the Ponte Vecchio.

Villa La Massa is an ideal way to experience the Tuscan countryside while remaining close to Florence's treasures.

The intimate villa has 24 exquisite guest rooms and 10 suites, all in classic Tuscan style. The main restaurant, Verrocchio, is located in Villa Vecchia, the oldest part of the house. Verrocchio serves all meals; focusing on regional and Mediterranean specialties. In warmer weather, guests may enjoy the views of the Arno while dining on the terrace. The pool bar, open

**VILLA LA MASSA**
Villa della Massa 24
Candeli Bagno a Ripoli
50012 Florence, Italy

# Villa San Michele

All travelers visit Florence for its splendid Renaissance art and history, but lucky visitors stay in one of Villa San Michele's 26 rooms or 15 suites.

Villa San Michele is located in the wooded hills of Fiesole, above Florence. Fifteen minutes or so from the center of the city, the hotel's vantage point allows you to admire Florence's glory in its entirety. It is said that Michelangelo designed the façade of this 15th century Franciscan monastery, now an Italian National Trust Monument.

The rooms and suites are handsomely appointed in Tuscan style with tiles and custom made walnut or

once used as a monastic retreat. Its wood-beamed ceiling is the only one in the entire hotel and the bathroom's vaulted ceiling is decorated with frescoes.

The stunning views of Florence and the Arno Valley and the Tuscan specialties make dining al fresco at the Loggia restaurant one of the most magical experiences at Villa San Michele. A formal, indoor restaurant and two bars provide alternatives for cooler months and late evenings.

Its monastic roots, Renaissance history and spectacular views make Villa San Michele one of the most delightful ways to experience Florence.

cherry wood furniture. The headboards, either hand-painted wood or intricate wrought iron, are delightfully unique. The Limonaia, where the monks once stored their lemon trees during winter, has been beautifully converted into two spacious suites with access to a secluded garden in an ancient quarry. Villa San Michele's most private suite is in the Chapel,

**VILLA SAN MICHELE**
Via di Doccia, 4
50014 Florence, Fiesole, Italy

# Four Seasons Hotel Milan

Four Seasons Hotel Milan sets a style of its own in one of the world's best-known fashion capitals.

The Four Seasons is located on Via Gesù, just off Via Montenapoleone in the heart of Milan's shopping district. One of the smaller hotels in the Four Seasons group, the Four Seasons Hotel Milan has an intimate character. The Neoclassical façade and cloistered courtyard hint at the building's former incarnation as a 15th century monastery. Bits of frescoes and vaulted ceilings also honor the history and have been carefully preserved.

However, it is the clean

lines and casual elegance of contemporary Italian design that dominate the interiors. Cassina furniture, Frette linens, Fortuny fabrics and burl cabinetry are a far cry from a spartan monastery and are used in the 77 serene rooms and 41 suites. My favorite rooms overlook the tranquil courtyard.

It is a mark of success when a hotel is enjoyed by its guests, but when the city's residents also make it their own, you know you have a special place. The notoriously hard-to-please Milanese adore the Four Seasons and regularly dine in its two restaurants and relax in its lounge. The leather upholstered walls and French walnut woodwork of Il Teatro set a stylish mood for a superb meal. La Veranda serves lighter fare and has a view of the garden and terrace. The lounge is a fashionable place for cocktails or a nightcap, where you can admire the fragments of original frescoes and the rare Peroni stage set drawings for La Scala.

Set your own style when you stay at the fashionable Four Seasons in Milan.

**FOUR SEASONS
HOTEL MILAN**
via Gesù, 8
20121 Milan, Italy

# Hotel Principe di Savoia

Principe di Savoia, a grand palazzo that opened in 1927, dominates Piazza della Repubblica in the heart of Milan's business district.

This Neo-Classical hotel has 266 rooms and 133 suites with turn-of-the-century décor. Rich wood paneling, wall coverings of damask, as well as rugs and curtains exclusive to the Principe di Savoia, give the rooms an elegant, but comforting touch. While all rooms are very spacious, it is the Presidential Suite that is particularly notable. With almost 5,400 square feet, it is one of the largest hotel suites in the world! The suite features a

The hotel has two restaurants and a winter garden bar. The five-star Ristorante Galleria serves delicious regional dishes overlooking the garden, or in summer in an open-air, gazebo setting. The less formal Café Doney will tempt you for breakfast, light lunch or afternoon tea.

Club 10, the hotel's fitness center and spa, is well equipped and perfect for those keeping in shape in this fashion capital.

Luxury, style and considerate service make the Principe di Savoia an excellent choice in Milan.

private spa with Pompeiian style frescoed walls containing a swimming pool, whirlpool, sauna and Turkish bath.

The grande dame of Milan, Hotel Principe di Savoia welcomes its female visitors with thoughtful touches, like bedtime herbal tea instead of the usual chocolates. A gloriously feminine décor is implemented in some rooms to make women feel more at home in this large city.

**HOTEL PRINCIPE DI SAVOIA**
Piazza della Repubblica, 17
20124 Milan, Italy

# Hotel Splendido & Splendido Mare

Once a simple fishing village, Portofino is now considered the jewel of the Italian Riviera.

Hotel Splendido rests high above the bay of Portofino. Situated within four acres of semi-tropical, terraced gardens of palm trees and olive groves, the hotel appeals to your senses with its fragrances and views of the azure Mediterranean Sea. Exceptionally private, the hotel has been a favorite of film stars seeking a retreat from their hectic lives for many years. Greta Garbo, Humphrey Bogart, Lauren Bacall and Elizabeth Taylor are just some of the luminaries that have vacationed here.

While the reception rooms feature antiques and Persian rugs, the mood is decidedly informal. The 44 guest rooms and 25 suites are decorated in a light, Mediterranean style with soft colors and pleasant fabrics.

The heated saltwater pool, the only one in Portofino, is an ideal place to soak up the sun and the scenery, and the poolside terrace serves light meals and snacks to satisfy your appetite.

Typical Ligurian cuisine of the region, including bountiful seafood, is served at Hotel Splendido; either open-air at La Terrazza or indoors overlooking the terraces and the sea.

Splendido Mare is an extension of Hotel Splendido and is located in Portofino's village overlooking the picturesque harbor. The traditional Ligurian style building is charming with 7 deluxe rooms, 9 suites and a delightful terrace restaurant. A shuttle service is provided between the two sister hotels.

Sophisticated while informal, Hotel Splendido & Splendido Mare personify Portofino.

## HOTEL SPLENDIDO
## SPLENDIDO MARE
Salita Baratta, 16
16034 Portofino, Italy

# Le Sirenuse

Located among the baroque houses of the hillside village of Positano on Italy's famed Amalfi Coast, Le Sirenuse is a special hideaway.

This 18th century summer house was transformed into a deluxe hotel in 1951.

Managed by the noble Neapolitan Sersale family that has owned the property for generations, Le Sirenuse is a luxury hotel while maintaining its soul as a private home. Guests are welcomed here as if they are members of the family.

Le Sirenuse takes it name from the enchanting islands it faces. These islands, the mythical home of the sirens that seduced Odysseus, will take your

family collection for years.

Sample the creations of an acclaimed chef here amid the bougainvillea-covered archways on the terrace. The kitchen serves delicious Neapolitan dishes - many are the family's own recipes. Relaxing by the pool with its terrific vantage point is one of my favorite pastimes, and a new spa was added just recently. Positano's location makes it ideal to visit bustling Naples, the ruins of Pompeii, the Amalfi Coast, or the magical island of Capri - only a hydrofoil away.

Le Sirenuse will welcome you with its friendly manner and enchant you with its beauty.

breath away while making you realize how easy it is to be tempted here.

The 62 rooms and suites, all facing the water, are beautifully decorated and provide a cool backdrop for the abundant sun and glittering sea. Floors are covered in handmade tiles from Vietri, and period furnishings and artwork provide more than adornment, as many have been part of the Sersale

**LE SIRENUSE**
Via Cristoforo Colombo, 30
84017 Positano, Italy

# Palazzo Sasso

Palazzo Sasso, a stunning 12th century villa, is in the medieval village of Ravello on Italy's Amalfi Coast.

With Moorish influences and staggering views, Palazzo Sasso offers an unforgettable experience. The 38 rooms and 5 suites are romantic, with period antiques and many full-length windows to enhance your enjoyment of the coastline. You will feel well taken care of here, with two staff members per room.

Palazzo Sasso's grounds are beautiful and the flowering shrubs, palm trees and peaceful fountains add to the inviting atmosphere. The enchanting shadows cast by the Moorish arches are alluring by day, and at night, both exotic and

mysterious. A swimming pool and hydromassage plunge pools are located on the rooftop terrace with equally stunning views.

The hotel originally belonged to the noble Sasso family. More than a century ago, Richard Wagner wrote a portion of the Parsifal here. It was home to Roberto Rossellini and Ingrid Bergmann on numerous occasions, as the restaurant's name might suggest.

The Italian haute cuisine at Rossellinis has earned it a

Michelin star and the flavorful food presented by the superb staff will surely earn it a place in your heart. The restaurant's setting, overlooking the fishing boats nearly 1,000 feet below, is one of the highlights of a visit to Palazzo Sasso.

The bar, terraces and library are all ideal spots for cocktails, snacks or fresh pasta dishes, or even cigars from the hotel's extensive collection.

Exotic yet familiar, Palazzo Sasso is a memorable place in an extraordinary setting.

**PALAZZO SASSO**
Via San Giovanni Del Toro, 28
84010 Ravello, Italy

# Hotel Eden

For more than a hundred years, Hotel Eden has romanced its visitors.

Hotel Eden is located in a quiet section of Rome at the corner of Via Porta Pinciana and Via Ludovisi. It enjoys a park-like setting with greenery from the nearby Ludovisi and Villa Borghese. The glamorous boutiques of Via Veneto and Piazza di Spagna are also within a few blocks. The historic treasures of the city are easily accessible from this peaceful location.

The Eden is perhaps best known for

its views above Rome, with its terrace restaurant and bar. Once you have seen Rome from above, you will fully appreciate its past and present glory. The city's adopted son, filmmaker Federico Fellini, was particularly enamored with the rooftop. Not only did he schedule most of his interviews and appointments here, but when his coat, hat, and red scarf were left in the cloakroom, it was a signal to the concierge that he would be expecting his usual table. Who can blame him, with views of the Spanish Steps, Villa Borghese and St. Peter's Basilica?

The hotel's 105 rooms and 14 suites are exceptionally decorated with gentle, appealing colors and have large windows for private enjoyment of the views.

Favorites are often found, and many guests choose to occupy the same room time and again when they visit Rome.

One visit to Rome and the Hotel Eden is never enough.

**HOTEL EDEN**
Via Ludovisi 49
00187 Rome, Italy

# Hotel Excelsior

Ah, Rome! In a city that exudes history and culture, the Hotel Excelsior stands out for its unique ability to blend the past with the present. Situated on Rome's fashionable Via Veneto, the Excelsior's prime location is across the street from the American Embassy and only steps away from the Borghese Gardens. For years, it has been the meeting place of choice for Romans and visitors alike.

The graceful world that is the Excelsior begins when you enter through the glass doors. The entry hall is full of sparkling chandeliers, gilded mirrors, breathtaking Oriental rugs, tapestries and paintings. While all rooms are

magnificent with walls and ceilings hand-decorated by artisans, furnished in Empire style with Bohemian crystal chandeliers, and modern amenities, the real centerpiece of the hotel is their new suite, Villa La Cupola. On the fifth and sixth floors of the hotel and under the building's signature cupola, this suite is beyond your wildest dreams with almost 11,700 square feet! It tastefully combines past and present by blending marbles, frescoes, elegant furnishings, and fittings inspired by Roman villas and palaces, plus every modern convenience - even an 8-person theater with teleconference capabilities.

The combination of excellence in size, location, décor, and technological equipment not only makes this suite unique, but also places it at the very top level of Italian and international hotel accommodations.

After a stay at the Hotel Excelsior, you will have a hard time saying, "Arrivederci Roma!"

**HOTEL EXCELSIOR**
Via Veneto, 125
00187 Rome, Italy

# Hotel Hassler

Many hotels offer proximity to sights, but Hotel Hassler in Rome has an especially enviable location at the top of the Spanish Steps.

Situated adjacent to the Church of Trinità dei Monti and a short walk to the Via Condotti for shopping, the Hotel Hassler has long been considered one of the world's best hotels. Marble columns, antique carpets, Murano chandeliers and brocade fabrics set a stately tone. Befitting a former palazzo, the 85 rooms and 15 suites are elegant. Original paintings by Titian and the Tintoretto Schools decorate the walls and original Louis XV furnishings are featured. The large bathrooms even include fabulous 23-karat gold-plated faucets!

declared that Hassler did not sound Italian enough, the hotel provides many choices for dining and relaxation. The cozy surroundings of the bar invite you to sample its popular Veruschka and Bellini cocktails. Salone Eva, traditionally serving afternoon tea, has recently expanded to include delicious all-day dining, including after-theater snacks. In the summer, enjoy the Palm Court, a delightful inner garden, for tasty offerings. For the best panoramic views of Rome in between bites of classic Continental and Italian specialties, I never miss dining at the Hassler Restaurant on the sixth floor.

Polished and esteemed, Hotel Hassler is the traditional choice in Rome.

Hotel Hassler takes its name from its founder, but the reputable Wirth family has owned and managed the hotel for more than 90 years. The Hassler has hosted memorable events for illustrious guests. Prince Rainier and Grace Kelly spent their honeymoon here and Princess Diana used to visit for the special Bellinis. These pedigreed "regulars" add to the mythical feel of the Hotel Hassler.

Often referred to as Villa Medici, thanks to Mussolini who

**HOTEL HASSLER**
Trinità dei Monti 6
00187 Rome, Italy

# Hotel de Russie

Refreshingly reinvented, Hotel de Russie is once again one of Rome's finest hotels.

A favorite of the Russian Imperial House, Stravinsky and Picasso in the 19th century, the hotel reopened in the spring of 2000 with an entirely new look. While you might expect turn-of-the-century décor in this venerable building, it is the mid-century style, with its juxtaposition of classical and modern, that dominates.

The striped carpets, high-back sofas and 1920's decorative steel panel of the sleek lobby create a lobby unlike any other in Rome. The 102 guest rooms and

garden's trees while staying here, and today's guests will enjoy a variety of ancient trees, fruit trees and flowering shrubs. The terrace, with its stairway slightly resembling the nearby Spanish Steps, is a peaceful spot for casual dining. The main restaurant and bar offer alfresco dining options as well as indoor seating.

Reflecting its modern sentiments, Hotel de Russie provides a health club and spa with hydropool, Jacuzzi, sauna, Turkish steam bath and beauty treatments.

Restored yet reinvented, Hotel de Russie makes Rome proud.

27 suites are eclectic and perfectly blend furnishings from different eras. The graceful decorative style of Olga Polizzi, sister of owner Sir Rocco Forte, can be seen throughout the hotel. Original photography, including the large color photographs of flowers by Robert Mapplethorpe, completes the contemporary look.

Once a modest vineyard, the hotel's garden is legendary. It is said that Picasso and Cocteau picked the oranges from the

**HOTEL DE RUSSIE**
Via del Babuino 9
00187 Rome, Italy

# St. Regis Grand

In Rome, another favorite of mine is the St. Regis Grand. It originally opened its doors in 1894, but recently underwent a multi-multi-million dollar renovation restoring it to its original glory. The hotel was founded by the successful hotelier Cesar Ritz, who built The Grand using the same founding principles of his other hotels; great attention to detail and superb service.

The St. Regis Grand is within walking distance of the Via Veneto and the Spanish Steps. The Coliseum, Piazza Navona, Trevi Fountain and the Roman ruins are just a few minutes away by taxi.

A visual link between the glorious history of Rome and

service, the St. Regis Grand now offers a butler floor for truly privileged pampering. The Salone Ritz, the first ballroom in Rome, is simply astounding with rich details, sparkling chandeliers and frescoed ceilings. It is marvelous for private events.

In addition to playing host for many years to the world's most fashionable and influential people, the St. Regis Grand was the first hotel to have electric lighting throughout and at no extra charge!

The St. Regis Grand has always been ahead of its time, while respecting, honoring and incorporating traditions.

the hotel has been established in each room with a hand-painted fresco-type decoration. Each is unique and represents a significant ruin, villa or area of Rome. The frescoes help provide the names that are assigned to the rooms. The lavishly appointed 136 rooms and 25 suites combine Empire, Regency and Louis XV decorative styles and all rooms have gleaming Murano glass chandeliers. Always dedicated to providing the best

**ST. REGIS GRAND**
Via Vittorio Emanuele
Orlando 3
00185 Rome, Italy

# Cala di Volpe

Sardinia, off the coast of Italy, is a wondrous island defined by its pristine beaches, glorious sunshine and infectious spirit. The Costa Smeralda, or "emerald coast," is a stretch of beautiful coastline in the northeast corner of the island. Named for its stunning water, it embodies the ideal European island destination.

One of the best ways to explore the Costa Smeralda is by boat, and Cala di Volpe can arrange boat hires for day trips to nearby islands and coves. A shuttle boat transports guests to the resort's private, sandy beach, though the seawater swimming pool may convince you to remain on the property. A 9 hole putting green keeps your game in shape and privileges to the Pevero Golf Club are extended to all guests.

Cala di Volpe is one of the Costa Smeralda's most intriguing resorts. Built in 1963, Cala di Volpe was designed to resemble an ancient fishing village. Resting on one of the most beautiful bays in Sardinia, the resort is an enchanting mix of porticoes, arches and a charming, covered bridge.

Cala di Volpe has a decidedly country ambience, particularly in its 111 rooms and 12 suites. Local crafts and furnishings, wrought iron and vibrant colors characterize the Sardinian décor. Beamed ceilings and split-levels make the rooms truly feel like part of an authentic village.

Two of the island's best restaurants are located at Cala di Volpe. International and Italian cuisine are the focus in the main dining room, while seafood and Sardinian specialties are served in the Barbecue Restaurant. Both restaurants have a relaxed ease with open-air arched windows, creative interior designs and fantastic views of the bay and swimming pool.

Savor Sardinia's natural charms at Cala di Volpe.

**CALA DI VOLPE**
Costa Smeralda
07020 Porto Cervo,
Sardinia, Italy

# Hotel Pitrizza

Hotel Pitrizza provides a different perspective on Sardinia's Costa Smeralda.

Hotel Pitrizza, located on a rugged stretch of coastline jutting into the bay, is for romantics. Sweeping views of the surroundings and the spectacular turquoise water can be enjoyed throughout the resort, whether you are lounging on the beach or napping in your guest room.

Villas nestled among wildflowers and native rocks contain 38 guest rooms and 13 suites. Pitrizza is an intimate hideaway where privacy is treasured. Handcrafted

furniture, native woods, granite and Cerasarda tiles typical of Sardinia define the natural, rustic style of all rooms. Large windows and an open-air atmosphere invite the glorious Sardinian sunshine indoors, and the views of the gardens or the bay are superb.

Fresh, local seafood and regional specialties are highlighted at Pitrizza's two restaurants. A simple, thatched-style roof serves as the only shelter for the main restaurant, allowing sea breezes to cosset you. Vibrant blue tablecloths and simple furnishings create a special Mediterranean ambience. The Barbecue

Restaurant is located on a terrace overlooking the swimming pool.

A private stretch of sandy beach is just outside your door, while the saltwater swimming pool, carved out of natural rocks, is particularly striking. A small jetty is convenient for docking small yachts. Pitrizza makes discovering the Costa Smeralda easy. The archeological site of Li Muri and the grottos of Ispinigoli and Bue Marino are worth the trip.

Delight in the unspoiled Costa Smeralda at Hotel Pitrizza.

## HOTEL PITRIZZA
Costa Smeralda
07020 Porto Cervo
Sardinia, Italy

# Hotel Romazzino

Hotel Romazzino, with its typical Mediterranean style, is a splendid resort on the Costa Smeralda.

Romazzino's whitewashed building is surrounded by lush, fragrant gardens of hibiscus, juniper, rosemary and olive trees and verdant lawns. A curvy path takes you down to the private beach of fine sand, or relax by the pool looking out to the sparkling water of the bay.

Based on local architecture, Romazzino is a brilliant white building with arched windows. The resort has 78 rooms and 15 suites, all with spacious, private balconies reaching out to the

water. Like the exterior, the rooms are painted a dazzling white that seems even brighter when the golden sunshine streams through the window. Brightly colored, hand-painted tiles from Cerasarda in Sardinia cover the floors and add a splash of color to the accommodations.

Water sports are plentiful at Romazzino, where the inviting sea is just outside your door. Windsurfing, water-skiing, sailing, fishing and scuba diving are all offered at

Hotel Romazzino. Tennis courts are located on the property, and golf is available just a short drive away.

Hotel Romazzino delights its guests with barbecues by the beach and buffets by the pool. Two restaurants serve a variety of local dishes. For a change of scenery, guests are granted special privileges at sister properties, Cala di Volpe and Hotel Pitrizza.

For active or lazy afternoons and sensual evenings, Romazzino is a perfect match.

**HOTEL ROMAZZINO**
Costa Smeralda
07020 Porto Cervo
Sardinia, Italy

# Il Borro

Stretching the concepts of a traditional hotel, Il Borro welcomes you to an authentic Tuscan estate owned by the Ferragamo family.

At Il Borro, a simple stroll along the stone path takes you back centuries, to a time when simple pursuits were relished. Imagine a place where you can hear the mocking call of the peacocks and the laughter of the pheasants just on your morning walk.

Unique lodging is offered at Il Borro. Seven farmhouses, varying in size, are scattered throughout the village. They remain true to their rustic origins in design,

but offer conveniences like operational kitchens and washing machines. Two grand farmhouses, set out on the estate's grounds, are divided into four apartments, perfect for couples on a romantic retreat or small families. The original barn has been converted to a special three-bedroom setting. Its elegantly rustic atmosphere defies its former incarnation. The old mill and miller's house, known as the Mulino houses, overlook the river and fields, and

a freshwater pool has been created from the original mill's dam.

The property lends itself to activities and fishing, horseback riding, hot air ballooning and gliding lessons are just some of the offerings at Il Borro. This charming place also offers weeklong courses in watercolor painting, Tuscan cooking and riding.

L'Osteria del Borro is located in the village and serves delicious Tuscan food and fine Italian wines. Many of the items grown on the property will be found at your table.

Immerse yourself in Tuscan culture and live like an Italian at Il Borro.

**IL BORRO**
Loc. Borro, 1/A
52020 San Giustino Valdarno
Tuscany, Italy

# Hotel Cipriani & Palazzo Vendramin

There are some places in the world where no description is needed and one word says it all, and Cipriani is one of those places.

Hotel Cipriani and Palazzo Vendramin are situated on Giudecca Island on the lagoon side of Venice. Away from the bustling crowds, yet close enough to enjoy the splendors of Venice, the island is only a five-minute boat ride to Piazza San Marco…of course provided by the hotel. Those five minutes make Cipriani different from any other property here. The hotel, surrounded by lush gardens and having the only swimming pool and tennis court in Venice, is a tranquil resort.

Venice. The Cipriani's ultimate personal service throughout is legendary.

Created by Giuseppe Cipriani, the Cipriani has a proud culinary tradition and fine reputation for superb Italian cuisine. Dinner is served in the restaurant or during much of the year on the terrace. Lunch and lighter meals are served at the poolside restaurant. Cip's Pizzeria and Grill at the Palazzetto faces Venice for delightful alfresco dining.

Cipriani is a truly romantic place that will capture your heart forever.

Though it might seem that the views of the lagoon or San Giorgio Maggiore or the walled gardens or pool from the 48 rooms, 27 junior suites and 13 suites in the main building would be enough decoration, the interiors are equally pleasing. Through the private gardens and linked by a loggia and ancient courtyard, Palazzo Vendramin is a 15th century residence that has been decorated in a Fortuny-inspired Venetian style. Most of the Vendramin's ten suites have views of St. Mark's Square. The historical Palazzetto, connected to the Palazzo Vendramin, has five junior suites overlooking spectacular

**HOTEL CIPRIANI &
PALAZZO VENDRAMIN**
Giudecca 10
30133 Venice, Italy

# Hotel Danieli

The opulent staircase that greets you as you enter the Hotel Danieli is a sure sign that you will be transported to a better way of living.

Since the 14th century, this palace has occupied a glorious site overlooking Venice's lagoon of the Grand Canal and adjacent to the Doge's Palace on St. Mark's Square. The palace was built for the noble Dandolo family, who accomplished such great feats as conquering Constantinople and bringing back the Four Horses that stand on the front of the Basilica di San Marco. The palace was converted into a hotel in 1822 after being purchased by Giuseppe Dal Niel. Danieli, Giuseppe's nickname, inspired the hotel's name.

Every light fixture is of Murano glass, but the lobby lounge is a marvel to behold with six huge sparkling Murano chandelier masterpieces. Both the lounge and the Bar Dandolo are terrific meeting places; whether for people watching, English tea in the afternoon or a drink before or after dinner. On the top floor, the Terrazza Restaurant features Italian cuisine and regional specialties for breakfast, lunch and dinner, but even better than the food is the view. In my opinion, the Hotel Danieli terrace has the best panoramic view of the splendors of Venice…a perfect place for a bellini, especially at sunset.

Live like a Doge at the Hotel Danieli.

Today's Danieli is composed of three buildings…the original Dandolo palace is linked by flying bridges to the adjacent palace, Casa Nuova, and the Danielino, constructed in 1948. In total, 233 rooms and 11 suites, many overlooking the lagoon, await your visit. Rich silk damasks, some woven with gold and silver thread, cover the walls, oriental rugs and frescoed ceilings reflect the Byzantine charm of this 14th century Venetian palace.

**HOTEL DANIELI**
Riva degli Schiavoni 4196
30122 Venice, Italy

# Europa & Regina

Europa & Regina is comprised of five 18th and 19th century houses with a splendid location on Venice's Grand Canal.

Each of the five palaces has a fascinating history. The oldest house, Palazzo Tiepolo, once belonged to the Tiepolo family who gave the city two doges and the 17th century painter Giambattista Tiepolo. Fine artists certainly take to this building; after it was transformed into a hotel, Claude Monet spent much of the autumn of 1908 here. An ancient squero, or workshop for gondola construction, once stood adjacent to Palazzo Tiepolo. Another one of the palaces was once the Minerva Theater, where the first opera composed by a young Rossini was performed.

Today, the five palaces blend perfectly to create one grand hotel. The public rooms have marble floors and walls, refined stuccowork and mosaic-framed mirrors. The 168 rooms and 17 suites incorporate Venetian and contemporary designs, some with lacquered furniture in pastel colors ranging from yellow to green to pink. The bathrooms of Portuguese pink, Alpine green or white Carrara marbles coordinate to match the color scheme of the room. The Europa & Regina also accommodates business travelers with ten "smart rooms," equipped with all modern office necessities.

La Cusina restaurant and terrace overlooking the Grand Canal is intimate with a menu based on the seasons and the market's freshest items. The Tiepolo Bar takes its design inspiration from Venetian salons and serves popular and distinctive cocktails. Don't ask for the recipes, though, because the bartenders will never reveal the secrets.

With hundreds of years of history from five buildings, Europa & Regina invites you to create your own history in Venice.

**EUROPA & REGINA**
San Marco 2159
30124 Venice, Italy

# Hotel Gritti Palace

The prestigious Hotel Gritti Palace is just as the "Doge" would want it.

The palace was home to the 77th Doge of Venice, Andrea Gritti. His formidable portrait hangs in the lobby, though you will not need a reminder that this hotel was once a palace. Everything here has an old-world elegance, from the fabrics and silks to the Murano glass.

The Gritti Palace is intimate, with only 82 rooms and 11 suites. The rooms are luxuriously decorated in Venetian style in pastel colors and period furnishings that truly sparkle. Located right on the Grand Canal and facing the Santa Maria della Salute Church, the Gritti Palace allows for terrific views.

A frequent guest of the hotel, Somerset Maugham said it well when he wrote, "there are few things in life more pleasant than to sit on the terrace of the Gritti." Take a table at the Terrace Restaurant and dine superbly while listening to the serenades of passing gondolas. Since 1975, the Gritti Palace has offered a four-day haute cuisine cooking school. Lessons covering the cuisine of the doges and cooking with fresh herbs are suitable for everyone, including beginners.

Venice's aura encourages you to spend time lingering over drinks in cafés and bars, and the Longhi Bar at the Gritti Palace is a perfect spot for an aperitif or after-dinner drink. Longhi, the 18th century Venetian painter, would be pleased to see the walls decorated with six paintings of his school.

Venice, in all of its resplendence, is epitomized at the Hotel Gritti Palace.

## HOTEL GRITTI PALACE
Campo Santa Maria
del Giglio, 2467
30124 Venice, Italy

# Hôtel de Paris

Dazzling visitors with its opulence, glamour and sophistication, Monte Carlo's Hôtel de Paris emanates the refinement of a bygone era. In this tiny principality, where yachts dot the coast and millionaires reside, the Hôtel de Paris symbolizes the Monegasque elegance and savoir faire.

Using only the best materials available and based on the design of the Grand Hôtel in Paris, the Hôtel de Paris opened in 1864 and quickly put Monte Carlo on the map. This renowned palace hotel has been a favorite of the rich and famous ever since. It became legendary for its lavish dinners and celebrations and for its

harbor or the splendid Royal Palace.

The Hôtel de Paris is closely linked to the world-famous Monte Carlo Casino in both location and spirit. It has been rumored that an underground tunnel connects the two and during the casino's renovations in 1878, the roulette wheel relocated to the Hôtel. The lobby's statue is also said to bring good luck to those who pat it.

Far from its simple origins as a deserted plateau with little more than lemon trees and olive groves, Monte Carlo and the Hôtel de Paris define elegance and luxury.

hosting of the world's elite in its 135 rooms, 19 junior suites and 43 apartments.

The Hôtel de Paris' tradition of great dining continues today. Alain Ducasse, the only 6-star chef in the world, presides over the Louis XV restaurant, which has garnered three Michelin stars. Or, sumptuously dine in the Grill on the top floor and gaze at the breathtaking

**HÔTEL DE PARIS**
Place du Casino
98000 Monte Carlo, Monaco

# Hotel Pulitzer

Hotel Pulitzer has been setting a stylish pace in Amsterdam for thirty years.

The Pulitzer is comprised of twenty-five 17th and 18th century narrow canalside buildings set on the Keizersgracht and Prinsengracht canals. Amsterdam's national treasures like Anne Frank's House, the Royal Palace, Dam Square and the Rijkmuseum are all within a short distance of the Pulitzer. Of course, the best way to explore this city is by boat on the famous canals and the hotel provides its own, moored directly in front of the hotel, for private tours.

of the hotel, original contemporary Dutch artwork is in all rooms. The hotel's art museum proves their commitment to art and maintains a significant collection of Dutch art.

Pulitzers Restaurant is chic and modern, with an intimate ambience and artistic design. Natural light floods the restaurant and natural partitions are created from the supporting walls of the many buildings. Artist Thierry de Cromieres created an original painting specifically for Pulitzers that will certainly catch your eye.

At once trendy and historic, Hotel Pulitzer is a special place in Amsterdam.

For guests' enjoyment, the Hotel also has a restaurant and bar, 3 courtyard gardens, an Art-Deco garden room and an art gallery.

The twenty-five buildings provide 223 guest rooms and 7 suites of different sizes and shapes with a unique Dutch character. The rooms' oak floors are fashioned in an Old Dutch block pattern and bathrooms are decorated with hand painted Dutch tiles. In keeping with the sleek style

**HOTEL PULITZER**
Prinsengracht 315-331
1016 Amsterdam,
The Netherlands

# Hotel Quinta do Lago

Quinta do Lago is the perfect playground in Portugal's Algarve region, known for its sandy beaches, temperate weather, championship golf and year-round sunshine.

The hotel is located within the 2,000-acre Ria Formosa Natural Park, overlooking the Atlantic Ocean. The 132 rooms and 9 suites, which overlook the landscaped gardens, golf course or the Atlantic Ocean, capitalize on the tropical setting with tiled terraces, natural wood and soft-hued fabrics.

Hotel Quinta do Lago provides so many activities that it is almost a crime to remain in

the room. Three championship golf courses are located within the hotel's grounds and five more are within a short distance. Two golf schools with multi-lingual, PGA-certified instructors will help you sharpen your skills, either with practice sessions or at the weeklong golf academy with instruction for all levels. The water sports center offers sailing, windsurfing, canoeing, deep-sea fishing and water skiing and swimmers will want to take advantage of the indoor and outdoor heated freshwater swimming pools. Guests seeking a retreat will be pleased with the short walk to the private, sandy beach with services like complimentary

mineral water, fruit kebobs, magazines and newspapers.

Hotel Quinta do Lago's dining options are as plentiful as its activities. The Ca d'Oro Restaurant specializes in Venetian cuisine and Brisa do Mar offers an international menu. The Poolside terrace and bar help satisfy your cravings while you relax in the sun and the Laguna Bar mixes sunset cocktails with live music.

Portugal's gold coast is blessed with sun, sand and golf, but mostly with Hotel Quinta do Lago.

**HOTEL QUINTA DO LAGO**
8135-024 Almancil, Algarve, Portugal

# Four Seasons Hotel The Ritz Lisbon

Prince Henry the Navigator, Ferdinand Magellan and Vasco de Gama explored the world in Portugal's name, but if they were alive today, they would need to look no further than Lisbon's own Four Seasons Hotel for treasure.

Located in the center of the city facing the Parque Eduardo VII, the Four Seasons Hotel The Ritz is just a short distance from Lisbon's major monuments and sights. The hotel has its own impressive and extensive collection of Portuguese artwork, carpets and tapestries. The collection's highlight is Pablo Picasso's *Girl with a Guitar*.

The hotel's 226 guest rooms and 58 suites are appointed in pleasant Portuguese colors and most have balconies with views of the gardens and park. Special suites include 18th century replicas by the Espirito Santo Foundation. Modern conveniences, like 24-hour business services and a spacious fitness center, make a visit to the Four Seasons comfortable for both business and leisure travelers.

Portuguese cuisine is served in the sophisticated setting of Varanda, with indoor and outdoor seating. Popular with Lisbon residents, it is considered to be one of the best restaurants in the city. The lobby lounge and terrace overlook the city skyline, while the bar provides an inviting and intimate setting.

At the Four Seasons Hotel, Lisbon's past and present join together.

**FOUR SEASONS HOTEL THE RITZ LISBON**
Rua Rodrigo da Fonseca, 88
1099-039 Lisbon, Portugal

# Lapa Palace

Located on a quiet street in Lisbon's exclusive Embassy district, Lapa Palace provides proximity to the city in a resort-like setting.

The mosaic-tiled circular driveway that welcomes arriving guests serves as a reminder of the hotel's past. Originally built as a private mansion for the Count of Valencas and his family in 1870, the building opened its doors as a hotel in 1992.

The traditional style of the Lapa Palace sets a refined tone in public and private rooms.

Richly painted tiles, or azulejos, enhance the interiors and are also used in the gardens and fountains. The 85 rooms and 9 suites are located in the main building and the poolside wing, and all have views of either the Tagus River or the hotel's gardens. Rooms in the main building are classically styled with 18th century furnishings, while rooms in the Palace wing are influenced by Art Deco.

The gardens provide a tranquil setting for the outdoor swimming pool where chirping birds and trickling fountains add to the serenity. The fully equipped fitness center provides an indoor pool, Turkish and Scottish baths and solarium.

Lapa Palace provides exquisite dining options from internationally recognized Ristorante Hotel Cipriani, with fine Italian and international cuisine, or the Rio Tejo Bar for informal gatherings. Barbecues and light snacks are served poolside during the summer months.

Luxurious and peaceful, the Lapa Palace feels like your own private mansion in the heart of Lisbon.

**LAPA PALACE**
Rua do Pau de Bandeira no. 4
1249-021 Lisbon, Portugal

# Reid's Palace

Four hundred miles off the west coast of Africa, Madeira is the closest sub-tropical island to Europe. This island that shares its name with its most famous export, Madeira wine, is home to one of the world's most famous hotels.

Reid's Palace was founded in 1891 by William Reid. Its clifftop location amid ten acres of sub-tropical gardens makes it an idyllic escape. Visitors have escaped to Reid's Palace since its opening. Winston Churchill spent time here recovering from a minor stroke and working on his war memoirs. Three swimming pools, including a tidal seawater pool, paragliding, parasailing and two golf courses keep guests active.

Trattoria Villa Cliff and Reid's Sandwich Bar.

The Edwardian traditions of Reid's Palace are maintained today, and afternoon tea is one of the joys of a stay here. This very British tea service is famous on Sundays, when it is enhanced by its renowned tango lessons on the lawn. Irish playwright and Nobel Prize winner George Bernard Shaw learned to tango while visiting Reid's. After his two-month visit, Shaw gave the instructor a signed photograph inscribed, "to the only man who ever taught me anything."

Come to Reid's Palace to share traditions and explore this unspoiled island.

The traditional 130 rooms and 32 suites also incorporate the island's decor with wicker furniture on the terraces. Updated with the conveniences of modern technology, the rooms enchant with their views of the lush gardens or the crashing sea below.

Tradition extends to dining, where formal dressing for dinner is revived in the main Victorian-style dining room. Casual dining is available at the

**REID'S PALACE**
Estrada Monumental 139
9000-098 Funchal, Madeira,
Portugal

# Hotel Baltschug Kempinski

The collapse of Communism has brought a new face to all of Russia, especially Moscow. Capitalism has replaced Iron Curtain-era bread lines and the city is pulsing with energy.

Hotel Baltschug Kempinski is a symbol of modern Russia. Its historical façade is complemented by a striking, contemporary interior. Standing on the banks of Moskva River, the hotel is directly across from Red Square, the Kremlin and St. Basil's Cathedral. This area, known as the Balchug Quarter, has

been favored for its central, yet removed, location since the time of the Czars.

Old and new Russia come together in the 220 rooms and 30 suites here. Distinctly Russian with the use of red tones and Bruyere wood, all rooms are also completely modernized, thanks to the exacting standards of Kempinski Hotels. The location near Moscow's cultural and business centers makes Hotel Baltschug perfect for leisure and business travelers alike. Travelers on business will appreciate the special care taken with efficient secretarial and translation services, as well as the state-of-the-art equipment.

Hotel Baltschug's signature restaurant has dramatic views of Red Square while the Restaurant Baltschug serves a la carte specials and nightly theme buffets. The hotel also has a stylish bar, vibrant lobby lounge and a coffeehouse with a tempting array of sweets.

Rediscover Russia's history while acquainting yourself with new traditions at Hotel Baltschug Kempinski.

**HOTEL BALTSCHUG KEMPINSKI**
Ulitsa Balchug 1
113035 Moscow, Russia

# Hotel Astoria

St. Petersburg is a magical and wondrous place. Founded by Peter the Great in 1703, the city's many islands linked by canals and bridges are reminiscent of Venice and much of the architecture hints at Paris. While European influences abound, it is St. Petersburg's Russian roots that make it so unique. The splendor of the Czars at the Winter Palace and Hermitage is simply beyond compare.

The stylish Hotel Astoria mirrors the city's sophistication and heritage. Its exclusive address places it ten minutes from the Hermitage and adjacent to another of St. Petersburg's famous landmarks, St. Isaac's Cathedral. It is one of the world's three largest domed cathedrals and is lavishly decorated with mosaics, malachite, lazulite, marble and other precious materials. Hotel Astoria blends contemporary sensibility with Russian tradition. The 192 rooms and 48 suites have been redecorated with an uncluttered, modern décor, yet the fascinating history of the city is never forgotten thanks to the terrific views of St. Isaac's Square and the monument of Nicholas I, which are available from most of the rooms.

Davidov's Restaurant, with its menu, entertainment, spectacular caviar and vodka display and fine Lomonosov porcelain, is a true Russian experience. Its romantic, chandelier-lit room overlooks St. Isaac's. Borsalino Restaurant emphasizes international cuisine and even provides a Japanese corner at breakfast. A delightful Russian tea service is served in the lobby lounge and the Rotunda Bar is a relaxing spot for cocktails.

With his taste for modernity, there is no doubt that Peter the Great himself would adore Hotel Astoria.

**HOTEL ASTORIA**
39, Bolshaya Morskaya
190000 St. Petersburg,
Russia

# Grand Hotel Europe

Grand Hotel Europe, St. Petersburg's oldest hotel, is an enduring legend.

In a city where every corner has a story to tell, the Grand Hotel Europe is a landmark in its own right. Founded more than 125 years ago, it has faced revolution, changes in political ideology and war while adjusting to the times. During the Bolshevik Revolution, the glorious hotel was transformed into an orphanage and it became a much-needed hospital during the 900-day siege of Leningrad.

The Grand Hotel Europe, a Kempinski Hotel, enjoys a prime location off Nevsky Prospect. In the heart of the historic district,

Seven restaurants and bars make the Grand Hotel Europe the center of attention in St. Petersburg. The Europe Restaurant is a glory to behold with stained glass ceilings and windows, five balconies and recessed dining areas. Relive the grandeur of the Czars here, where the menu is inspired by traditional Russian recipes and ingredients. Chinese dishes, Italian and Mediterranean specialties and vegetarian dishes are also to be enjoyed in a variety of settings, while the Caviar Bar encourages you to sip champagne or vodka while tasting the best caviar.

Experience the glory of St. Petersburg while staying at the Grand Hotel Europe.

the hotel is near the Church of the Spilled Blood, where Czar Alexander II was assassinated, and within walking distance of the Hermitage within the Winter Palace and numerous other historic landmarks like Yusopov Palace. The 228 guest rooms and 73 suites cater to discriminating travelers with a graceful combination of precious antiques, Art Nouveau designs and modern amenities. Tchaikovsky, Pavlova and Dostoyevsky all once graced the halls here.

## GRAND HOTEL EUROPE KEMPINSKI
Mikhailovskaya 1/7
191011 St. Petersburg, Russia

# Gleneagles

Located one hour northwest of Edinburgh, Gleneagles gloriously rests within 850 acres in the misty Perthshire countryside.

Opened in 1924, Gleneagles was built by the Caledonian Railway Company and had its own railway station. It quickly earned a reputation as "the Riviera in the Highlands." With its grand tradition and wealth of aristocratic country pursuits, Gleneagles indeed feels like an exclusive private club. Three world-renowned championship golf courses, The Queen's Course, The King's Course and The Jack Nicklaus Centenary Course, have hosted prestigious tournaments throughout the years and make Gleneagles a top destination for all golfers. A fourth course, the 9 hole Wee Course, is provided for beginners. The exceptional golf academy provides individual or group instruction that is guaranteed to improve your swing or lower your handicap.

Gleneagles is not just for golfers, however. Choose from the centuries-old sport of falconry, or sharpen your skills at the world-class Jackie Stewart Shooting School. The Equestrian Center is one of the world's best, while the terrain just outside of Gleneagles is perfect for off-road driving enthusiasts. Among other activities, a fitness center and spa with beauty and relaxation treatments are also available.

After a day of activity, you will be pleased to retire to one of the lovely 219 rooms and 14 suites. The rooms are spacious and soothing, with subtle colors, traditional Scottish patterns, and unobstructed views of the estate. The restaurants offer a tempting array of choices, from the hearty fare at The Dorny Clubhouse to casual, Mediterranean cuisine at The Club and the exquisite fine dining at the Strathearn Restaurant.

The fantastic experiences offered at Gleneagles will make you want to head for the Scottish Highlands.

GLENEAGLES
Auchterarder, Perthshire,
PH3 1NF, Scotland

# The Balmoral

Edinburgh, Scotland's capital city, is home to the charming and inviting Balmoral. The regal, Edwardian-style hotel opened in 1902 at the top of Princes Street, the city's main shopping promenade. Though Edinburgh's most famous landmark is the imposing castle built upon an ancient volcano, The Balmoral's clock tower is a close second. You may not choose to set your watch by it, though, as it is always set two minutes fast to ensure guests catch their trains on time!

The hotel's 165 rooms and 21 suites are

traditionally Scottish in their use of colors and patterns and are elegantly furnished. The one-of-a-kind Scone & Crombie suite is spacious and sumptuous. Rooms offer views of Edinburgh Castle, the gardens or the rolling hills beyond the city.

The Balmoral's restaurants range from casual and contemporary at Hadrian's Brasserie to formal and sophisticated at Number One. The fitness center has the largest swimming pool in Edinburgh and the spa provides a pleasant retreat. On the edge of the city, 22 golf courses and two trout streams tempt athletic-minded guests. The cultural capital of Scotland, Edinburgh hosts the latest West End productions and ballets, and the world-famous Military Tattoo every August. Of course, there are numerous historical sites to explore, from the Castle to Hopetoun House, one of Scotland's finest 18th century Adam architectural masterpieces, to the Palace of Holyrood House, a royal residence and one-time home to Mary, Queen of Scots.

In the center of it all, The Balmoral is the correct choice for experiencing Edinburgh at its best.

**THE BALMORAL**
1 Princes Street
Edinburgh EH2 2EQ,
Scotland

# Hotel Arts Barcelona

Barcelona is a feast for the eyes, with some of the world's most fascinating and fanciful architecture. Though it is best known for Gaudi's often outrageous buildings, one of the city's finest hotels is also one of its architectural landmarks.

The 44 stories of exposed glass and steel make Hotel Arts Barcelona the tallest building in Spain and an impressive feature on Barcelona's skyline. This contemporary building sits waterfront in the Olympic Village area, and commands astounding views of the port and Mediterranean. It is minutes away from the wide boulevards and busy social scene of Las Ramblas and the medieval intimacy of the Gothic Quarter, yet Hotel Arts is also its own exciting world.

The interiors of the 397 rooms, 58 suites and 27 private duplex apartments reflect the exterior of the hotel, with modern furnishings and 21st century technology. All rooms are equipped with sleek Bang & Olufsen audio equipment and bedside panels control the room's lighting. Large windows showcase Barcelona's natural beauty and marina.

Hotel Arts provides all the services expected of a hotel in the acclaimed Ritz-Carlton group. Two bars, one lounge and three diverse restaurants serve varied cuisine in a variety of settings. Fitness and business facilities are well equipped and staffed by professionals.

Hotel Arts Barcelona towers above the rest with its fine service and chic simplicity.

**HOTEL ARTS
BARCELONA**
Carrer de la Marina, 19-21
08005 Barcelona, Spain

# Kempinski Resort Hotel

The playful and sunny stretch of Spanish coastline known as the Costa del Sol is blessed with sandy beaches, blue water and time for relaxation.

Occupying a prime, beachfront location, Kempinski Resort Hotel Estepona extends a warm welcome. Set within lush, secluded gardens with cascading waterfalls, the resort feels far away from the many homelands of its guests. Not far from Gibraltar on the Costa del Sol, the resort offers distant views of the African coast from its rooms. The 131 rooms and 17 suites are classically inviting and open onto large, terracotta-tiled terraces that overlook

the sea. The vibrant works by artist Stefan Szczesny can be enjoyed throughout the hotel, from indoors at reception to the large painted amphoras in the garden.

The resort's location allows for numerous activities, both on and off the property. Thirty golf courses are within close proximity, and tennis facilities are provided on the grounds. The sandy beach is just outside your door and the water

sports facility ensures your aquatic enjoyment. The resort's fitness center includes an indoor pool and gym, while Turkish baths, Thalasso water treatments, Rasul bath, Bio Steam and massage treatments are available at the wellness center.

The restaurant offers fresh, and sometimes exotic, Mediterranean cuisine in a relaxed setting and the poolside restaurant has authentic regional Spanish food. The two bars add spice to your nights.

Kempinski Resort Hotel Estepona is a perfect Spanish vacation retreat.

**KEMPINSKI RESORT HOTEL ESTEPONA**
Ctra. de Cadiz, km 159
29680 Estepona, Spain

# Hotel Ritz

Once the center of a far-reaching global empire, Madrid is a thriving city with a regal past. Its Golden Age splendor is shared in the city's museums. In fact, there are more masterpieces per square mile in Madrid than anywhere else in the world.

Hotel Ritz, facing the famous Prado and Thyssen Museums, is the city's most prestigious address. Necessity is the mother of invention, and the Hotel Ritz is no exception. When preparing for his daughter's marriage, King Alfonso XIII realized that no hotel in Madrid was fit for hosting the illustrious wedding guests. Inspired by the grand monuments and resplendent palaces he visited on his travels, Alfonso XIII set about constructing a grand hotel, hired the best architects and personally oversaw the entire project. This Belle Epoque masterpiece opened in 1910 and continues to be one of the most glamorous hotels in Europe today.

The 129 rooms and 29 suites are truly fit for royalty. The décor is refined and lavish, yet never garish. Beautiful handmade carpets, period furniture, antique accessories and embroidered linens lend a regal touch. Rich colors imbue warmth. Many rooms overlook Lealtad Square or the Prado Museum. Outside your room, the hotel is centrally located and most of Madrid's major points of interest lie just a short walk from here.

The richly decorated Goya Restaurant defines elegant dining. The acclaimed menu focuses on international cuisine, though Spanish specialties, like Madrilenian cocido, are also offered. All of Madrid comes to the Ritz Terrace and Gardens for typical Spanish tapas in a refreshing setting. The lobby serves an intimate afternoon tea, while the cocktails at the Bar Velazquez are delightful.

Hotel Ritz celebrates timeless elegance.

**HOTEL RITZ**
Plaza de la Lealtad, 5
28014 Madrid, Spain

# Beau-Rivage

Geneva, with its French style and Swiss sensibility, is a polished and well-heeled city. Set on Lake Geneva's southwestern tip, the city enjoys staggering views of the Alps and Mont-Blanc.

Beau-Rivage, located directly on the shores of the lake, is a luxurious hotel and a city institution. Founded in 1865, Beau-Rivage is the oldest privately owned hotel in Geneva. The fourth generation of the Mayer family runs the hotel today with the same exacting standards, dedication and pride of their great-grandfather.

Beau-Rivage's 91 rooms and 6 suites are luxurious without ostentation. The suites are regally appointed with period furnishings, while the guest rooms exude intimacy with warm colors and lake views. L'Atrium Bar is a nice spot for traditional English afternoon tea or cocktails. The food will tempt and the setting will enchant at Beau-Rivage's restaurant, Le Chat-Botte, which has won accolades for its superior cuisine.

Beau-Rivage delights with its tradition and unique character.

Beau-Rivage has a storied past. Visiting royals often selected Beau-Rivage as their temporary home because of its luxurious interiors and sterling service. Though many illustrious guests passed through these doors, it is Empress Elizabeth of Austria's tragic visit that is most often remembered. After being stabbed in the city's streets by an anarchist, the Empress was rushed back to her suite where she was unable to be saved. A beautiful suite pays tribute to her today.

BEAU-RIVAGE
13, Quai du Mont-Blanc
1201 Geneva, Switzerland

# Mandarin Oriental Hotel du Rhône

Mandarin Oriental Hotel du Rhône is a fashionable choice in the heart of Geneva.

Situated on the right bank of the Rhône River, the Mandarin Oriental is only minutes from the city's flourishing businesses, exclusive boutiques and cultural attractions. The early Modernist and Art Deco design influences reflect its history as the first hotel built in Europe following World War II.

The 180 rooms and 12 suites are elegant, but understated. Luxurious materials like parquet floors and marble complement the simple lines of the Swiss-made furnishings. Comfort is a priority in all rooms, even amenities like heated bathroom floors.

While the hotel's design harkens back to the 1950's, the technology is decidedly 21st century. All rooms are equipped with fax machines and each guest is assigned a private number for the duration of their stay. Two telephone lines, as well as four handsets, are provided for guests' use.

Two terrific restaurants are located within the hotel. Le Neptune, as you would suspect, specializes in seafood and changes seasonally.

Neptune, the Roman god of the sea, is depicted in the murals and in summer, the pleasing restaurant extends to the terrace with views over the river. The Café serves a light seasonal menu in a pleasant, informal setting.

For a stylish choice in Geneva, stay at the contemporary Mandarin Oriental Hotel du Rhône.

**MANDARIN ORIENTAL HOTEL DU RHÔNE**
Quai Turrettini 1
1201 Geneva,
Switzerland

# Le Richemond

The sumptuous interiors and club-like atmosphere of Le Richemond have attracted guests for over 125 years.

Gracing the shores of Lake Geneva, Le Richemond overlooks the greenery of Jardin Brunswick in the heart of the business district. Le Richemond's 19th century glamour and signature crimson red are seen throughout the private and public rooms. The hotel's 67 rooms and 31 suites are individually decorated and lavishly appointed with rich, jewel tones, refined furniture and distinctive antiques. Beautiful views of Lake Geneva, Jardin Brunswick or the charming courtyard can be enjoyed from all rooms.

Founded by A.R. Armleder, Le Richemond has been home to

many artists, including Charlie Chaplin, Marc Chagall and Colette, who lovingly described the hotel in her writings. A stunning suite pays tribute to her today. Since 1989, the Armleder Foundation has awarded a literary prize, known as the "Prix Colette," to honor her memory as well as the art of writing.

A city landmark, Le Richemond is also a favorite of Geneva's citizens who regularly dine in one of the three restaurants. Italian and Mediterranean influenced cuisine is served at Le Jardin, which lives up to its name with a gorgeous flower-decked terrace. Its striking Art Deco décor makes it a favorite of prominent members of society. Gourmet food in a clubhouse setting is offered at Le Gentilhomme. The charming pavilion of The Cottage is tucked amidst the greenery of the Jardin Brunswick in front of the hotel. This haven right in the middle of the city is perfect for lunch, dinner or an afternoon refreshment.

Return to the elegance of a bygone era at Le Richemond.

**LE RICHEMOND**
Jardin Brunswick
1201 Geneva, Switzerland

# Victoria-Jungfrau Grand Hotel & Spa

Nestled between Lake Thun and Lake Brienz in the scenic Bernese Oberland, Interlaken is the Swiss capital of year-round sport adventure. Its mountainous setting makes for terrific hiking and paragliding in summer, while winter months are perfect for snowboarding and skiing.

For over 135 years, Victoria-Jungfrau Grand Hotel & Spa has been keeping up with trends while honoring rich traditions. The 118 rooms and 94 suites are in Swiss contemporary design. Bright splashes of color used on a chair or a swag

add a lively touch. Superb views of the snow-capped or green mountains top off the pleasant surroundings. Three restaurants are located within the hotel, and gourmet cuisine, Swiss favorites and specially created spa menus are offered.

The sleek Victoria-Jungfrau Spa is one of Europe's best. The fitness facility provides advanced equipment and stimulating lessons, like gymnastic instruction and sport-specific training. Not restricted to four walls, the spa ventures outside to offer river rafting and canyoning, among other sports. The spa caters to sports enthusiasts and non-athletes alike with a variety of soothing and relaxing treatments. Whether you ski or indulge in a body treatment, you can be assured that the staff of doctors, nutritionists, physiotherapists and sports coaches will provide expert advice.

The genuine hospitality and variety of thrilling adventures make Victoria-Jungfrau Grand Hotel & Spa the epitome of Interlaken and Switzerland.

**VICTORIA-JUNGFRAU GRAND HOTEL & SPA**
3800 Interlaken, Switzerland

# Beau-Rivage Palace

Beau-Rivage Palace invites you to trace the steps of Russian archdukes, English lords and other nobility who have visited this esteemed hotel since 1861.

Beau-Rivage Palace occupies an idyllic spot on the shores of Lake Geneva in Lausanne's residential area of Ouchy. Surrounded by ten acres of park-like greenery and private gardens, the hotel affords picturesque views of the Alps.

Beau-Rivage Palace's tradition of excellence coupled with its stunning scenery makes it one of Switzerland's finest hotels. The 140 guest rooms and 29 suites are traditional in feel, yet distinctive. Each room's individual character is defined by glittering chandeliers, exquisite Persian rugs and glorious fabrics. State-of-the-art communications and glorious views of the grounds and lake round out the experience.

Outdoor activities abound at Beau-Rivage Palace. Enjoy the pleasures of the lake on one of the spectacular lake cruises or take an excursion to the Swiss Alps. An 18 hole golf course is nearby, fabulous skiing is just 40 minutes away, while the hotel provides its own tennis courts and a stunning indoor/outdoor pool. The fitness center has a sauna, Turkish baths, solarium and beauty salon with Guerlain and Chanel booths.

The dining choices at Beau-Rivage Palace are plentiful and delectable. La Rotonde is renowned for its gourmet cuisine in a beautiful setting complete with marble floors and potted palms. Café Beau-Rivage is based on a Parisian brasserie with a contemporary informal atmosphere, while the Grill Piscine features lunch by the pool or dinner by candlelight. The Wine Bar features international and Swiss wines, and the English Bar has a cozy, clubby ambience ideal for extending your evening celebration.

Distinguished and classic, the Beau-Rivage Palace is a wonderful place for a relaxing holiday.

**BEAU-RIVAGE PALACE**
1006 Lausanne, Switzerland

# Palace Luzern

Set on the banks of Lake Lucerne within private gardens, the luxurious Palace Luzern is a peaceful retreat.

Located in central Switzerland, Lucerne is an idyllic Swiss Alpine city complete with covered bridges, medieval chapels and narrow streets. This storybook setting makes it an ideal spot for a restful holiday, while five golf courses and a wide variety of year-round sporting activities provide many leisure opportunities.

The city's most distinguished hotel, Palace Luzern, has elegantly greeted guests since 1906 except during World War II. During the war it was used as a military ambulance station and military commissariat. After complete renovation, it reopened its doors in 1946. Even with constant innovations and improvements, its classic atmosphere and tradition evoke old-world Europe.

The 178 guest rooms and suites pay homage to the past with traditional style furniture and materials. Many rooms maintain the hotel's original Art Nouveau decor. The historic character of the hotel is complemented by the latest technology. At Palace Luzern, antique chandeliers are at home with ISDN lines.

Palace Luzern's restaurants combine spectacular settings with superb dining. Le Mignon is renowned for its French cuisine. In summertime an attractive terrace right on the lakeside promenade complements this formal dining room. Also located on the lakeside promenade, Le Maritime has a charming garden terrace with a pleasing atmosphere for more casual fare. Le Gourmet is particularly inviting with panoramic lake views.

The Wellness Corner is relaxing with saunas, steam baths, a solarium and massages. Boating excursions on the lake are popular, as are hiking, mountain climbing, golf and world-class skiing.

Palace Luzern is a perfect blend of old and new in scenic Switzerland.

**PALACE LUZERN**
Haldenstrasse 10
6002 Lucerne, Switzerland

# Badrutt's Palace

Switzerland's St. Moritz is the ultimate ski resort, and Badrutt's Palace is the ultimate hotel in St. Moritz.

Caspar Badrutt opened Badrutt's Palace in 1896. Though it is managed by Rosewood Hotels, it still belongs to the Badrutt family today and they are actively involved in running the property. Badrutt's Palace looks like a majestic palace set on six acres of private grounds with spectacular views of the mountains and lake.

St. Moritz is a winter wonderland and a summer paradise. In winter, skiing is the most popular alpine sport, and Badrutt's has one of the best ski schools, as well as a ski shop for all necessary equipment. The ice rink on the property

has a resident pro, and other outdoor activities will be arranged at your request. In warmer months, Badrutt's guests may take lessons with the tennis pro on one of the courts, swim in the indoor or outdoor pools or play golf at the nearby course. Badrutt's is also the official home of the St. Moritz Polo Club. An exclusive shopping gallery, home to internationally recognized names like Giorgio Armani, Versace, Cartier and Louis Vuitton, is located within the hotel.

The 170 rooms and 39 suites are tastefully decorated in a traditional style and are mood enhancing with their bright colors and flowered fabrics. Rooms overlook the lake, mountains or the grounds. Badrutt's Palace has a large variety of lounges and restaurants to suit all preferences. During the winter, the Moorish style King's Club Disco is one of Europe's most popular clubs. Additionally, the rustic Chesa Veglia offers even more dining options. Located two minutes from the hotel and owned by the Badrutt family, it is one of the oldest houses in St. Moritz in a casual, country style and features Engadine and Swiss specialties.

Far from a simple ski lodge, Badrutt's Palace entertains you in a grand style.

## BADRUTT'S PALACE
7500 St. Moritz, Switzerland

# Park Hotel Vitznau

With its gabled roofs and stone tower, the romantic Park Hotel Vitznau is like a fairy tale castle.

The hotel majestically rests on the shores of Lake Lucerne in Vitznau, a picturesque hamlet just over one hour from Zurich. This Alpine wonderland is complete with snow-capped mountains and verdant pastures. In Vitznau, the soothing ring of the cowbells is the only audible noise.

The distinguished Park Hotel is a far cry from its simple origins as a boarding house that hosted Victor Hugo and Mark Twain. The 71 rooms and 33 suites evoke repose with their pastel colors and large balconies that open to the gardens and lake. Asian-inspired decorative objects delightfully grace the traditional furnishings and exceptional flowers grown in the hotel's greenhouse are thoughtfully placed throughout the spacious rooms.

Taking advantage of the great outdoors is something that guests at the Park Hotel Vitznau must do. You can play a game of tennis, swim in the indoor and outdoor pool or take an excursion on the lake. You can even ride Europe's first cogwheel railway to the summit of Mt. Rigi, where you can take in the breathtaking views of the Alps.

Three restaurants offer exquisite food in equally exceptional surroundings. Quatre Cantons is commended for its gourmet menu and incomparable setting overlooking the garden. The Panorama Restaurant offers international and Swiss cuisine in a romantic ambience complete with musicians and lake views. The poolside restaurant is convenient and casual.

Storybook memories are to be made at Park Hotel Vitznau.

PARK HOTEL VITZNAU
6354 Vitznau, Switzerland

# Grand Hotel Zermatterhof

Zermatt is an idyllic Swiss village. The air is especially pristine here because there are no cars, only horse drawn carriages. This year-round resort at the base of the Matterhorn is blessed with high altitudes and excellent snow conditions in winter, making it a skier's paradise. During summer months, the region is ideal for glacier skiing, hiking along pine-scented trails, or simply relaxing.

dome, transforming it into a winter garden, and Le Jardin is open in the summer months for alfresco dining. Make sure to try the Swiss cheese raclette!

In addition to the recreational activities available outdoors in Zermatt, the Grand Hotel has a fitness facility with a semi-Olympic-size swimming pool as well as a sauna, solarium and exercise room.

Grand Hotel Zermatterhof is the ideal choice for an active holiday.

Grand Hotel Zermatterhof has been welcoming visitors since 1879. Though the hotel's private gardens may deceive you with their secluded feel, the Grand Hotel is located on the village's main street. Awaken each

morning to the sound of tinkling bells as a small group of goats is herded through town to the hills. The Matterhorn, Zermatt's centerpiece, is visible from most of the 61 rooms and 25 suites. While some rooms resemble a ski chalet with vaulted, wooden ceilings and country fabrics, others are more contemporary with pastel colors and blonde wood.

Gracious hospitality extends to the hotel's restaurants. Restaurant Prato Borni is ideal for creating special memories. Its gourmet five-course dinners are a celebration of the culinary arts. The rotisserie La Broche has a wonderful glass

**GRAND HOTEL ZERMATTERHOF**
Bahnhofstrasse
3920 Zermatt, Switzerland

# Hotel Baur au Lac

Having the world's fourth largest stock exchange, Zurich is Switzerland's business capital and one of the world's leading banking cities. It is a beautiful combination of the modern and old world, with very charming, cobblestone streets and Alpine clocktowers of the Old Town mixing with the exclusive boutiques of the modern Bahnhofstrasse. In the center of it all is the Hotel Baur au Lac.

The Baur au Lac delightfully rests within private grounds overlooking the lake. Resembling a large villa, this aristocratic hotel was founded in 1844 by Johannes Baur and has always been a favorite

of a powerful, international set. Richard Wagner gave the world premiere of the first act of his *Die Walkure* at the hotel and the idea for the prestigious Nobel Prize was formulated here.

The Baur au Lac's style is greatly influenced by its international clientele. The 83 rooms and 42 suites are individually decorated in various styles, including Louis XVI, Directoire, Empire, Regency and Chippendale. The furnishings are carefully selected to enhance the beauty of the room while considering the

needs of all visitors. Of course, modern technology is available in every room.

Some of Zurich's finest food can be found within the Baur au Lac's four restaurants. Whether you seek fine dining or a simple snack within the fragrant garden, the restaurants will not disappoint. An exclusive nightclub, available only to hotel guests and club members, keeps you dancing all night.

Traveling for business or leisure is always a pleasure at the Hotel Baur au Lac.

**HOTEL BAUR AU LAC**
Talstrasse 1
8001 Zurich, Switzerland

# Dolder Grand Hotel

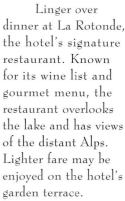

For over 100 years, the landmark Dolder Grand Hotel has rested on a wooded hill overlooking the city of Zurich.

The Dolder Grand's site offers a unique way to experience Zurich. The businesses and attractions of the city are just a short funicular ride away, yet the natural setting provides a tranquil alternative to the bustling city. A beautiful 9 hole golf course sits outside the hotel's entrance, and clay tennis courts are located nearby. In winter, rent skates at the ice skating rink or swim in the special swimming pool with artificially produced waves. The forests that shade this exclusive residential area are perfect for exploration, whether you choose to hike or jog.

The Dolder Grand's architecture of turrets and gables is incredibly romantic. The 144 rooms and 35 suites are warmly decorated. Rooms in the main building are traditional with formal furnishings, while rooms in the newer wing use soft pastels and white as the main palette. It is not uncommon to find a fawn and its mother grazing outside the forest-view rooms. Other rooms offer terrific city and lake views.

Linger over dinner at La Rotonde, the hotel's signature restaurant. Known for its wine list and gourmet menu, the restaurant overlooks the lake and has views of the distant Alps. Lighter fare may be enjoyed on the hotel's garden terrace.

With its secluded setting, yet convenient location to the city, the Dolder Grand Hotel offers a romantic and peaceful way to visit Zurich.

**DOLDER GRAND HOTEL**
Kurhausstrasse 65
8032 Zurich, Switzerland

# Ciragan Palace Hotel Kempinski

Founded in 330 AD as Constantinople, Istanbul straddles the Asian and European continents and offers an intoxicating blend of cultures. The city has a dizzying pace and its sounds and sights intensify your experience, whether you are haggling in the Grand Bazaar or watching the Muslims heed the muezzin's call to prayer.

The city was home to the Byzantines, Romans and Ottomans, but it is the last great civilization that we have to thank for one of the city's most glorious hotels, Ciragan Palace Hotel Kempinski. The hotel is a former palace of the last Ottoman sultan. Rebuilt several times over two centuries, it sits right on the Bosphorus, the waterway that divides Europe and Asia. Though a devastating fire consumed the building in 1910, it was carefully restored to its original splendor.

Ciragan Palace defines opulence. The 284 rooms and 20 suites are lavish with Ottoman décor and fabrics, and are decidedly romantic with incomparable views of the Bosphorus. The Sultan Suite is extraordinary, from its ornate decoration to its pool-size sunken marble bath. Even the original marble hamam has been restored for use as a private function room. Do ask to see it!

Committed to preserving the hotel's history, the Tugra Restaurant serves traditional Ottoman cuisine recreated from genuine Palace recipes. Of course, other choices are available...from Italian, Continental and nouveau cuisine to Turkish delights...and all with incredible views.

Leisurely hours may be spent at Ciragan Palace's Turkish bath or on Istanbul's only putting green and infinity swimming pool on the shores of the Bosphorus.

Live like a sultan at the Ciragan Palace Hotel Kempinski.

**CIRAGAN PALACE HOTEL KEMPINSKI**
Ciragan Caddesi 84
Besiktas, 80700
Istanbul, Turkey

# Four Seasons Hotel Istanbul

You must look closely at the Four Seasons Hotel to discover its history. A few tiles and marble columns remain, but the building's layout with an enclosed courtyard is the largest clue to its former life as the Sultanahmet prison. Built eighty years ago to house Turkey's dissident writers and politicians, today it attracts guests of a different nature.

The Neo-Classical building is located in Istanbul's historic quarter with its wonderful and exotic attractions. Everything is within walking distance and the Blue

Mosque and Hagia Sofia are visible from the hotel. The Four Seasons Hotel mixes its renowned standards with a true sense of locale. Whether you are relaxing in the lounge or lobby, or luxuriating in one of the 54 guest rooms and 11 suites, there is never a doubt that you are in Turkey. Ottoman antiques, kilim carpets and tapestries decorate private and public rooms. The softly painted walls are distressed, following methods used by artisans in the Ottoman palaces.

As a city, Istanbul echoes one of its many great attractions, the Grand Bazaar. Full of energy, the city's colors and sounds compete for your attention. In comparison, the Four Seasons Hotel has a decidedly uncluttered feeling throughout. Dining is equally peaceful at the two restaurants. While those incarcerated once desired to flee from this building, you will undoubtedly hope to never leave.

Let the Four Seasons Hotel Istanbul hold you captive.

**FOUR SEASONS HOTEL ISTANBUL**
Tevkifhane Sokak No. 1
34490 Sultanahmet-Eminönü,
Istanbul, Turkey

# The St. David's Hotel & Spa

The Welsh waterfront capital of Cardiff is a new destination. Its boom can be felt throughout the city, from the thriving business center to the new homes for the Welsh Assembly and the Welsh National Opera to the revitalized waterfront community of Cardiff Bay. This exclusive area is home to the newly minted St. David's Hotel & Spa.

The St. David's Hotel & Spa is thoroughly modern. Its lobby and atrium will astonish you with their dramatic flair. The clean, simple lines of glass and steel welcome you at reception. The 116 rooms and 20 suites use contemporary Italian furnishings to complete the sleek décor and the panoramic views are best enjoyed from the private balconies available in all rooms.

Sophistication is paramount at the St. David's Hotel, and Tides Restaurant & Bar reflects that principle. Floor-to-ceiling views of Cardiff Bay are accompanied by a wide variety of dishes based on fresh and local produce. Spa visitors seeking lighter meals need only ask at the restaurant.

Visitors to the spa at St. David's will quickly forget their woes. This health facility and spa is the first of its kind in Wales. Cardiff's aquatic setting influences the spa's philosophy and treatments, with hydrotherapy serving as the main focus. The saltwater hydro-pool massages the tensions away with its warm water treatments, while the swimming pool affords bay views.

Conduct your business in style at The St. David's Hotel & Spa.

**THE ST. DAVID'S HOTEL & SPA**
Havannah Street
Cardiff 10 5SD Wales

# Africa & Indian Ocean

BOTSWANA

EGYPT

KENYA

MAURITIUS

MOROCCO

SEYCHELLES

SOUTH AFRICA

# Chobe Chilwero & Chief's Camp

Botswana's glories are shared at Abercrombie & Kent's Chobe Chilwero and Chief's Camp.

Chobe National Park is home to an abundance of wildlife, although it is best known for having the world's largest elephant population. The region's diversity assures a fabulous safari. Translated to "place of high view," Chobe Chilwero is an intimate, stylish safari lodge overlooking lush plains and river islands on the edge of Chobe National Park. The 15 safari cottages are decorated in an eclectic African style with unique artifacts. Somali headrests, Makonda combs, a pygmy shield from the Congo and a honey gatherer's ladder from Zambia are just some of the intriguing objects you will discover. The bathrooms are exceptional with handmade free-form bathtubs and outdoor showers. Dining at Chobe Chilwero is a far cry from rustic with Western and African cuisine and fine South African wines.

Many years ago, a chieftain of Botswana's Batawana tribe discovered a place so rich and beautiful, he made it his private hunting ground. What was once only explored by him is now available to all at Chief's Camp, on Chief's Island in the Mombo concession of the Moremi Game Reserve. This untamed and unexplored region of the Okavango Delta is home to a large number of predators and plains game animals like cheetah, lion, leopard, and painted wild dog plus a prolific bird life. Set in a natural bushveld setting, the 12 secluded tents blend perfectly with the surroundings. These luxury en suite "camp bedrooms under canvas" warmly welcome you to this fascinating world. By day, take a safari walk or a game drive with one of the expert guides, but be sure to experience the mystical African night on one of the night drives.

For the Botswana safari experience of a lifetime, visit both Chobe Chilwero and Chief's Camp.

**CHOBE CHILWERO
CHIEF'S CAMP**
Abercrombie & Kent
1520 Kensington Road
Oak Brook, IL 60523

# Four Seasons Hotel Cairo

Home to the only surviving ancient Wonder of the World, Cairo is a hypnotic city. Modern skyscrapers and ancient pyramids define this city of contrasts, and its blend of Islamic, Jewish and Coptic cultures is intoxicating.

Just minutes from downtown Cairo and with extensive views of the Nile River and the Pyramids of Giza, the Four Seasons Hotel is setting new standards for perfection. The centerpiece of The First Residence, Cairo's most prestigious residential and shopping complex, the Four Seasons enjoys an exclusive location on the west bank of the Nile. Opposite the zoological and botanical gardens, the hotel is a true oasis in this bustling city.

Cairo's Belle Epoque is celebrated in the interiors at the Four Seasons. Rich reds,

greens and golds are used in the public rooms and contemporary furnishings in the French Empire style dominate throughout the hotel. The 228 rooms and 43 suites are the largest-sized accommodations in Cairo and all are handsomely appointed in soothing color tones. Handwoven textiles, Egyptian antiques and decorative objects enhance the Neo-classical décor.

Though influences from around the world are evident at the Four Seasons, great care is taken to share Cairo's traditions with guests.

The fabulous spa incorporates ancient rituals practiced by the pharaohs – you will never forget the foot treatment that begins every massage. Experience the ancient art of reading the future at the bottom of an Arabic coffee as demonstrated at the hotel, or relax by the pool. North African and Lebanese flavors and influences will be discovered while dining with a view of the Nile in the hotel's restaurant.

With its soothing ambience, lush interiors and extraordinarily attentive staff, the Four Seasons Hotel Cairo is a modern wonder of the world.

**FOUR SEASONS
HOTEL CAIRO**
At The First Residence
35 Giza Street
Giza, Cairo, Egypt 12311

# Mena House Oberoi

Mena House Oberoi in Cairo is steeped in history.

Originally a royal lodge for the King of Egypt, Mena House opened as a hotel in 1869. Named for the first pharaoh listed on the Tablet of Abydos, Mena House is set within 40 jasmine scented acres with the ancient pyramids looming nearby. Not many hotels can claim an ancient wonder of the world in their backyard! The view of the Pyramids from your room or while lounging at the pool is hard to beat. Indeed, many of Egypt's treasures are easily explored from Mena House. The legendary Sphinx keeps eternal guard just across from the hotel's 18 hole golf course.

Mena House honors its place in Egyptian history with traditional décor, including arabesque furniture inlaid with mother of pearl, handcrafted mosaic tiles and intricately carved wooden doors. Victorian-era works of art and antiques are abundant at Mena House. The hotel's 84 rooms and 13 suites are equally traditional in décor, while modern amenities ensure comfort and convenience.

Though Mena House enjoys a distinguished history, a lively spirit pervades the hotel's restaurants, bars and casino. Six restaurants celebrate the culinary arts with menus based on Indian, Continental, Mediterranean and Asian cuisines. In addition to delicious food, the restaurants provide intimate and exotic atmospheres. Nightly entertainment includes belly dancing and local music, and the nightclub is one of the hottest in Cairo.

Cairo's heritage is alive at Mena House Oberoi.

**MENA HOUSE OBEROI
AN OBEROI HOTEL**
Pyramid's Road, Giza
Cairo, Egypt

# The Oberoi, Sahl Hasheesh

The Oberoi, Sahl Hasheesh on the Red Sea offers an unforgettable experience.

Facing the sparkling sea and surrounded by majestic mountain ranges, The Oberoi, Sahl Hasheesh sits on 48 beachfront acres. Just opened in early 2001, this all-suite luxury resort exceeds your expectations with its breathtaking scenery and imaginative architecture. Share the mysticism and romance of Islamic architecture at The Oberoi, where a series of domes, columns and arches combine to create a stunning effect.

Similar to the Oberoi properties in Bali and Lombok, The Oberoi, Sahl Hasheesh is comprised of a series of villas backed by surrounding walls, ensuring complete privacy for each guest. The resort's 86 deluxe suites and 18 royal and grand suites are incredibly spacious; each accommodation has a living room, bedroom and bathroom. The gorgeous bathrooms overlook private landscaped gardens and have sunken bathtubs. The royal suites feature elevated dining pavilions as well as a central courtyard with a private swimming pool. The interiors share The Oberoi's ethnic pride with fabrics indicative of the region and local furnishings.

Two restaurants serve Continental and Oriental cuisines. The informal dining room captures magical views of the brilliant blue sea, while the formal dining room is enclosed within a courtyard and features nightly entertainment.

In addition to the beach club, The Oberoi, Sahl Hasheesh offers a glorious infinity swimming pool, tennis facilities and a fitness center with spa treatments. The Oberoi's prime location on the Red Sea, known for its abundant marine life, allows you to delight in the wonders of the deep.

Share in the magic of The Oberoi, Sahl Hasheesh.

## THE OBEROI, SAHL HASHEESH
Red Sea, Hurghada, Egypt

# The Ritz-Carlton, Sharm el Sheikh

A dramatic mountainous landscape juxtaposed with the clear blue water of the Red Sea defines the southern Sinai Peninsula, known for its rich history and spectacular underwater exploration.

Opened in 2000, The Ritz-Carlton, Sharm el Sheikh has brought great style to the Red Sea. As you enter, your eyes feast on a modern Egyptian glass temple complete with gold capped columns and marble. Within this building are the reception and concierge services, elegant Lobby Lounge and bar, four of the resort's restaurants and the spa. The accommodations are located in two story buildings blended perfectly within the landscaped

grounds of bougainvillea, cacti, palm trees, fountains and serpentine pools.

The Ritz-Carlton's 259 rooms and 48 suites are influenced by Egyptian design with a neutral palette. All feature private terraces and offer views of the gardens or sea.

The restaurants dazzle your senses with their cuisine and capture your attention with their décor. Fayrouz serves Middle Eastern food in an exotic setting, while inventive Asian cuisine is available in Blue Ginger, La Luna has delicious Italian food and The Café and Waves feature casual dining.

This region is one of the world's best for diving, and the resort directly overlooks the Amphora Reef with its rare coral and fish.

The spa services are influenced by the region and many of the products contain the same elements as those used by the pharaohs. The massages are out of this world. Timed to coincide with sunrise or sunset, they can be enjoyed in a beachside Arabian tent.

Experience Egypt's Red Sea at The Ritz-Carlton, Sharm el Sheikh.

### THE RITZ-CARLTON, SHARM EL SHEIKH
Om El-Seed
Sharm el Sheikh
South Sinai, Egypt

# Olonana

Enjoy the spectacular wildlife of Kenya at Abercrombie & Kent's remarkable Olonana.

A permanent tented bush camp in East Africa, Olonana, is situated on the banks of the Mara River in the Masai Mara Game Reserve. The Mara, Kenya's portion of the Greater Serengeti ecosystem, is world renowned for its incredible wildlife; see lion, elephant, cheetah, giraffe, wildebeest, gazelle and zebra here.

Named after one of the Maasai's great leaders, Olonana is unrivaled for its luxurious and unique style. Environmentally conscious, Olonana is powered by solar electricity. Giving back to its environment is a hallmark of the camp. Twelve bush pavilions, each with a terrace built on wooden platforms, overlook the river. The spacious interiors are defined by an uncluttered African décor; beds swathed in sheer netting complement traditional African patterns and unusual decorative objects.

Lacking a strict, rigorous schedule, Olonana's game viewing excursions and other activities are scheduled around guests' desires and the changing patterns of animal activity. No two days are ever the same here, making for a truly extraordinary safari. Guided game drives for only four people in custom made, open top Land Cruisers and escorted bush walks provide memorable experiences. Located in the midst of Big Game country, you can even see game without ever leaving the camp. A pod of hippos laze in the river opposite Olonana and the salt lick across the river is host to a bevy of ever-changing animals.

Stylish and sophisticated meals are served at Olonana, and bush breakfasts and sundowner cocktails on the nearby Siria Escarpment are popular outings.

Conjure up thoughts of *Out of Africa* while living out your dreams of Africa at Olonana.

OLONANA
Abercrombie & Kent
1520 Kensington Road
Oak Brook, IL 60523

# The Oberoi, Mauritius

Mauritius is divine. Surrounded by the turquoise waters of the Indian Ocean, the island is blessed with sandy beaches and golden sunshine. It is a wonderful vacation destination.

Opened in late 2000, The Oberoi, Mauritius is the island's premier resort. Its location on the northwest coast is private and exclusive. Surrounded by a turquoise lagoon, guests can also look out to the majestic range of green mountains on the horizon. The Oberoi, Mauritius perfectly blends Mauritian culture and heritage while incorporating Chinese, French, Indian and African cultures. The 76 villas are luxurious and most have private swimming pools set within sub-tropical gardens. Natural fabrics in subtle colors are used in the interiors, and original Mauritian artwork abounds. Elevated dining pavilions, featured at all villas, have fantastic views of the Indian Ocean and lagoon and make private dining even more exceptional.

Water sports are abundant, and two public swimming pools delight swimmers and sunbathers alike. Two restaurants expertly blend Creole, Asian and European flavors. A bar, with a beachfront setting that includes an 18th century ruin, is an exotic place to unwind.

Like the resort, The Oberoi's spa is tranquil and serene. Each treatment room overlooks its own private garden. A strong commitment to holistic therapy is evident at the spa, and many Mauritian fruits and vegetables are used in the treatments. You will leave the spa feeling rejuvenated and with a special glow.

Come enjoy the luxurious and caring service at The Oberoi, Mauritius.

**THE OBEROI, MAURITIUS AN OBEROI RESORT**
Baie aux Tortues
Pointe aux Piments, Mauritius

# La Mamounia

You need not look past the rose-colored ramparts of Marrakech to find a mystical and enchanting place. The city is the centerpiece of Morocco, with an alluring blend of Berber, African and Arab cultures. Vibrant colors, heady aromas and fascinating street theater of snake charmers and raconteurs compete for your attention as you wind your way through the labyrinthine medina.

La Mamounia completes Marrakech's seductive picture. Just outside the Kasbah, La Mamounia is a masterpiece of ornate Moroccan and Art Deco architecture set within twenty acres of luscious grounds. Intoxicating scents and over two centuries of history attract visiters to the gardens where each guest finds a favorite spot. Loyal

My favorites are the Moroccan suites complete with arches, fountains, tiles, oriental rugs, inlaid furniture and colorful pillows.

Five restaurants span the globe with their menus based on traditional Moroccan, French and Italian cuisines. Le Marocain is noteworthy for its seductive, traditional Moorish interior design, refined Moroccan cuisine and nightly entertainment with ethnic music, colorful dancers and a belly dancer. A selection of bars and the grand casino will keep you entertained until dawn, but you may not want to sleep in with all the available leisure activities.

Explore Marrakech from the legendary La Mamounia.

visitor Winston Churchill favored the secluded olive groves, where he spent many hours painting.

La Mamounia's 171 rooms, 57 suites and 3 villas provide a variety of refined accommodations. Seven suites are themed and offer unique touches. The Churchill Suite is properly English with Chesterfield furniture. Churchill's easel decorates one corner of the room, with an unfinished painting of the gardens atop. The glamour of a luxury train compartment can be relived in the Orient-Express suite.

**LA MAMOUNIA**
Avenue Bab Jdid
40 000 Marrakech, Morocco

# Frégate Island Private

Frégate Island's secluded location in the Seychelles, off the eastern coast of Africa, made it the perfect hideaway for 17th century pirates seeking rest between raids. Today, it provides a luxurious and idyllic escape from the world.

Total privacy is guaranteed at Frégate Island, with only 16 villas and a maximum of 40 guests at one time. Nestled among the bamboo, banyan and wild fig trees, the villas are influenced by Indonesian and Balinese architecture. Fourteen are clifftop, and the views of the turquoise and emerald waters of the Indian Ocean are breathtaking. Each villa features a deck with Jacuzzi, perfect for listening to the sounds of the sea and enjoying the sweet fragrances of the frangipani and ylang ylang. The villas' interiors are far from "roughing it," with luxurious accommodations enhanced by Thai silk, Egyptian cotton and Asian art.

A restored plantation house is home to one of the resort's two restaurants and serves Creole delicacies in a historic, colonial setting. The main dining room specializes in gourmet cuisine and has staggering views of the water.

Giant tortoises, exotic birds and other wildlife populate this 740 acre island, and the coral reef is home to a wide variety of marine life, making scuba diving and snorkeling two popular activities at Frégate Island. Seven white sand beaches, some of the most beautiful in the world, are worth the steep walk from your villa. A magnificent infinity pool is built into a natural rock basin, and offers terrific views of the Indian Ocean.

Frégate Island is paradise for modern-day Robinson Crusoes.

**FRÉGATE ISLAND PRIVATE**
Victoria Rahe, Seychelles

# Mount Nelson Hotel

Cape Town, with miles of beaches and mountains that edge the sea, is undoubtedly one of the world's most enchanting cities. For over three centuries, Cape Town has served as the link between Europe and the East.

The Mount Nelson Hotel has embodied Cape Town's gracious hospitality for over 100 years. The hotel is legendary, from its superb taste and manners, to its incredible guest list that has included high society, dignitaries and explorers from all ports of call. The hotel was originally built to accommodate passengers from the Union-Castle steamships, and

the history that has unfolded within these walls is astonishing.

Affectionately nicknamed "the Nellie," the Mount Nelson elegantly rests within seven acres of manicured gardens. This grande dame's signature pink color is custom-designed to fade to just the right shade, and the gardens even contain special roses in the same pink hue.

The 145 rooms and 75 suites have a refined country décor, with flowered fabrics and soft colors. In addition to the main building, four separate wings present unique, luxurious accommodations and are set in private gardens. The Churchill Suite is one of my personal favorites. It is easy to imagine the pensive Churchill here, gazing out

at majestic Table Mountain from its huge bay window.

The Mount Nelson has two restaurants, with the Cape Colony Restaurant being of particular note. It has been voted one of the top ten hotel restaurants in the world and its blend of Cape Malay, Thai, and Mediterranean flavors is superb.

The Mount Nelson Hotel, steeped in history and wearing its finest regalia, is without a doubt one of the world's finest establishments.

**MOUNT NELSON HOTEL**
76 Orange Street
Cape Town 8001, South Africa

# Saxon

Saxon celebrates South Africa's heritage.

Situated in an exclusive suburb of Johannesburg, Saxon is set on six acres of lush, indigenous gardens. It enjoys a soothing and welcoming atmosphere. Upon his release from prison, Nelson Mandela chose Saxon as the home where he would enjoy his first days of freedom. Mandela also edited his autobiography, *Long Walk to Freedom*, while residing here.

An impressive collection of African art and artifacts, as well as contemporary African décor, define Saxon's design philosophy. Local flavor abounds, and the soft, muted tones and animal prints so indicative of Africa are present throughout

the hotel. Indeed, Saxon feels like a stylish private home rather than a hotel.

Spacious and dramatic, all 20 Egoli (Gold) Suites, 4 Presidential and 2 Platinum Suites – the Mandela and Mbeki suites are 4,500 square feet - display handcrafted South African art alongside state-of-the-art technology. Latticed shutters shade large bay windows that look out over tranquil gardens or the beautiful pool areas. Monochromatic colors like ochre, ivory and earth tones evoke serenity while highlighting the fantastic decorative objects.

World-class chefs work behind the scenes to create delightful, personalized cuisine. The dining room's

casual elegance is the perfect complement to the kitchen's concoctions. The marvelous wine collection is displayed in an appealing manner.

If the calming tones and restful pace of Saxon haven't relaxed you, the Clarins spa and fitness center with lap pool will assuage you. Massages can also be arranged under the shaded gazebos next to the pool.

Celebrate South Africa and live freely at Saxon.

**SAXON**
36 Saxon Road
Sandhurst, Johannesburg
Saxonwold 2132, South Africa

# The Westcliff

Since its opening in 1998, The Westcliff has been Johannesburg's leading hotel.

Located in an exclusive suburb, The Westcliff resembles a village with Mediterranean style buildings dotting the landscape. This private, walled estate is built into the side of a hill, affording terrific views of the Zoological Gardens below. Set within formal, landscaped gardens, The Westcliff enjoys a resort-like atmosphere while retaining its city address. The interior is cool and elegant. Distinctive touches, like the use of animal print fabrics in the lobby, add a

regional, ethnic touch to the hotel. The 106 rooms and 14 suites are equally personalized and many have balconies. Guests with balconies may be lucky enough to view the strolling elephants below!

The Westcliff is committed to physical fitness and well-being with two outdoor pools, a modern fitness center and spa. Three of Johannesburg's most prestigious golf clubs are nearby and the hotel's tennis courts are supported by a full range of services, including coaching from a well-known tennis personality. The two restaurants are popular for their spectacular settings and fine North Mediterranean dishes. The atmosphere at the Polo Lounge Bar and Terrace is fun. The decorative photographs and equipment celebrate the sport of polo. It is one of the city's most fashionable meeting places.

Though located in a northern suburb, The Westcliff is easily accessible from the city center and the hotel's shuttle service makes transfers even easier. Shuttles are also available to the elegant shopping districts of Sandton, Hyde Park and Rosebank.

The Westcliff provides a tranquil home in Johannesburg.

**THE WESTCLIFF**
67 Jan Smuts Avenue
Westcliff, 2193, Johannesburg
South Africa

# *Asia & Pacific*

AUSTRALIA

CHINA

FIJI

INDIA

INDONESIA

JAPAN

MALDIVES

NEW ZEALAND

SINGAPORE

THAILAND

# Hayman

Lying off the coast of northern Queensland in the scenic waters of the Whitsunday Passage, Hayman is one of the islands of Australia's magnificent Great Barrier Reef.

A luxurious private yacht whisks you to Hayman, the only resort on the entire island. The island's rugged landscape, deserted beaches and amazing array of flora, fauna and marine life beg to be explored.

Hayman offers a myriad of activities and services. You will never tire of the resort's six restaurants, where Japanese, Australian and Asian specialties are just some of the cuisines that you may sample. Golf, tennis, squash and cinema screenings are some of the activities here, with watersports being the most popular. If a romantic picnic on a deserted island is more your speed, the resort will arrange that in a snap. However, the biggest attraction at Hayman is the abundant marine life of the nearby Great Barrier Reef. The resort provides boat, seaplane and helicopter tours of the reef, as well as snorkeling and diving instruction.

The resort's fabulous west wing pool is truly a sight. This saltwater pool is seven times the size of an Olympic pool and is one of the largest in the Southern Hemisphere! Set within exotic tropical gardens, the east wing pool offers a more secluded atmosphere.

The guest rooms and suites are contemporary, with soft, natural tones and international decorative objects. Hayman's extensive collection of contemporary Australian art can also be enjoyed in the private rooms. Eleven penthouses are individually themed and take their inspiration from other cultures. Morocco, Greece and Japan are just some of the countries represented in the suites.

Quite simply, Hayman is one of the world's best resorts.

HAYMAN
Great Barrier Reef
Queensland 4801, Australia

# Lilianfels Blue Mountains

Only ninety minutes from Sydney in Australia's picturesque Blue Mountains, Lilianfels is a special hideaway.

This historic property has an awe-inspiring location on an escarpment overlooking the eucalyptus-scented Blue Mountains. Set amidst two acres of English-style gardens, Lilianfels was built in 1889 for Sir Frederick Darley, Chief Justice of New South Wales. The original residence now houses the sensational Darley's restaurant, while the adjacent country house welcomes guests with its gracious 81 rooms and 4 suites. The freestanding cottage suite, once the servants' quarters, is a beautiful and spacious accommodation

Mountains. Seasonal produce is highlighted in the European-influenced menu at Darley's Restaurant. The wine list is exclusive to Australian wines and is continually lauded for its excellent selection. Located in the country house, Lilians is a slightly more casual setting with a focus on Australian cuisine.

Aside from its own stunning vistas, Lilianfels is a five-minute walk from one of Australia's largest natural attractions, the rock formation known as the Three Sisters.

Lilianfels will wow you with its majestic views and welcome you with its comforting, country house style.

with a private garden. All rooms maintain the property's Victorian heritage while adding contemporary touches.

The peaceful region inspires reflection, yet activities abound. Fishing, horseback riding and bush walking are just a few of the options located nearby. Lilianfels has its own excellent health club with indoor pool, exercise facilities and spa.

The two restaurants echo the relaxing setting of the Blue

**LILIANFELS BLUE MOUNTAINS**
Lilianfels Avenue
Echo Point, Katoomba
NSW 2780, Australia

# The Windsor

Melbourne is a wonderful city filled with wide boulevards, sidewalk cafés and lush greenery. Considered one of the most livable cities in the world, Melbourne exudes elegance and is Australia's cultural capital.

No other hotel captures Melbourne's Victorian-era charms and romance like The Windsor. Opened as The Grand in 1883, the hotel's name was changed to The Windsor after a visit by the Duke of Windsor in the 1920's. The Windsor reflects Melbourne's elegant character and heritage. A grand staircase, featuring wrought iron banisters, Persian carpets and rare Stawell sandstone steps, leads all guests to their accommodations. Each

landing even has hand-painted mosaic tiles. The Victorian décor is authentic and is listed by the National Trust of Australia. Indeed, much of the hotel is protected by the Trust.

The 160 guest rooms and 20 suites are plush with refined furnishings and floral patterned fabrics. Some have views over the Parliament House, while the Windsor Suites also look out to the Princess Theatre and Exhibition Building. Once used as private residences, the Victorian Suites are spacious and grandly decorated. Comfort at The Windsor is paramount – special pillow menus

are offered to ensure your rest.

Victorian draperies, Persian rugs, parquet floors and large windows make 111 Spring Street an enchanting spot to dine. Exquisite meals are served throughout the day, though it is especially famous for its traditional afternoon tea, a Melbourne ritual since 1883. Melbourne is the country's sporting capital, and The Windsor has hosted many leading sports figures, including cricket's greatest players. The Cricketer's Bar honors the sport with an extraordinary assortment of sports memorabilia.

Welcome to the genteel world of The Windsor.

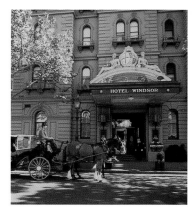

**THE WINDSOR, MELBOURNE**
103 Spring Street
Melbourne 3000, Australia

# The Observatory Hotel

Sydney is a terrific city. Its style and sophistication are well complemented by its sandy beaches and friendly residents. Nestled near the harbor in the Rocks district, The Observatory Hotel has a tasteful style like that of a private home.

The Observatory Hotel is located on a quiet side street, yet remains close to Sydney's bustling business district, as well as museums, shops and restaurants. The hotel takes its inspiration from the historic Elizabeth Bay House and it was named after the Sydney Observatory. Australian antiques, oil paintings

fireplace is an elegant spot for afternoon tea.

The Observatory Hotel boasts an outdoor tennis facility, health club and spa. The indoor pool is spectacular, with a ceiling of fiber optic lights recreating the constellations of the Southern Hemisphere.

Known for its superb service, The Observatory meets every guest's request with a warm, friendly greeting.

The Observatory Hotel is an impeccable choice for visitors to Sydney.

and fine tapestries add to the ambience of a private residence. This feeling is intensified when you wander into the Globe Bar, where rare books on travel, natural history and astronomy can be found on the shelves. The 79 rooms and 21 suites are beautifully appointed, and terraces offer views of Observatory Hill and historic Walsh Bay.

Galileo Restaurant's modern Australian cuisine with an Italian influence continually wins awards and the drawing room with an antique

THE OBSERVATORY HOTEL
89 Kent Street
Sydney, NSW 2000,
Australia

# The Regent Sydney

All of Sydney is within reach while staying at The Regent.

Its prime location in the historic Rocks district right on Sydney Harbour places it within a short distance from major museums, shops and just ten minutes from the business district. The 36 story tower built in 1982 is Sydney's first true luxury modern hotel. Reopened after a complete top to bottom renovation, The Regent is once again in a class by itself.

Watch Sydney pass you by while you lounge in The Regent's dramatic lobby. The

contemporary décor of The Regent extends throughout its public areas to all 417 guest rooms and 114 suites. Large windows display fantastic harbor views and the corner rooms look out over the instantly recognizable Sydney Opera House.

In a city known for its superb cuisine, The Regent is no exception. Kable's, the hotel's signature restaurant, is a spectacular sight with soothing color schemes and clean, simple lines. The menu capitalizes on Australia's abundant seafood and local produce and game, including Mandalong lamb, Tasmanian scallops and Wallis Lake oysters. The Wine Bar at Kable's invites you to enjoy a wide variety of

Australia's best boutique wines. Meet the locals for wood-fired pizzas and beers at GSB, or pull up a chair in the Bar located in the lobby. Cabana caters to guests relaxing by the outdoor pool with snacks and drinks.

Committed to excellence, The Regent features a state-of-the-art fitness center and swimming pool deck that provides a unique vantage point for experiencing Sydney.

Keep up with Sydney at The Regent.

THE REGENT SYDNEY
199 George Street
Grosvenor Place
Sydney, NSW 1200, Australia

# The St. Regis Beijing

For six centuries, Beijing has been a historical, political and cultural capital. Contemporary Beijing is a fascinating combination of old and new, with tai chi enthusiasts and bearded old men alongside young Chinese clad in Gucci and Prada.

The St. Regis represents the finest of Beijing and is the most luxurious hotel in this exhilarating city. The city's business and shopping areas are nearby, as are Beijing's major sites, including Tiananmen Square, the Forbidden City and the Silk Market. The St. Regis, in the exclusive embassy district, neighbors the historic Beijing International Club, the famed meeting place of dignitaries,

foreign correspondents and government officials. Beijing's imperial history inspired The St. Regis' unparalleled levels of service and attention to every detail.

The hotel honors the city's glorious past while instilling new traditions. All 134 rooms and 139 suites are incredibly inviting in classical contemporary design with subtle color schemes. My personal favorites are the elegant and spacious Statesman Suites. In St. Regis style, there are helpful butlers on every floor.

Eastern and Western culinary tastes blend in the world-class restaurants. The Garden Court is a lovely brasserie with all-day dining and a superb buffet, while Danieli's concentrates on the cuisine of northern and central Italy in its chic setting.

Savor Cantonese cuisine with local variations in the Celestial Court, or enjoy authentic Japanese dishes, like sushi and tempura, at Tokyo Aoyama Mangetsu. Popular with the local residents, the Garden Lounge and Press Club Bar have enticing atmospheres to enjoy afternoon tea or cocktails.

The St. Regis Beijing encourages you to explore the city's past while enjoying its exciting future.

**THE ST. REGIS BEIJING**
No 21 Jian Guo Men Wai Da Jie
Beijing 100020, China

# Mandarin Oriental, Hong Kong

Deeply rooted in Asian culture, the Mandarin Oriental, Hong Kong is one of the world's finest hotels.

The Mandarin Oriental is situated in the heart of Hong Kong's financial district while overlooking Victoria Harbour. The entire island and mainland are easily explored from here, with mass transit just outside the door and the Star Ferry just a few minutes away by foot.

A fabulous fitness center, spa, beauty salon and Roman-style indoor swimming pool are located within the hotel. Four restaurants, two of which are located on the top floor, have an amazing array of menus, including French, Cantonese, Continental and International. Three bars, including the Cohiba Cigar Divan, also provide entertainment. Don't miss afternoon tea with the Mandarin's famous rose petal jam!

Experience time and place at the Mandarin Oriental, Hong Kong.

The Mandarin Oriental preserves its Chinese heritage and has an impressive collection of Chinese art. Many rare and unique pieces grace the public and private rooms. Most of the 486 guest rooms and 55 suites have balconies, a rarity in Hong Kong. Rooms come complete with binoculars for sharper viewing of the city's skyline as well as across Victoria Harbour. The rooms establish a sense of place with Chinese porcelain light fixtures and Chinoiserie fabrics copyrighted especially for the Mandarin Oriental. Twelve themed suites offer individualized décor. The Mandarin suite is particularly notable for its antiques…like the two Taoist vases from the Sung Dynasty, a Qing Dynasty court robe and a 19th century Shansi lacquer chest which blend with five-star amenities like satellite television and Internet access.

**MANDARIN ORIENTAL, HONG KONG**
5 Connaught Road, Central
Hong Kong

# The Peninsula Hong Kong

Not just a hotel, The Peninsula is a Hong Kong landmark. Opened in 1928, The Peninsula's genteel surroundings and superb service are world-renowned. It is a perennial favorite.

The privileged lifestyle that The Peninsula shares with its guests begins at the airport, where a Rolls Royce greets you. Those visitors in more of a hurry may choose to arrive by helicopter – the hotel's tower has twin helipads for such occasions. The Peninsula is located in the heart of Kowloon's business and shopping area overlooking the Harbour.

Chinese decorative objects are interspersed among the classic European décor of the hotel's sumptuous 246 rooms and 54 suites. Floor-to-ceiling glass walls

for enjoyable occasions. Gaddi's is a Hong Kong institution, notable for its elegant setting and gourmet French cuisine. Specializing in Pacific Rim cuisine, Felix occupies the top two floors of the tower and has a trendy décor styled by Philippe Starck. The Peninsula Academy, a series of master-class vacations, is a unique opportunity at the hotel. The Chinese Cultural Experience offers insight into Chinese traditions, including feng shui, tai chi, Cantonese cooking and medicine. Participants in The Lifestyle Experience enjoy true pampering with stylish sightseeing and dining, while gourmets jump at the chance to participate in the Culinary Experience.

Become a part of the Hong Kong legend at The Peninsula.

in the tower allow guests uninterrupted views of the harbor, while specially commissioned telescopes help you take advantage of the staggering views.

With a retractable glass screen and full harbor views, The Peninsula's swimming pool is stupendous. Its magnificent setting is linked to a sun terrace and the health club. Of course, an exceptional spa is also located within the hotel.

Three bars and eight restaurants provide elegant settings

**THE PENINSULA HONG KONG**
Salisbury Road
Kowloon, Hong Kong, China

# The Ritz-Carlton, Hong Kong

The Ritz-Carlton, Hong Kong has an intimate and inviting atmosphere. Located just minutes from major international businesses in Central's financial district, The Ritz-Carlton takes advantage of sweeping harbor and city views.

The Ritz-Carlton was the first post-modern building constructed in Hong Kong. Hong Kong's British influence is highlighted in the hotel's 216 rooms and 29 suites with 18th century English antiques and oil paintings. Chinese silks and furniture in rich mahogany, walnut and rosewood add to the luxurious accommodations. The Ritz-Carlton's club

floor, comprised of 19 rooms and 5 suites, is ideal for guests seeking an even more exclusive atmosphere. The club floor has its own concierge and private lounge, where special presentations like mid-morning snacks and afternoon tea are provided.

East meets West in the wonderful restaurants and bars. The Café is open all day for a la carte specialties and elaborate buffets. Northern Italian cuisine is highlighted at Toscana, the Cantonese restaurant serves superb local delicacies and the Japanese sushi bar includes private

tatami rooms. Shanghai-Shanghai is great fun in a refined Art Deco setting. Nightly, singers perform songs from 1930's Shanghai.

The Ritz-Carlton accommodates business travelers in this financial capital with business support. Translation and secretarial services make your meetings more efficient and the private rooms are well-equipped to handle all technology needs.

Seek a new experience while enjoying the comforts of The Ritz-Carlton, Hong Kong.

**THE RITZ-CARLTON, HONG KONG**
3 Connaught Road
Central, Hong Kong

# Grand Hyatt Shanghai

The Grand Hyatt Shanghai is the tallest hotel in the world. Occupying floors 54 through 87 of this impressive tower that is China's tallest and the world's third largest building, the Grand Hyatt is a welcome addition to Shanghai.

Jin Mao Tower respects Shanghai's heritage while introducing contemporary design principles to the city. Naturally, its views of Bund and Huang Pu rivers are unmatched. The tower has 88 floors — an auspicious number representing great wealth and prosperity in China.

Though located on the top floors of the building, the Grand Hyatt's six high-speed elevators whisk you to the lobby in a mere 47 seconds. The lobby commands staggering panoramic views with its

floor-to-ceiling glass walls.

The Grand Hyatt's 510 rooms and 45 suites are equally breathtaking. The sleek, contemporary design of the exterior is softened by its interiors. A careful blend of ancient Chinese design and Art Deco creates a pleasing décor. Ming-style cabinets house televisions while antique red lacquer screens with gold calligraphed Tang Dynasty poems serve as headboards. The top seven floors comprise the Grand Hyatt's Regency Club, an exclusive space with private boardroom, lounge and special services.

The Grand Hyatt's elegant functions rooms are the preferred location for the city's most prestigious social engagements and influential business meetings. Twelve restaurants and bars welcome city residents and hotel guests with a variety of atmospheres and menus. Club Oasis is the highest fitness center in the world, with a fantastic sky swimming pool.

Grand Hyatt Shanghai towers above the city.

**GRAND HYATT SHANGHAI**
Jin Mao Tower
88 Century Boulevard
Pudong, Shanghai 200121

# The Portman Ritz-Carlton, Shanghai

Don't just visit Shanghai; experience it. The city's legendary hustle and bustle is right outside your door when you stay at The Ritz-Carlton, Shanghai. Located on Nanjing Street, in the heart of the city, the hotel is the shining star of the prestigious Shanghai Centre complex.

The hotel's entrance is incredibly dramatic. A 3,000 pound stacked glass and fiber optic threaded "moongate" creates a dazzling display of color and movement. The 486 rooms and 78 suites are equally colorful, with inventive designs and intriguing decorative objects.

Though Chinese in design, the standards are purely Ritz-Carlton. Technology butlers are on call at all times.

The Portman Ritz-Carlton has one of the largest fitness facilities in the city. The complex includes indoor/outdoor pools, courts for tennis, squash and racquetball and lessons in t'ai chi and aerobics. Pilates, the latest trend in physical fitness,

is also offered at the health club. With six restaurants at the hotel, you may want to join the class!

Shanghai's attractions are not to be missed, but join Mark De Cocinis, the hotel's general manager, in the sidecar of his limited edition Chang Jiang 750cc motorcycle, for an eye-opening tour of the city's landmarks. It is unlike any other tour available!

Let The Portman Ritz-Carlton dazzle you.

**THE PORTMAN RITZ-CARLTON, SHANGHAI**
Shanghai Centre,
1376 Nanjing Xi Lu
Shanghai 200040, China

# Vatulele Island Resort

Vatulele Island Resort is a secluded hideaway on one of Fiji's southern islands.

This unspoiled island in the South Pacific provides the perfect setting for this casual resort, where the pressures of the world quickly fade. No telephones, radios, televisions or newspapers can be found here and footwear is optional, even at dinner.

Vatulele is comprised of 18 villas, or bures. The bures are nestled within a dense jungle, providing natural privacy. Spacious and beautiful, the bures have a unique architecture with distinctive, handmade

touches. They enjoy easy access to the water and each has its own stretch of sand. The warm, gracious staff attends to your every need and makes you feel at home in this exotic land.

Vatulele Island is protected by a barrier reef, and snorkeling and scuba diving are particularly rewarding here. Jungle hikes with one of the resort's experts offer insight into native plant medicines. You may also swim in underground caves or explore archaeological sites on the island.

Fresh ingredients from Australia and New Zealand are flown in daily and dining is terrific here. Among other influences, the chef enjoys preparing Californian, Thai and Japanese cuisine; but no matter what his fancy, you are sure to have a superb meal. Nothing quite matches the feeling of dining under the stars on a remote Fijian island.

Vatulele Island Resort is heaven in the South Pacific.

**VATULELE ISLAND RESORT**
Vatulele Island, Fiji

# Amarviläs

Few things in this world can compare to the Taj Mahal in Agra. It is the most romantic symbol of eternal love - a monumental tribute by Shah Jehan to his beloved wife, Empress Mumtaz Mahal.

Opened in early 2001, Amarviläs brings you the Taj Mahal like no one else can. This latest addition to the Oberoi Group is a marvel to behold within landscaped gardens of terraced lawns, geometric pools and pavilions. In an area known for having the largest collection of world heritage monuments in one region, Amarviläs stands out gloriously with its stately five story Indian palace defined by graceful arches

and domes. Enter through its courtyard of 64 fountains and arched colonnade decorated with Mughal murals. The domed lobby is decorated with cobalt blue and gold leaf, reviving the ancient traditions of local craftsmen.

Amarviläs bears the distinction of having unobstructed views of the Taj Mahal from all 99 rooms and 7 suites, the restaurants and the lobby. Most of the accommodations have private terraces and all have exquisite bathrooms. Polished teakwood floors, inlaid furniture and rich fabrics reflect the region's history and heritage.

The resort's two restaurants are delightful, whether you dine at Esphahan with its Mughlai and

Indian food or enjoy the Continental and Indian fusion cuisine at Bellevue. Dining alfresco at Amarviläs is not something that you will easily forget as you view the Taj Mahal.

The heath club and outdoor swimming pool encourage you to unwind in their splendid surroundings, while the spa treatments take inspiration from the gentle beauty of the region.

With the Taj Mahal as the background, fall in love with Amarviläs.

**AMARVILÄS, AGRA
AN OBEROI RESORT**
Taj East Gate Road
Agra 282001, India

# The Oberoi, Bangalore

Dating back to the First Century AD, Bangalore has enjoyed a long history. Constantly reinventing itself, the city was once known as "Little England in India." Widely recognized for its lush gardens in the middle of steamy southern India, Bangalore's most recent reincarnation is as India's Silicon Valley.

The Oberoi, Bangalore opened in the heart of the city in 1992. Close to the busy commercial center of Brigade Road and Commercial Street, The Oberoi enjoys a park-like setting of tended lawns, manicured gardens, rock gardens and fish ponds. Built around a 75 year old rain tree, The Oberoi is committed to preserving

data port connections in every room, as well as cellular phones upon request for everyone.

The Oberoi, Bangalore shares a variety of cuisines with its guests. Authentic Thai cuisine is the focus of Rim Naam, while Le Jardin features Indian and Continental dishes along with nightly themed buffets, including Italian and Mexican food. The Polo Club is an English-style pub with wine and cheese, malts, cigars and rosti, a Swiss specialty shared on Friday and Saturday evenings. Szechwan Court specializes in cuisine from the Chinese province of Szechwan in a dramatic setting with cascading waterfalls and bamboo shoots.

The Oberoi, Bangalore brings you the best of modern day India.

India's fragile environment and Bangalore's reputation as the "garden city."

The gardens are the hotel's centerpiece and all 149 rooms and 9 suites have balconies overlooking the grounds. The rooms are a testament to the Oberoi Group's dedication to excellence with Burmese teak floors, Italian marble bathrooms and 24-hour personalized butler service. The hotel caters to business guests with two telephone lines and

**THE OBEROI, BANGALORE**
37-39 Mahatma Gandhi Road
Bangalore 560 001, India

# Oberoi Grand

Calcutta is a place of dizzying proportions, where extreme poverty and prodigious riches live alongside each other. Its rich history is evident in its streets, from its fading mansions to its street markets that tell stories of the modern Bengali culture. Under British rule, Calcutta was the capital of the British Raj and the most important city under the Crown.

Inextricably linked to Calcutta's rich history, Oberoi Grand is legendary. Once a simple boarding house for war veterans, Oberoi Grand was transformed into one of the country's finest hotels during the Victorian era. Nicknamed "the Grand Old Lady on Chowringhee," the hotel's gleaming white facade and manicured grounds epitomize the glamour of turn-of-the-century Calcutta.

The finest materials, fabrics and furnishings are used in the hotel's 207 guest rooms and 6 suites. The suites feature parquet floors covered with Kashmiri carpets and specially crafted canopy beds. Pictures from the albums of Jahangir, the Mughal emperor, enhance the walls. The wooden furniture in the rooms is typical of India, with bone and ivory inlay.

Oberoi Grand is home to Calcutta's finest restaurants. La Terrasse resembles a French café with its louvered doors and French windows which overlook bird cages and beyond to the swimming pool. Baan Thai serves some of the best Thai food outside of Thailand in a traditional setting complete with Khumtoke, or typical Thai seating with a sunken area for leg space. The fine dining of royal India is revived at Gharana, where the ambience mimics a palace courtyard. The menu, based on the seasons, includes dishes created by the royal chefs.

For a true historical experience, stay at Oberoi Grand.

**OBEROI GRAND**
15 Jawaharlal Nehru Road
Calcutta 700 013, India

# The Oberoi, New Delhi

The Oberoi, New Delhi is in a class by itself in India's capital city.

Opened in 1965, The Oberoi brought unparalleled standards of luxury and service to New Delhi. The hotel overlooks the prestigious Delhi Golf Club, though it remains close to the city's business center, shopping districts and major monuments.

The Oberoi welcomes guests with a refined tone set by Oriental carpets and crystal chandeliers. Large windows look out over tranquil landscaping, providing a relaxing ambience. Magnificent works of art adorn the walls throughout the hotel, whether it is in the lobby, restaurants or even guest corridors. The richness and diversity of Indian art and culture is celebrated in the hotel's collection which includes antique Chogas worn by Mughal royal gentry and contemporary sculptures by world-renowned artist, Amarnath Sahgal.

The 256 guest rooms and 31 suites are elegantly appointed with a blend of European influences and Indian decorative objects and furnishings. All rooms overlook the fairways of the golf course or the historic tomb of Mughal Emperor Humayun. Business travelers need never leave their rooms, with multi-line telephones, individual fax machines and Internet access. When the time does come to leave, The Oberoi features a telephonic express check-out, perfect for harried executives.

The Oberoi promises a culinary journey with its five restaurants and two bars; Thai, Continental, Indian and Chinese are just some of the cuisines that can be sampled here.

Let the tranquility of The Oberoi, New Delhi share the delights of the capital with you.

**THE OBEROI, NEW DELHI**
Dr. Zakir Hussain Marg
New Delhi 110003, India

# Rajvilas

Even in a country full of mysticism, romance and cultural heritage, Jaipur stands out among India's cities. Nicknamed the "Pink City" because of its pink-hued buildings, Jaipur is a showpiece for Rajasthani architecture and a fascinating fusion of a legendary royal past merged with the frenetic pageantry of today's city streets.

Just outside Jaipur is Rajvilas, a 72 room resort set on 32 acres of gardens, pools and fountains. Honoring the traditions of the region's architecture and reviving the majestic lifestyles of the Rajput princes, Rajvilas recreates a traditional Rajasthani fort. Deluxe rooms are a blend of traditional flat-roofed houses and havelis, or courtyard mansions, and are

clustered in groups of four and six around courtyards. The 54 deluxe rooms are richly furnished with colonial and traditional regional influences and have sunken marble baths that overlook private walled gardens. Three private villas feature individual swimming pools, though perhaps more distinctive are the 14 private tents, which are set apart in two corners of the estate. In sharp contrast to anything called a conventional tent, they come with teak floors, embroidered interior canopies, furnishings covered in lavish cotton fabrics and sumptuous bathrooms.

If the lush surroundings haven't soothed you, a day of pampering at the spa certainly will. Its broad range of holistic, ayurvedic and western relaxation and beauty treatments will calm both body and mind. Dine elegantly on interpretations of traditional Rajasthani dishes, as well as Continental cuisine at the resort's restaurant.

Rajvilas offers unique explorations of the Rajasthani countryside by elephant safari…atop a decorative wooden howda you will wind along the riverbeds.

From its proximity to Jaipur to its luxurious style, Rajvilas is the perfect oasis.

**RAJVILAS, JAIPUR
AN OBEROI RESORT**
Goner Road
Jaipur 303 012, India

# Wildflower Hall

Wildflower Hall, beckons to you from its lofty position high in the Himalayas.

Located 45 minutes from Shimla, Wildflower Hall, An Oberoi Resort, is in the picturesque town of Mashobra in the lower Himalayas. Wildflower Hall captures your imagination with its stunning scenery of snowcapped mountain peaks, green meadows and cedar forests on its 22 acres of unspoiled land with a forest cover of 3,000 trees. The former home of British Commander-in-Chief Lord Kitchener, Wildflower Hall opened as a luxury resort in April 2001.

This six-story hotel retains the original spirit of a country retreat in its architecture, interior design and attitude. Teak paneling, rich woods and Oriental carpets create an old world ambience. Large, arched windows invite the natural light and breathtaking natural scenery inside. The 81 rooms and 6 suites are equally delightful with gracious furnishings.

Wildflower Hall presents a veritable culinary tour with its restaurants. The Brasserie, a lovely greenhouse with a large terrace for warmer days, serves pan-Asian and Continental cuisine. Or, opt for traditional favorites, local delicacies and cuisine inspired by the Raj period at the inventive Indian restaurant. Children are treated to their very own restaurant at Wildflower Hall, where special menus and entertainment keep little faces smiling.

If the inspirational and serene setting hasn't set you at ease, the meditation and yoga practiced at the fitness center certainly well. Wildflower Hall's spa is superb and is guided by traditional Indian Ayurvedic principles of herbal treatments, aromatherapy and holistic health maintenance.

Wildflower Hall is a blissful mountaintop retreat.

**WILDFLOWER HALL, MASHOBRA
AN OBEROI RESORT
IN THE HIMALAYAS**
Mashobra
Shimla 171012, India

# The Oberoi, Mumbai

It is a city of many names. Alternatively known as Bombay, Mumbai is affectionately called Bollywood for its status as the world's largest producer of films. Stylish and fast-paced, Mumbai is also India's most Westernized city, though its location facing the Arabian Sea serves as a constant reminder of its Indian roots.

Opened in 1986, The Oberoi, Mumbai is a sleek tower in the city's business center of Nariman Point. Designed with the business traveler in mind, The Oberoi was built on 20th century ideals. Superb, efficient service is a hallmark of the hotel. The 315 guest rooms and 22 suites accommodate the needs of visitors on business with separate work areas, laptop and fax connections in all rooms and serene décor that soothes while never distracting the minds of preoccupied guests. Personal butlers are assigned to each room, ensuring a warm welcome and a satisfying stay. An entire floor is dedicated to hosting women travelers, who are attended by female butlers.

The Oberoi, Mumbai features stylish dining options. The Brasserie is straight out of the Alsace region with its etched glass and traditional menu. The Rotisserie & Sea Grill offers grilled and roasted meats, game and poultry in a stylish setting with pastel upholstery and topped off by a gold dome. Delicious tandoori and charcoal grilled specialties from the Northwest frontier of India are the focus at Kandahar, while the Tea Lounge is a relaxing spot for a bit of the familiar.

The Oberoi brings great modern style to Mumbai.

### THE OBEROI, MUMBAI
Nariman Point
Mumbai 400 021, India

# Vanyaviläs

One of the world's most majestic creatures, the tiger is also one of the most elusive. These animals of the forest once aggressively hunted as prized trophies neared extinction, but thanks to conservation efforts like the Ranthambor Tiger Reserve, they are thriving once again.

The Oberoi Group's newest resort is also one of its most exotic. Opened in the autumn of 2001, Vanyaviläs, which means "jungle palaces," is India's first luxury jungle camp. Adjacent to the Ranthambor Tiger Reserve, Vanyaviläs is completely unrivaled. Where else can you stay in luxurious tents at night and spot the mysterious tiger by day?

The 25 tents and public

areas comprise only 5% of the total 20 acres in an effort to preserve the delicate environment of India. The accommodations in this exotic locale are simply remarkable. Extremely spacious, the tents have an area of 790 square feet. Despite its proximity to the jungle, the tents are appointed with teak floors, fine fabrics, air-conditioning and marble bathrooms recalling a grander era.

Vanyaviläs has two restaurants specializing in Continental and Indian cuisine. Whether you choose to dine indoors or out, you will be

satisfied. The swimming pool provides a refreshing alternative to the Indian heat, especially after a day of exploration.

Home to a wide variety of wildlife, the Ranthambor Reserve is best known for its tigers. Notoriously difficult to spot, sightings in Ranthambor are very frequent. In the spring of 2000, former President Bill Clinton had four sightings in just a few hours. Noted tiger expert Mr. Fateh Singh Rathore is the resident wildlife expert at Vanyaviläs. Considered the father of the Ranthambor Reserve, Mr. Rathore's lectures and insight are priceless.

For a one-of-a-kind experience, visit Vanyaviläs.

**VANYAVILÄS
AN OBEROI RESORT**
Ranthambhor Road,
Sawai Madhopur
Rajasthan, India

# Cecil

The majestic peaks and forests of the Himalayas surround this inspired land that was a dense forest just two centuries ago. Discovered in 1824, Shimla was named the summer capital of British India shortly thereafter.

Cecil, an Oberoi Resort, shares Shimla's strong tradition of gracious living in the Himalayas. The place to be seen both before and after independence from Britain, Cecil began as a single storied house known as the Tendril Cottage in 1884. Now a part of the hotel, the cottage hosted many well-known guests, including Rudyard Kipling, who spent several summers here.

after extensive renovations, Cecil's accommodations feature state-of-the-art equipment and services.

The Atrium Bar is a lively place to soak up Cecil's culture, while the Lounge is ideal for a quiet drink. Both Asian and European specialties are served in the restaurant.

Cecil never ceases to amaze its visitors, even more than a century later. The newly opened spa caters to guests with beauty and relaxation treatments based on western and ayurvedic principles, while the indoor swimming pool is the only one of its kind in the Himalayas.

Relive India's British Empire heritage at Cecil.

Located at the quiet end of the Mall, yet not far from downtown Shimla, Cecil is classically elegant in every way. The Atrium lobby speaks of the Colonial past with its warm wood and European furnishings. European influences dominate the elegant 71 guest rooms and 8 suites. Oriental carpets, beautiful fabrics and luxurious furniture lend an air of refinement, while windows share views of India's revered Himalayas. Reopened in 1997

**CECIL, SHIMLA
AN OBEROI RESORT**
Chaura Maidan
Shimla 171004, India

# Udaiviläs

Northern India's Udaipur is a city of alluring palaces, havelis and temples built around a series of shimmering, clear blue lakes. Expertly blending Mughal design influences with Rajput intricate craftsmanship, Udaipur's architecture captivates and inspires.

Opening in late 2001, Udaiviläs welcomes you to a magical world. Situated on Udaipur's famous Lake Pichola, Udaiviläs replicates a traditional Rajasthani palace. Its 30 acres of grounds are filled with landscaped gardens, fountains and pavilions and its views toward the City Palace, one of Udaipur's major landmarks, are sensational.

The 91 rooms and suites are elegantly appointed, combining traditional Indian furnishings with European influences. The bathrooms, made entirely of marble, look out over private, walled gardens. Most rooms have uninterrupted views of Lake Pichola and the City Palace, and all rooms feature terraces. The Deluxe Suites and Maharaja Suite even have private swimming pools.

Two restaurants, including one specializing in Rajasthani food in a traditional setting, complete the enchanting experience. Two outdoor swimming pools offer recreational options, while the spa brings an unprecedented level of treatments and relaxation to Udaipur.

Certainly, you have never experienced anything quite like a romantic sunset cruise on picturesque Lake Pichola while aboard a Gangore Nav, a traditional boat similar to those used during the famous Gangore festival 150 years ago.

Explore the legendary city of Udaipur while enjoying the pleasures of palace life at Udaiviläs.

## UDAIVILÄS, UDAIPUR AN OBEROI RESORT
Haridasji Ki Magri
Udaipur 313001, India

# Four Seasons Resort Bali at Jimbaran Bay

Exotic and mystical, Bali awakens your senses.

The Four Seasons Resort at Jimbaran Bay is located on the southern tip of Bali on the northeastern slopes of the Bukit peninsula. This superb location affords views of Jimbaran Bay and across to Mount Agung, the physical and spiritual center of Bali. Taking tradition from its home nation, the Four Seasons Resort is built as a series of villages on the side of a hill. Clustered into squares of 20, the resort's 147 villas are influenced by traditional Balinese pavilion design. Each villa has three separate pavilions within for bathing, dining and sleeping. Set within courtyard walls, the villas also feature

landscaped courtyards with private plunge pools.

Local tradition abounds at the Four Seasons, where 500 handmade shrines can be found throughout the property and Indonesian furnishings decorate the rooms. Bathing becomes a magical ritual here, where you may choose from an invigorating outdoor shower or a scent infused soak in your oversized bathtub.

Three restaurants will delight your senses with tempting food and exotic locations, including secluded gardens and beachside pavilions. All meals and snacks may also be served in your villa's dining pavilion.

Catering to individuals and couples, the spa's program is dedicated to providing traditional island treatments with an emphasis on natural elements from the sea. The Lulur Jimbaran is a relaxing way to soak up Balinese culture. This centuries-old Javanese ritual is performed daily for 40 days prior to a bride's wedding day. With enticing spices and cooling flowers, you need not be a bride to enjoy.

The Four Seasons Resort Jimbaran Bay is a fitting tribute on this "island of the gods."

**FOUR SEASONS RESORT BALI AT JIMBARAN BAY**
Jimbaran, Denpasar
80361 Bali, Indonesia

# Four Seasons Resort Bali at Sayan

The Four Seasons Resort Bali at Sayan is situated in the central highlands of Bali overlooking the Ayung River. This riverside retreat rests on 17 acres of green terraced rice slopes and is just 10 minutes from Ubud, Bali's artistic and cultural center.

The resort's architecture blends perfectly with the natural surroundings while casting a contemporary glance. The three-level main building is dramatic – an elliptical lotus pond rests on the roof and guests descend a staircase that cuts through the pond to enter reception.

the interiors, and many of the decorative objects and furnishings are from Ubud.

The spa is influenced by the sacred Ayung River and focuses on earth elements. Clay and spices are combined with leaves, flowers and herbs to create heavenly treatments.

Two restaurants offer delicious menus, but for a behind-the-scenes look at ceremonial Balinese cuisine, take one of the daily classes offered by the resort's chef. His insight into local culture is invaluable.

Let the Four Seasons Resort at Sayan inspire you.

The resort also features an organic, paddy-field shaped swimming pool. Extensive use of flowing water, integral to Balinese culture, can be seen throughout the resort.

Suspended teak walkways lead you to the resort's 18 suites and 36 villas. The bi-level villas offer an upper level lounging area with lily pond, while the lower level includes the living areas and private plunge pool. Locally woven textiles and indigenous artwork dominate

**FOUR SEASONS
RESORT BALI
AT SAYAN**
Sayan, Ubud, Gianyar
80571 Bali, Indonesia

# The Oberoi, Bali

The Oberoi, Bali is situated within 15 acres of tropical gardens on Seminyak Beach, Bali's most beautiful beach.

Built on the site of an ancient village, The Oberoi, Bali has pampered guests in the finest style since 1978. Mr. M.S. Oberoi created the first villa resort concept in the world here. It resembles a traditional Balinese village of 15 secluded villas with 60 luxurious lanai cottages. The resort's extensive use of local materials and authentic Balinese architecture has earned worldwide acclaim. The beautifully landscaped gardens include fragrant frangipani and tropical flowers.

The villas are spacious and have courtyard

gardens with rock ponds. Floral themed names are assigned to each villa. Individually designed bedrooms reflect the themes with oil paintings and handcarved wooden headboards. Nine of the villas have private swimming pools. Secluded and romantic, The Oberoi is a favorite.

The resort's primary swimming pool enjoys a superb location right on the golden sand of Seminyak Beach. The fitness center's traditional architecture provides inspiration for staying in shape. Open-air pavilions, overlooking the lily ponds, are blissful spots for relaxation. The Oberoi also has all the other amenities expected of a five-star resort; a beauty salon,

boutiques, business center, the sea facing Kayu Bar, open-air Frangipani Café and Kura Kura, a Balinese restaurant. Traditional Balinese performances that combine dance, music and song with brilliant costumes, masks and headdresses are offered regularly at the hotel for your enjoyment. Every aspect is intimate and spiritual.

The Oberoi, Bali is far more than a beach resort; it is a memorable experience.

**THE OBEROI, BALI
AN OBEROI RESORT**
Seminyak Beach, Jalan
Laksmana, Denpasar
80033 Bali, Indonesia

# The Ritz-Carlton, Bali

Perched on a cliff overlooking the Indian Ocean in southwestern Bali, The Ritz-Carlton, Bali is incredibly dramatic as you look upon the terraced water gardens, temple-like Balinese structures and lush, verdant foliage.

All 287 rooms and suites in the main building have splendid views of the gardens and the ocean beyond. Thirty-six private Balinese villas have traditional alang-alang thatched roofs, intricately carved doors, Indonesian décor and fabulous bathrooms with walled gardens. Many villas feature private plunge pools and bale bengongs, or open-air lounging pavilions, for relaxing moments.

Balinese and Javanese cultural concepts of well being meet at The Ritz-Carlton's spa. A foyer from an 1800's private residence (believed to be owned by the royal family of Demak) serves as the spa's reception area. Traditional carvings and art decorate the complex.

Flower baths may be enjoyed in the privacy of your own room or villa. Native flowers and essential oils provide natural healing properties, and glorious scents like frangipani and lavender will fill your room.

The Ritz-Carlton's adventure tours allow guests to bicycle through the hunting grounds of Balinese kings or sail along the rugged Bukit coastline. The resort's children's program introduces Balinese art, drama and traditions to the smallest guests.

Enjoy the sounds of traditional instruments while dining or relaxing in one of the resort's open air restaurants or bars, where international and local flavors may be sampled.

The Ritz-Carlton, Bali will enchant you.

**THE RITZ-CARLTON, BALI**
Jalan Karang Mas Sejahtera, Jimbaran
80364 Bali, Indonesia

# The Oberoi, Lombok

Lombok, a neighboring island of Bali, is one of Indonesia's gems. This exotic place is blessed with mountainous rainforests, golden beaches and gentle people.

Opened in 1997, The Oberoi, Lombok is a romantic beach resort. Its lush 24 acres rest on Medana Beach on the island's northwest coast. As you enter the temple inspired reception area, you are left breathless. When you see the terraced, reflecting infinity pools dotted with palms and secluded bale bengongs, as well as the sea and Gili Islands beyond, you know you have reached paradise.

This picturesque and peaceful haven has 30 terrace pavilion rooms and 20 luxurious villas. The terrace pavilion rooms offer a beautiful setting with your choice of garden or ocean views. Each thatched-roof villa is set within stone walls and is extremely spacious with beamed, vaulted ceilings and fabulous modern bathrooms looking upon private rock pond gardens. In addition, they have raised dining pavilions, terraces and courtyard gardens, plus many have private swimming pools. Indonesian furnishings and decorative objects are used throughout The Oberoi.

Lumbung Restaurant serves an International and Asian menu in a relaxed outdoor setting. The Tokek Bar serves the pool and recreational areas, while the Sunbird Café is beachside. Dining by the peaceful reflective pools or in the privacy of your own villa is a treat.

Pamper yourself at the resort's spa. The open pavilions offer massages and soothing beauty treatments. The Mandi Lulur, one of the resort's most popular treatments, includes a massage and relaxing tropical floral bath. Tennis facilities, health center and a PADI-certified Dive Center also offer diversions.

Romantic and exotic, The Oberoi, Lombok transports you to paradise.

## THE OBEROI, LOMBOK
## AN OBEROI RESORT
Medana Beach, Mataram
83001 Lombok, Indonesia

# The Ritz-Carlton, Osaka

Osaka represents modern Japan with its impressive skyline of contemporary architecture. A trading center since the 16th century, it has emerged as one of the world's most influential commerce centers.

Nishi-Umeda, the hub of Osaka's commerce and culture, is home to the city's finest hotel. The Ritz-Carlton, Osaka occupies the top floors, 24th to 37th floors, of Umeda's tallest building, thus affording panoramic views of the city. With the most spacious guest rooms available in Osaka, The Ritz-Carlton entertains its guests in style.

Honoring the tradition of Ritz-Carlton hotels, The Ritz-Carlton, Osaka is furnished

with Kyoto-style Kaiseki dishes, teppanyaki, tempura and sushi prepared in the authentic Edomae culinary style. Mediterranean-influenced dishes will be savored at Splendido, while La Baie serves French seafood delicacies in a Continental atmosphere. Xiang Tao, the Cantonese restaurant, has a tantalizing menu and is the home of many rare Asian antiques, including Ching Dynasty embroidery, a Tang horseman statue and rare snuff bottles. The Ritz-Carlton even has a gourmet take-out shop filled with delicious goodies.

With its warm welcome, sensational service and world-class style, The Ritz-Carlton brings a little bit of Europe to Osaka.

in grand European style with silk wall coverings and 19th century art and antiques. The 262 rooms and 30 suites are welcoming and offer the most modern amenities for business and leisure travelers. Wooden and stone floors, tatami mats, shoji screens and traditional Japanese bathrooms with granite tubs complete the serene décor in two Japanese themed suites.

The Ritz-Carlton has exceptional dining selections. Hanagatami introduces four Japanese culinary styles to guests

**THE RITZ-CARLTON, OSAKA**
2-5-25 Umeda, Kita-Ku
Osaka 530-0001, Japan

# Four Seasons Hotel Tokyo at Chinzan-so

Just on the edge of the financial and business centers, the Four Seasons is located in the exclusive residential neighborhood of Bunkyo-ku. Situated within the 17 acre historic Chinzan-so Gardens, the Four Seasons offers serenity in a bustling world capital.

The Chinzan-so Gardens were established over a century ago by Japanese royalty. This tranquil haven, open to hotel guests and locals, is home to a wide variety of monuments, shrines and artifacts. A sacred Pasania tree, over 500 years old, is located within the gardens. Chinzan-so even has its own mineral spring well, and the water is bottled and offered exclusively to hotel guests. The centerpiece of the gardens is the 1,000 year-old Pagoda brought from Hiroshima in its original form. It is perhaps most dramatic at night, when it is lit for all to enjoy.

The Four Seasons Hotel's décor is primarily European, but an extensive Japanese art collection reflects Asian culture and heritage. Antique porcelain vases, glazed pottery, Japanese screens, ancient scrolls, hand-carved chests and other valuable pieces of art can be enjoyed throughout the hotel.

The 228 rooms and 55 suites are decidedly traditional; though two suites are dedicated to Japanese design. All rooms are spacious and most feature large V-shaped bay windows. The one-of-a-kind Imperial suite is the hotel's most extravagant accommodation.

The hotel's fitness center and spa include a heated indoor pool, sauna, steam bath and Guerlain spa. The Onsen bath offers a traditional Japanese mineral bath with water from the famous Itoh Hot Springs.

The Four Seasons Hotel blends old and new Tokyo in one magnificent setting.

**FOUR SEASONS
HOTEL TOKYO
AT CHINZAN-SO**
10-8 Sekiguchi 2-Chome,
Bunkyo-ku
Tokyo 112-8667, Japan

# Four Seasons Resort Maldives at Kuda Huraa

Off the coast of India in the middle of the Indian Ocean, the Maldives are a collection of 1,200 tiny islands that dazzle your senses. It just doesn't get much more exotic than this, where only 70 islands are inhabited and most are occupied by a single resort.

The Four Seasons Resort Maldives indulges your fantasies with white sand beaches and perpetually warm turquoise waters. Occupying an entire coral island, this secluded resort is luxury at its finest. The resort's 106 thatched-roof bungalows are located on the beach and over the water. The 38 water bungalows, perched on stilts above the blue lagoon, have an appealing atmosphere with sun decks and steps leading directly down to the water. Beach villas have splendid garden showers or private plunge pools. Rattan and wicker furniture and natural fabrics lend a casual ease.

The Four Seasons Resort offers a multitude of dining choices. Baraabaru, in the main pavilion or at the lagoon's edge, serves exotic dishes from rice biriyanis to delicacies from the tandoori oven. Mediterranean dishes are highlighted at the Reef Club, and its deck is terrific for sunset cocktails. Café Huraa is housed within one of the resort's signature open-air, thatched-roof pavilions.

One of the largest in the Maldives, the blue-tiled pool is a magnificent sight. In one of the world's top ten diving destinations, active guests will delight in the water sports, including a dive center, the fitness facility and tennis courts. Take advantage of the soothing spa services with a tropical, Asian flair.

Delight in the private luxury at the secluded and exotic Four Seasons Resort Maldives.

**FOUR SEASONS
RESORT MALDIVES
AT KUDA HURAA**
North Malé Atoll
Republic of the Maldives

# Soneva Fushi Resort & Spa

Sheltered from the rest of the world, Soneva Fushi is tucked away on one of the seventy inhabited glorious private islands in the Maldives.

A blend of the owners' names, Sonu and Eva, Soneva Fushi is an unusual home away from home. The 62 accommodations, 25 sea-facing bungalows and 37 villas are nestled within the lush, dense greenery of the island. Indigenous woods, subtle fabrics and touches of sand create havens of serenity while showcasing a relaxed, regional decorative style. Each villa is fortunate enough to have its own stretch of pristine, powdery sand.

Soneva Fushi is dedicated to establishing

harmony with its natural environment. Most of the villas were constructed around existing vegetation; only two trees were removed to make way for the resort. Guests receive faxes in bamboo canisters, rather than wasting paper envelopes, and guests are encouraged to protect the ecology.

The spa is an integral part of the experience at Soneva Fushi. Taking a holistic approach to personal well-being, each guest is assessed by the staff to determine specific needs, rather than choosing from a menu of beauty treatments. Traditional treatments like Swedish massage and reflexology are offered alongside newly-developed programs like detoxification massage and kinesiology.

Dining at Soneva Fushi is delightfully fun and romantic in the open-air restaurant, but you should experience the lantern-lit dinner on a private beach or picnic on a deserted island.

Soneva Fushi is surrounded by a private shallow lagoon and enclosed by a coral reef, making it a perfect spot for scuba diving and snorkeling. Both beginners and more advanced divers will benefit from the PADI dive school.

Soneva Fushi is barefoot chic at its best.

**SONEVA FUSHI**
Malé
Republic of the Maldives

# Huka Lodge

On the banks of the Waikato River with the mighty cascades of Huka Falls just below, Huka Lodge shares New Zealand's pristine landscape of verdant fields and crystal clear water with its guests.

Huka Lodge was established more than half a century ago by Alan Pye, an Irishman who came to Taupo after hearing it was an angler's paradise. Though early guests encountered a simple lodge and slept in canvas tents, Huka Lodge's reputation as an idyllic retreat grew. While the original spirit remains, today's guests are treated to luxurious accommodations and fine cuisine.

Welcoming you with its roaring log fire and panoramic views, the Main Lodge is the perfect spot to enjoy a good book or an evening cocktail. The greens and blues of the forest and river come alive in the Lodge's décor, while touches of red add warmth.

With superb cuisine, fine wines and varied settings, dining at Huka Lodge is a truly memorable experience. The wine cellar, library and trophy room provide elegant settings, while the terrace, garden and riverbank are ideal for alfresco dining.

Twenty secluded guest suites are tucked along the riverbank and enclosed by trees. Rich wood floors and antique country furniture set an understated elegance in the rooms. Influenced by the natural setting, bathrooms feature glass ceilings for unique views of the towering trees.

No time spent at Huka Lodge would be complete without casting a fishing line or enjoying the natural beauty of the park-like grounds or the area.

Sleep well at Huka Lodge, but wake each morning to the gentle sounds of the out of doors.

**HUKA LODGE**
Huka Falls Road
Taupo, New Zealand

# Four Seasons Hotel Singapore

The Four Seasons Hotel is a contemporary building located on tree-lined Orchard Boulevard, just around the corner from Orchard Street, Singapore's Fifth Avenue. The hotel is convenient to all key business and financial districts.

The 214 rooms and 40 suites have a distinctive European character. The executive suites are perfect for informal business meetings, while the Presidential and Royal suites are ideal for gracious entertaining. Over 1,500 pieces of Asian and International art grace the walls of the hotel.

The Four Seasons offers two wonderful dining choices. Jiang-Nan Chun has a gourmet Cantonese menu and serves traditional dim sum along with Cantonese delicacies. One-Ninety specializes in cuisine from all over the world. Have no fear - the expert staff will guide your every selection. At tea time, One-Ninety continues the tradition of a bygone era when Singapore was a significant British Empire colony by serving "high tea."

The elegance and tradition at the Four Seasons Hotel Singapore will satisfy your every whim.

Many important pieces are counted among their impressive collection.

With two outdoor pools and the country's only air-conditioned tennis courts, the Four Seasons feels more like a resort than a hotel in a city. The well-equipped health club covers two floors and includes fantastic recreational and relaxation facilities. Here at the Four Seasons, stress relief can include massages, body wraps or sessions in the flotation tank or mind gear syncro-energizer.

**FOUR SEASONS HOTEL SINGAPORE**
190 Orchard Boulevard
Singapore 248646

# The Ritz-Carlton Millenia, Singapore

Dominating more than seven acres on Marina Bay, Singapore's newest business and entertainment center, The Ritz-Carlton Millenia is a modern architectural landmark.

The hotel's extensive art collection, which includes American artists like Frank Stella, Andy Warhol, David Hockney and Dale Chihuly, comprises 4,200 pieces and is considered one of Southeast Asia's finest. The hotel's commitment to art is instantly recognizable in the lobby. See Frank Stella's striking three-ton roof sculpture suspended from the ceiling and in the Lobby Lounge gaze at Dale Chihuly's magnificent glass "Sunrise" sculpture. Intriguing pieces can be found throughout the hotel.

The Ritz-Carlton's 528 deluxe rooms and 80 suites are a

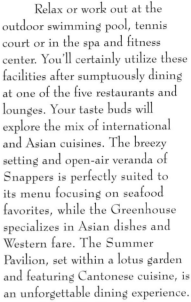

vision of contemporary elegance. The city and marina views are astounding and even extend to the magnificent bathrooms, voted among the sexiest in the world by *Tatler*. All rooms feature Guestnet, an infra-red wireless keyboard system that allows guests to check their email, access the Internet and watch the latest Hollywood releases. The Ritz-Carlton is world-renowned for its exceptional and thoughtful service, and deservedly so as everything is attended to here.

Relax or work out at the outdoor swimming pool, tennis court or in the spa and fitness center. You'll certainly utilize these facilities after sumptuously dining at one of the five restaurants and lounges. Your taste buds will explore the mix of international and Asian cuisines. The breezy setting and open-air veranda of Snappers is perfectly suited to its menu focusing on seafood favorites, while the Greenhouse specializes in Asian dishes and Western fare. The Summer Pavilion, set within a lotus garden and featuring Cantonese cuisine, is an unforgettable dining experience.

Stay at The Ritz-Carlton Millenia, Singapore for a scintillating experience.

**THE RITZ-CARLTON MILLENIA, SINGAPORE**
7 Raffles Avenue
Singapore 039799

# The Oriental

Established 125 years ago on the banks of the Chao Phraya River, the ancient River of the Kings, The Oriental is legendary. This magical hotel has been the source of inspiration for generations of writers, including Somerset Maugham, Graham Greene, Noel Coward and James Michener.

The Oriental is one of the world's most acclaimed hotels. Its 360 rooms and 35 suites are exquisite with the shimmer of Thai silk and furnishings from the Orient. All guests are regally pampered with personal butler service.

The Oriental provides a complete dining experience with ten different cuisines. You will

It is a celebration of ancient Siam, from its traditional dishes to its entertainment of classical Thai dance and music.

The Oriental encourages you to take home a greater understanding of Thailand's rich traditions through its cooking and culture programs, run by top chefs and leading Thai scholars. Be sure to take the daily cruise on the Oriental Queen, which takes you to the majestic ruins of Ayudhaya, Thailand's capital between the 14th and 18th centuries. After a long day of working or sightseeing, luxuriate at the pool or spa for health and beauty treatments.

Let The Oriental of Bangkok inspire you.

never forget dining at the Riverside Terrace, where the long tail boats and rice boats pass you by. Named for one of Joseph Conrad's characters, Lord Jim's prepares magnificent seafood, while the riverside buffet encompasses more than a hundred courses! Certainly the most unique, the Sala Rim Naam is one of the treasures of The Oriental. Located directly across the river from the hotel, the Sala Rim Naam is housed in a pavilion made of teak, bronze and marble.

**THE ORIENTAL**
48 Oriental Avenue
Bangkok 10500, Thailand

# The Peninsula Bangkok

**B**angkok is a mystical city of palaces and shrines. Its incredible sense of timelessness and fascinating history make it one of Southeast Asia's most alluring cities.

The Peninsula blends European and Thai style on the west bank of the Chao Phraya River. This 39-story building echoes its riverbank setting with its wave-shaped architecture. All of Bangkok's major sights are nearby, including The Grand Palace and the Reclining Buddha Temple, and the hotel's unique green-roofed boat provides easy transportation across the busy river.

All of The Peninsula's gracious 305 guest rooms and 65 suites face the river. With just 10 rooms and 2 suites located on each floor, The Peninsula offers incredible space. After a day out on Bangkok's crowded streets, you will be delighted with the extra room! The rooms combine European and Asian design, and five of the suites are themed. The Peninsula Suite is the hotel's showpiece in size and view with warmth and beauty. The Thai suite expertly blends contemporary Bangkok with traditional Siamese.

The Peninsula's recreational facilities are astounding. The fitness center has two floodlit tennis courts and a full gym with river views. The three-tiered outdoor swimming pool is the hotel's crown jewel, though. Stretching toward the river, the pool's terraces have waterfalls, bridges and abundant tropical flowers. Intricately carved wooden pavilions known as salas are located poolside. Six restaurants tempt guests with choices of Asian and international specialties.

Pamper yourself at The Peninsula in Bangkok.

**THE PENINSULA BANGKOK**
333 Charoennakorn Road, Klongsan
Bangkok 10600, Thailand

# The Sukhothai

Borrowing its name from the 13th century capital regarded as the first true Thai kingdom, The Sukhothai recalls the grandeur of the finest palaces and salons of Bangkok's golden age.

Away from the bustle of Bangkok's famously frenetic streets, The Sukhothai is on a quiet, tree-lined street in the city's embassy district. Its six acres of flower gardens, lily ponds and reflection pools are atmospheric and serene. Though opened in 1991, The Sukhothai shunned the modern architecture of glass towers and skyscrapers for uncomplicated four and nine story buildings capped by simple pitched roofs. The Sukhothai's statement is exquisitely Thai.

20th century comforts and technology. Magnificent teak floored bathrooms are enormous and equal the size of many standard hotel rooms. Private balconies overlooking the tranquil lily ponds or inner courtyards grant peace to all guests.

As one would expect from a hotel whose name means "dawn of happiness," The Sukhothai offers some of Bangkok's finest dining. Surrounded by a lotus pond, the traditional Thai salas at Celadon offer a unique and spectacular setting for one of the city's finest Thai restaurants. Three other restaurants serve terrific French, Italian and Asian dishes.

Let your happiness abound at The Sukhothai.

The Sukhothai's use of fine Thai fabrics, teak, granite and mirror is artful, and more than 750 years of Thai art and architecture influence all public and private spaces. Serene courtyards, located throughout the property, are home to reflecting pools with 13th century stupas and glorious pagodas. The lobby courtyard has a stunning reflection pool.

The 146 rooms and 80 suites echo traditional Thai design philosophies while incorporating

**THE SUKHOTHAI**
13/3 South Sathorn Road
Bangkok 10120, Thailand

# The Regent Resort Chiang Mai at Mae Rim Valley

A one hour flight from Bangkok brings you to the magical world of the Mae Rim Valley, a mountainous landscape dotted with terraced rice paddies and lush vegetation. The Regent Chiang Mai's reputation for sterling service and luxurious accommodations has put the Mae Rim Valley on the map for all discerning travelers.

The Regent Chiang Mai, a Four Seasons Resort, is a glorious world of its own with 64 Lanna-style pavilions. Built with indigenous materials, the suites are accented with Siamese art and rich Thai fabrics. Eleven suites are especially palatial, with multiple bedrooms, private plunge pools and rooftop penthouses. These suites even come with your own Mae Baan, or live-in housekeeper.

A comprehensive spa is set within the gardens. Thai herbs and aromatic oils are sourced from traditional rural origins and serve as the influence for many of the soothing treatments. Other facilities include a swimming pool and lighted tennis courts.

The two restaurants and bar highlight Thai cuisine, and picnic baskets with local and Western specialties may be ordered for excursions. Though the resort's sweeping views, breathtaking scenery and attentive service may encourage you to spend all of your time within, venture beyond to enjoy the local culture. Orchid, snake and butterfly farms are nearby, and elephant trekking is a great way to see the countryside. Hill tribe villages, untouched by the demands of the 20th century, offer fascinating insight into this region. River rafting and mountain trekking to the Golden Triangle, Laos and Burma can also be arranged.

The Regent Resort Chiang Mai entices and mesmerizes.

**THE REGENT RESORT CHIANG MAI AT MAE RIM VALLEY**
Mae Rim-Samoeng Old Road
Mae Rim, Chiang Mai 50180,
Thailand

# North America
# &
# South America

CANADA

UNITED STATES

MEXICO

ARGENTINA

BRAZIL

PERU

VENEZUELA

# The Ritz-Carlton, Montreal

Montreal's intimate character and European flavor make it one of Canada's most enchanting cities. This 350 year-old city is the second largest French-speaking city in the world and its first-class restaurants, museums and festivals continue to attract the world's most discerning visitors. In the center of it all is The Ritz-Carlton, Montreal.

Built in 1912, this landmark hotel combines old-world charm and modern amenities as one of the first properties of the Ritz-Carlton Hotel Company. Since the hotel's opening, Canadian history has unfolded here. The first transcontinental phone call was placed from the original Ritz-Carlton.

delightful and romantic; perhaps one of the many reasons that Elizabeth Taylor and Richard Burton chose the hotel for one of their weddings.

One of the pure delights of a stay at The Ritz-Carlton, Montreal is an afternoon at Le Jardin du Ritz; enjoy its manicured gardens and duck pond with an adorable family of ducklings. The formal dining room, Café de Paris, serves fine French food in a classic setting.

The Ritz-Carlton, Montreal will thrill you with its grand tradition and impeccable service.

After Vancouver replied that it could hear the caller from Montreal, champagne corks were popped in celebration.

The Ritz-Carlton, Montreal has a timeless style. Persian carpets line the floors and even the ordinary act of opening a door becomes extraordinary with gold-plated doorknobs. The 185 deluxe rooms and 45 suites are

**THE RITZ-CARLTON, MONTREAL**
1228 Sherbrooke Street West
Montreal, Quebec H3G 1H6, Canada

# Four Seasons Hotel Toronto

Toronto is Canada's melting pot. It is home to one half million Italians, the largest Chinese population in Canada, and the largest Portuguese colony in North America. The city thrives on its diversity, especially in arts and culture. Toronto's theater scene is the world's third largest!

Opened in 1972, the Four Seasons Hotel Toronto not only set new standards in Toronto, but also revolutionized the industry as the first Four Seasons Hotel. Today, the impeccable standards set in Toronto can be appreciated in 51 hotels throughout the world.

The Four Seasons Hotel Toronto is an ideal base for visitors to this vibrant metropolis. Located in Yorkville, a neighborhood renowned for

its fabulous entertainment, you will discover inventive restaurants and fine shopping just outside your door. The Royal Ontario Museum is just a few yards away from the hotel, and the business district is just a five minute walk.

The 230 rooms and 150 suites live up to your expectations with fine furnishings and creature comforts like in-room exercise

equipment, multiple phone lines and CD players. Of course, there is a health club and pool.

Toronto's dining scene is well represented at the Four Seasons. The Studio Café has a gallery style space with an eclectic collection of Canadian arts and crafts. Its extensive menu has something for everyone. The formal dining room, Truffles, will transport you to the French countryside with Provencal cuisine. The people-watching at La Serre is extraordinary; *Newsweek* recently named it as one of the world's best bars.

Both trendy and traditional, the Four Seasons Hotel Toronto is tops.

**FOUR SEASONS
HOTEL TORONTO**
21 Avenue Road
Toronto, Ontario M5R 2G,
Canada

# Four Seasons Hotel Vancouver

Vancouver is bursting with energy. It is the commerce and culture capital of British Columbia in Western Canada and its dramatic mountainous landscape immediately catches your eye. With a prime location and renowned service, the Four Seasons Hotel is the finest in Vancouver.

Whether you are visiting Vancouver on business, pleasure, or prior to or after taking an Alaskan cruise, the Four Seasons is sure to please. It occupies an ideal location atop the fashionable boutiques of the Pacific Centre; and the popular Market area, Gastown and famous

Stanley Park are just minutes away. Vancouver's lively arts and entertainment scene is a must for every visitor, and is just a short walk away. Though there are many terrific dining choices in Vancouver, the hotel's own Chartwell Restaurant has an inventive and delicious menu that will persuade you to stay close to home.

The 318 rooms, 65 suites and 2 split-level penthouse suites are soothing after a long day. The décor has a relaxed ease and the harbor view accommodations are picture-perfect.

An efficient and professional

business center will bring smiles to harried executives needing assistance in an unfamiliar city, and the hotel's health club will delight all guests. With free weights, advanced exercise machines and an indoor/outdoor pool with an oasis-like outdoor terrace, there is something for everyone here.

Experience the energy of Vancouver while enjoying the serenity and service of the Four Seasons Hotel Vancouver.

**FOUR SEASONS
HOTEL VANCOUVER**
791 West Georgia Street
Vancouver, British Columbia,
Canada V6C 2T4

# Arizona Biltmore Resort & Spa

Arizona's largest resort, the Arizona Biltmore Resort & Spa is also one of the country's best.

Set in the foothills of Squaw Peak in Phoenix's exclusive Biltmore district, the Arizona Biltmore bears the distinction of being the only existing hotel touched by the hand of architectural visionary Frank Lloyd Wright. Thirty-nine acres of flowering gardens invite you to unwind while savoring the desert landscape.

Opened in 1929 and owned for 44 years by chewing gum magnate William Wrigley, the Arizona Biltmore established a reputation for being the favored spot of business tycoons and celebrities.

The 730 guest rooms, suites and private villas all reflect Frank Lloyd Wright's distinctive style. Mission-style furnishings and 1930's lamps complete the interior design while a desert palette of beige, sand and ivory is used in all accommodations.

The Arizona Biltmore offers a wealth of recreational opportunities, from water sports and tennis to croquet and lawn bowling. Two PGA championship golf courses are adjacent to the property, and with eight swimming pools, the hot Arizona sun is never a concern. A 92 foot water slide makes the Paradise Pool great fun, while the Catalina pool, named for its tiles that originate from California's Catalina Island, is a more intimate setting. It was Marilyn Monroe's favorite.

The resort's sensational spa takes its influence from the Native Americans who once inhabited this region with treatments like raindrop therapy and cactus flower wraps.

Four distinctive restaurants serve an exquisite blend of New American cuisine that combines French, Southwestern and Asian flavors. This property has it all, from informal cafés to more formal dining.

Arizona Biltmore Resort & Spa is always a sunny choice.

**ARIZONA BILTMORE RESORT & SPA**
24th Street & Missouri
Phoenix, Arizona 85016 USA

# Royal Palms Hotel & Casitas

The northern edge of the Sonoran Desert, known as the Valley of the Sun because of its 330 plus days a year of sunshine, is home to the seductive Royal Palms Hotel & Casitas.

Royal Palms, named for the glorious palms that line the driveway, is a resort in the Mediterranean style with charming stone walkways, courtyards with trickling fountains and Spanish Colonial architecture. The mansion, once the winter home of Cunard steamship executive Delos Cooke, serves as the resort's inspiration. The original owner's presence is still felt at Royal Palms. Avid world travelers, the Cookes often brought mementos home

from their trips. Many of the exotic palms, flowers and cacti in the garden were brought home from abroad, and the interiors are enhanced by items acquired during their travels.

The 116 guest rooms and casitas are furnished in a rustic Mediterranean style. Jewel tones are complemented by southwestern themes, and many rooms have fireplaces and private patios. The rooms speak of a private home, no doubt due to the unusual artifacts and individualized styling found in each accommodation.

The romantic vaulted ceilings and warm glow of the fireplace at T. Cooke's provide an inviting and romantic spot for dining. T. Cooke's gourmet Mediterranean menu is

punctuated by dishes from Barcelona and Tuscany.

Guests at Royal Palms may venture beyond to the resort communities of Scottsdale and Phoenix to play a round of golf or enjoy a scenic hike, though you may choose to remain by the pool or enjoy an in-room fireside massage.

Royal Palms Hotel & Casitas is an intimate enclave with the panache of the Mediterranean and the spirit of the Southwest.

**ROYAL PALMS
HOTEL & CASITAS**
5200 East Camelback Road
Phoenix, Arizona 85018 USA

# Four Seasons Resort Scottsdale at Troon North

For a golfer's mecca, head to the Four Seasons Resort Scottsdale at Troon North. Though this region is home to over 130 golf courses, Troon North's two championship courses are considered among the best desert courses in the world. Fairways wind through the rugged landscape scattered with cactus forests and giant boulders and abundant sunshine helps make playing conditions ideal.

The Four Seasons, adjacent to the two courses, is the official resort of Troon North. Half the tee times are allotted for Four Seasons guests, and all guests are given priority when selecting times. Southwestern,

adobe-style casitas are clustered around the grounds dotted with Native American pottery and saguaro cacti. The 188 guest rooms and 22 suites are housed in 26 casitas, and 23 villas are also located on the property for those needing a bit more room. The suites have private plunge pools, outdoor garden showers and outdoor kiva fireplaces. A definitive southwestern theme is used in the interiors and many rooms have sensational views of Camelback Mountain.

The Four Seasons is a treat for all guests, including non-golfers. Focusing on Native American traditions, the spa offers a soothing way to spend an afternoon.

Indigenous materials, like yellow clay and algae mud from the nearby Mojave Desert and rocks from the Salt River, are used in the relaxing treatments. The swimming pool, carved out of the desert, is a serene spot. The three restaurants create lively atmospheres for delicious dining.

The Four Seasons Resort Scottsdale at Troon North is a hole in one.

## FOUR SEASONS RESORT SCOTTSDALE AT TROON NORTH
10600 Crescent Moon Drive
Scottsdale, Arizona 85255 USA

# The Phoenician

The Phoenician, with 654 guest rooms and suites, 11 restaurants and 9 pools, is the epitome of a grand resort.

Nestled at the base of Camelback Mountain in the Sonoran Desert, The Phoenician maintains the intimacy of a boutique hotel while offering the services of a mega-resort. The property truly has something for everyone. Play a round of golf on the spectacular 27 hole course or meet your match on the championship tennis courts. The Centre for Well-Being is renowned for its sessions including body treatments, massages and other relaxation techniques. Nine pools and a waterslide will cool you down after a hard day's play.

Guest accommodations are situated within two buildings, private casitas and villas. In the heart of it all, the main building offers 454 rooms and 14 suites with a central location near the pools and restaurants. The Canyon Building has only 20 rooms and 40 suites and is set back against Camelback Mountain. A bit more secluded, the casitas and villas offer 107 rooms and 19 suites with even more privacy and space. Casual elegance, muted colors, rattan furniture and Berber carpets are found in all rooms. The 8 million dollar art collection may be enjoyed throughout the resort.

Food is taken very seriously at The Phoenician. Bedtime chocolates are flown in three times a week from Belgium and the resort boasts an in-house butcher. Pastries, bread and ice cream are made fresh daily. Mary Elaine's is the star of the resort, with award-winning cuisine and a multi-million dollar wine cellar.

Rising from the desert, The Phoenician is superb.

**THE PHOENICIAN**
6000 East Camelback Road
Scottsdale, Arizona 85251
USA

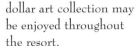

# Ventana Inn & Spa

Ventana Inn & Spa, on California's Big Sur coast, is truly uplifting.

Perched 1,200 feet above the Pacific Ocean, Ventana Inn enjoys a peaceful setting amid 240 acres of meadows, redwoods and flowering shrubs. Twelve buildings, carefully designed to blend with the landscape, contain just 59 rooms and suites. Polished cedar used in the interiors is complemented by personal touches like curtained beds, handmade quilts and handpainted headboards. Some accommodations feature fireplaces, wet bars and hot tubs.

Peace and quiet is paramount at Ventana, making it the perfect place to rekindle or begin a romance, or take time for reflection. The Allegria Spa, translates to happiness both literally and figuratively. The spa's philosophy of connecting the mind and body to nature is present in many of the treatments and programs. Two heated outdoor pools with bathhouses containing Japanese hot baths and sun decks, and guided hikes leading up the Santa Lucia Mountains entice you to get back to nature.

Cielo, Ventana's restaurant, is nestled at the top of the bluff, linked by a wooded trail to the guest accommodations. Though the inn provides shuttle service, the fifteen minute walk past towering redwoods and oaks is worth it. The fresh seafood, game and traditional fare is matched only by the panoramic views of the unparalleled Pacific.

The romantic Ventana Inn & Spa is a California dream.

**VENTANA INN & SPA**
Highway One
Big Sur, CA 93920 USA

# Four Seasons Resort Aviara

Four Seasons Resort Aviara offers the best of both worlds. San Diego's attractions are just 30 minutes away, yet the resort's serene setting is worlds apart from everyday distractions.

Situated within 200 landscaped acres, the resort shares southern California's natural beauty with its guests. Resting on a plateau, the resort overlooks the Batiquitos Lagoon, Pacific Ocean and a nature preserve home to a wide variety of wildlife, including blue herons, great egrets and even endangered western snowy plovers.

The Four Seasons celebrates southern California's Spanish influences in its colonial architecture. The resort's 287 rooms and 44 suites are located in the main

Spanish Colonial building. Rooms create a sophisticated setting with elegant furnishings and modern amenities. Once you are ensconced in your room, it will be easy to understand why this is the San Diego area's finest resort. Villas, nestled near the lagoon, provide an even more exclusive experience.

Golf is a major highlight at the Four Seasons Resort Aviara. Designed by Arnold Palmer, who took great pains to preserve the natural wetlands, the 18 hole golf course is a challenging delight. If the breathtaking views of the

lagoon and ocean make it difficult to focus on your game, try a lesson at the Aviara Golf Academy. Its innovative techniques for teaching the game and honing skills are making it a destination in itself.

In addition, a tennis program, fitness facility, full-service spa and walking tours of the gardens keep visitors active during their stay at Aviara. Or, lounge on the multi-tiered deck with two swimming pools and enjoy poolside frozen strawberries. Five restaurants create special memories.

The Four Seasons Resort Aviara is southern California at its best.

**FOUR SEASONS RESORT AVIARA**
7100 Four Seasons Point
Carlsbad, CA 92009 USA

# Quail Lodge Resort & Golf Club

Carmel's fabled charms are best enjoyed at Quail Lodge Resort & Golf Club.

This scenic resort is bestowed with 850 acres of lakes, gardens and rolling hills. Situated on the golden side of Carmel, away from its notorious fog, Quail Lodge enjoys sunshine and temperate weather for most of the year.

With its stunning 18 hole golf course, it is no wonder that golf is a favored pursuit at Quail Lodge. The Carmel River snakes along the course and its gentle gurgle calms even the most preoccupied golfer. Home of the annual California Women's State Amateur Championship, Quail Lodge consistently wins praise for its efforts to encourage women to play the game.

Quail Lodge's inviting 86 rooms and 14 suites set a graceful mood with warm colors and soft lighting. Listen to the chirping of the birds from your room and set your mind at ease.

Covey Restaurant provides delightful dining. Resting beside Mallard Lake, Quail Lodge's signature and favored spot, the restaurant has romantic views of the lighted fountain and charming footbridge. Swans glide past as you dine on imaginative cuisine, and the wine cellar offers a comprehensive selection of California wines, including the best from Monterey County.

Quail Lodge is an ideal base for exploring the California coast. Hot air ballooning and helicopter trips over Big Sur and the Monterey Peninsula and tours of Carmel Valley wineries can be arranged. Carmel-by-the-Sea is just a few minutes away. Monterey's Fisherman's Wharf and the famous 17 mile drive along the Pacific coast are also great ways to enjoy the region.

Quail Lodge Resort & Golf Club is a tranquil spot in California.

**QUAIL LODGE RESORT & GOLF CLUB**
8205 Valley Greens Drive
Carmel, CA 93923 USA

# The Ritz-Carlton, Laguna Niguel

Perched on top of a dramatic 150-foot bluff overlooking the crashing surf of the Pacific Ocean, The Ritz-Carlton, Laguna Niguel is the perfect blend of romance, luxury and natural beauty.

The location, halfway between Los Angeles and San Diego, is a delightful destination. Explore Southern California's sights, such as the charming artists colony of Laguna Beach, or escape your routine and relax at the award-winning Ritz-Carlton, Laguna Niguel.

Since opening in 1984, more than 4,000 weddings and innumerable marriage proposals and anniversary celebrations

have occurred at the resort. It is impossible to forget the glorious sunsets in this magnificent setting. The four story Mediterranean style building houses 363 rooms and 30 suites, all with private balconies. The comfortably elegant décor blends perfectly with views of the courtyard pool, garden, coastline or ocean. Of course, my favorite accommodations have sweeping views of the Pacific. In keeping with Ritz-Carlton tradition, the gracious staff is superb and the service is impeccable.

At this full-service resort, guests may choose to play golf on the adjacent oceanfront Robert Trent Jones, Jr. course, practice their serve on the tennis courts, swim in one of the two heated outdoor pools, work out in the fitness center or simply unwind on the two mile stretch of sandy beach.

Dining at the hotel is a delightful experience. Californian cuisine, interspersed with French and Mediterranean specialties, is served at the hotel's restaurants. Sip afternoon tea in the Library, and sample light meals or cocktails in the Lobby Lounge while gazing out at the soothing Pacific Ocean.

Bathed in sunshine and cosseted by ocean breezes, The Ritz-Carlton, Laguna Niguel is an idyllic resort.

**THE RITZ-CARLTON, LAGUNA NIGUEL**
One Ritz-Carlton Drive
Dana Point, CA 92629 USA

# Miramonte Resort

Experience the Tuscan countryside in the heart of California's desert at Miramonte Resort.

Located just minutes from the resort capital of Palm Springs in exclusive Indian Wells, Miramonte enjoys a majestic setting at the base of the Santa Rosa Mountains. The groves of olive trees and earth-toned buildings with expertly crafted stonework and graceful arches exude Italian charm. Roses interspersed among fountains and bougainvillea that twists its way along balconies and arches also speak of Italy.

Fourteen buildings in the Mediterranean style house 217 spacious rooms and 5 suites decorated with wrought iron headboards and soothing colors. Windows look out to the Santa Rosa Mountains and the surrounding golf courses. Miramonte epitomizes intimacy; even room service arrives by bicycle!

Miramonte, surrounded by three championship golf courses, is a golfer's dream. A special golf concierge handles all the details, from arranging custom clinics or lessons to developing golf itineraries based upon your skill, budget and schedule.

Tennis, horseback riding, hot air ballooning and rock climbing are just some of the other recreational opportunities available at Miramonte. Two sparkling swimming pools create the perfect setting for an afternoon of relaxation in the desert, while the comprehensive spa can take you to an even higher level of relaxation.

Miramonte's all-day restaurant, Brissago, concentrates on northern Italian cuisine with a focus on fresh fish and pasta. The Lobby Bar and Pool Grille offer more casual settings with equally delicious food.

Miramonte, with Tuscan charm and a stunning desert landscape, makes for a memorable vacation.

**MIRAMONTE RESORT**
45-000 Indian Wells Lane
Indian Wells, CA 92210 USA

# La Valencia Hotel

The charming seaside village of La Jolla may only be a seven mile stretch of coastline, but its spectacular scenery, variety of sporting activities and quaint mix of museums, galleries and shops makes it a wonderful vacation spot.

La Jolla's brightest gem is La Valencia Hotel. Opened in 1926, the hotel has a patina that contemporary hotels lack. Its history is closely tied to the community, and even today, La Valencia hosts as many local residents in its lounge and restaurants as out-of-towners. Affectionately known as "the pink lady of La Jolla," the hotel is instantly recognizable and its mosaic-tiled tower can be seen for miles. In fact, during World War II, residents and guests climbed the tower on the lookout for enemy planes!

La Valencia's position on a bluff overlooking the Pacific Ocean gives it a breezy atmosphere. Sea breezes and scents of tropical flowers waft through the 90 rooms, 10 suites and 15 villas. Rare antique furnishings enhance the individualized old-world style of all the rooms and suites. Newly opened, the villas are appointed with bright colors appropriate for the seaside. Handpainted Mexican tiles and white fir beamed ceilings, along with black granite sinks and baths, give the villas a luxurious ambience.

La Valencia's three restaurants are as unique as its accommodations. With only 12 booths and tables, The Sky Room Restaurant overlooks the cove and lights of the shore. The Mediterranean Room features an outdoor patio and scenic oceanview terrace for all-day dining. The Whaling Bar, with nautical murals and authentic harpoons and lanterns, is a real treat!

La Valencia Hotel is the jewel in the crown in La Jolla.

**LA VALENCIA HOTEL**
1132 Prospect Street
La Jolla, CA 92037 USA

# The Beverly Hills Hotel & Bungalows

You can't get more legendary accommodations in Hollywood than at the Beverly Hills Hotel & Bungalows.

Affectionately known as the "pink palace," the Beverly Hills Hotel has been one of the city's landmarks since 1912. Hovering above Sunset Boulevard, the hotel epitomizes Hollywood's history and glamour. Since opening, it has been the playground, meeting place and home for film's biggest stars. Marilyn Monroe and Yves Montand stayed here while filming *Let's Make Love*, and Katharine Hepburn once dove fully clothed into the pool. Clark Gable and Carole Lombard used to rendezvous in the bungalows before their marriage.

privacy and resembling private homes, they are favored among the stars and those seeking refuge from the world.

The hotel's well known restaurant, the Polo Lounge, continues its long standing as one of the city's hottest spots, and the newly created menu tempts with its offerings. Strolling in here while wearing a pair of trousers, Marlene Dietrich forever changed the rules dictating women's fashion.

The Beverly Hills Hotel & Bungalows is a Hollywood classic.

The hotel's almost three year facelift has freshened it without stripping it of its traditional charms. The monkeys that have stood guard at the entrance are still there, and the trademark banana-leaf wallpaper still decorates the hallways and coffee shop. The Beverly Hills Hotel's 203 guest rooms, suites and bungalows revive the glamour of 1940's Hollywood with handsome, plush furnishings. Of course, it is the 22 bungalows, nestled among banana palms, that are the most famous. Providing the utmost

**THE BEVERLY HILLS HOTEL & BUNGALOWS**
9641 Sunset Boulevard
Beverly Hills, CA 90210 USA

# The Peninsula Beverly Hills

Close to both Rodeo Drive and Century City, The Peninsula is an oasis in Beverly Hills.

The refined French Renaissance-style building is further enhanced by glorious gardens filled with an extraordinary selection of flowers, trees and shrubs. Exotic plants from as far as the Amazon and Hawaii are also included. Jacaranda trees and giant birds of paradise infuse the gardens with color. The gardens possess a distinctly European flavor, reinforced by trellises and fountains found throughout. The tranquility is astounding, considering the Peninsula is located in one of the world's busiest cities!

The Peninsula extends consideration to guests with pampering and unique services. Understanding today's travelers, especially those on business, the hotel features 24-hour check in/out services. A fleet of Rolls Royces is at your beck and call for local transportation while staying at the hotel.

The 164 rooms, 32 suites and 16 villas are sumptuously appointed with antiques, artwork, rich fabrics and marble floors. Luxurious villas are hidden within the gardens and filled with handwoven carpets, imported raw silks and custom furnishings. Loyal villa guests will discover their own monogrammed bathrobes, pillowcases and stationery on return visits.

The rooftop garden pool and terrace have terrific views of the city skyline and feature 12 private cabanas. Indulge yourself at the superb spa with one of the special treatments. The Bar is one of the hottest places in town. Belvedere Restaurant is a magnet for gourmands with its eclectic West Coast cuisine and beautiful garden-view ambience. After sampling the delicious cuisine at The Peninsula, you won't want to leave without ordering from Pen Air to Go. This service allows you to take tantalizing meals with you when you board your plane.

The Peninsula shines in Beverly Hills.

**THE PENINSULA BEVERLY HILLS**
9882 So. Santa Monica Boulevard
Beverly Hills, CA 90212 USA

# The Regent Beverly Wilshire

Head to The Regent Beverly Wilshire for a glimpse of sheer glamour.

You will walk a gilded path at The Regent Beverly Wilshire, where the temptations of Rodeo Drive are just outside your door. Located at the intersection of Rodeo Drive and Wilshire Boulevard, The Regent Beverly Wilshire encourages you to live the glamorous life in the heart of Beverly Hills. The hotel has always been adored by Hollywood's greatest stars. Elvis Presley, Steve McQueen and Warren Beatty all resided at The Regent Beverly Wilshire for periods of time.

The Italian-Renaissance landmark hotel is comprised of two wings with two very different personalities. The historic Wilshire wing dates to 1928 and features 147 rooms with a classic décor, while the contemporary Beverly wing has 248 rooms with sleek designs. Bridging old and new, the Regent Beverly Wilshire has something to suit your every mood.

The rich mahogany paneled walls and frescoed ceilings of the Dining Room set an elegant tone, while the California cuisine with Italian accents pleases your palate. Just off the Wilshire's main wing, the Lobby Lounge is a trendy venue for all-day dining. The hotel's pastry chef shares his English heritage with a traditional afternoon tea. The sultry lighting and intimate quarters of the Bar are scripted straight from a movie scene.

Even pets are regally pampered at The Regent Beverly Wilshire, where biscuits are served on silver trays and bowls are filled with Evian water. Your dog will surely know the best places in town after a walk with the concierge, customary for all four-legged friends.

Live the luxe life at The Regent Beverly Wilshire.

**THE REGENT BEVERLY WILSHIRE**
9500 Wilshire Boulevard
Beverly Hills, CA 90212 USA

# Hotel Bel-Air

Cross the arched bridge and enter the unhurried, romantic world of the Hotel Bel-Air.

Hotel Bel-Air's eleven acres of lush grounds, intimate courtyards, trickling fountains and wrought-iron balconies have been cosseting guests for over 50 years. Its intimate and serene atmosphere in the wooded canyons near Beverly Hills has made it a favorite of celebrities seeking anonymity and other guests seeking tranquility or romance.

Pink stucco 1920's Mission style buildings graciously house 52 distinctive rooms and 40 suites. Spread throughout the grounds, the rooms and suites offer incredible privacy. Flowered fabrics of the finest quality, European

The centerpiece of the gardens is certainly the graceful pond complete with elegant swans.

Delightful French-California cuisine is the focus at the main restaurant. Influenced by the seasons, the dishes feature fresh produce and herbs straight from the chef's garden. The outdoor terrace, overlooking the gardens and signature Swan Lake, is an exceptional spot for intimate dining. Additionally, Hotel Bel-Air features the only private in-kitchen dining room in Los Angeles. Eight guests are treated to a behind-the-scenes look at the chef's award-winning kitchen. Whether you remember the pointers or not, this is an experience to cherish.

Let Hotel Bel-Air envelop you in its romance.

furnishings and individual entrances from the hotel gardens, fountain courtyards or swimming pool area, create magical private settings.

Ten gardeners tend to the gardens and waterfalls at the Hotel Bel-Air. The gardens are a horticultural masterpiece. Home to a collection of more than 200 botanical species, the gardens also feature rare species and plants rarely seen in southern California. Glorious flowers and blossoms represent every color of the rainbow, and the scents are intoxicating.

HOTEL BEL-AIR
701 Stone Canyon Road
Los Angeles, CA 90077 USA

# Four Seasons Hotel Los Angeles at Beverly Hills

The Four Seasons Hotel Los Angeles at Beverly Hills is a star.

The sixteen-story hotel affords panoramic views of Beverly Hills, the Hollywood Hills, Bel Air and Century City. Located on a quiet residential street, the Four Seasons exudes calm.

The hotel's 188 rooms and 97 suites are luxuriously appointed with European panache. In keeping with the city's fast-paced nature, guests at the Four Seasons never have to worry about missing a call. Calls are transferred to personal cellular telephones, and for those guests who do not have a phone, the hotel will loan you one.

The spa at the Four Seasons is sensational. Exceptional treatments, like the European body kur and tequila massage, are offered here, yet it is the technological advances that make this spa a standout. Treatment rooms are equipped with advanced stereo systems for personalized selections and DVD players with soothing videos are attached to massage tables. The spa's signature aromatherapy products incorporate seasonal influences. Orange, rose and jasmine remind you of summer, while cinnamon, pink pepper and vanilla hint of autumn. The fourth floor has a lovely terrace with a heated swimming pool, Jacuzzi and poolside café.

The Windows Lounge is the place to be seen in Los Angeles. Hollywood's "A-list" comes here for the chic setting and the inventive drinks. Eleven different martinis are on the menu, and all pay tribute to the film industry with names like The Indie and The Starlet. Fine dining is adjacent to the lounge at Gardens Restaurant, a Florentine-inspired space showcasing California-Pacific cuisine.

The Four Seasons is a stylish selection in Los Angeles.

**FOUR SEASONS HOTEL LOS ANGELES AT BEVERLY HILLS**
300 South Doheny Drive at Burton Way
Los Angeles, CA 90048 USA

# The St. Regis Los Angeles

At last, The St. Regis brings its legendary standards and service to Los Angeles, the world's entertainment capital.

Located on the fashionable west side, The St. Regis is close to the businesses of Century City, yet Rodeo Drive and Beverly Hills are just one mile away. The hotel is also within walking distance of the city's top stores, restaurants and the famous Shubert Theatre.

The 257 rooms and 40 suites are elegantly appointed with a contemporary elegance. All rooms have private balconies to enjoy the fabulous views of the downtown skyline, Santa Monica coastline, the

estates of Bel-Air and the Hollywood Hills. Rooms are equipped with state-of-the-art technology, yet the warm décor ensures that all guests feel right at home. Grand deluxe rooms feature signature St. Regis butler service.

French elegance meets California ease at Encore, where creative Provencal cuisine is the focus. Parquet floors and palm trees set a refined tone, while floor-to-ceiling windows allow views of the surrounding landscaped gardens. Proper

English tea with delicate finger sandwiches and delectable pastries is served in the afternoon at the St. Regis Lounge.

The hotel's rooftop heated pool is topped off by whirlpool spas and private cabanas. Health conscious guests will be pleased to dine on spa cuisine by the pool. The health club is fully equipped with the latest cardiovascular equipment, while personal trainers and yoga instructors are available for private sessions. The spa also provides a full range of beauty and relaxation treatments.

All of Los Angeles is within your reach while staying at The St. Regis.

**THE ST. REGIS
LOS ANGELES**
2055 Avenue of the Stars
Los Angeles, CA 90067 USA

# The Ritz-Carlton, Marina del Rey

The Ritz-Carlton, Marina del Rey is only minutes from the Los Angeles Airport, but it is worlds apart spiritually.

The Ritz-Carlton stands at the edge of the world's largest manmade marina on over five waterfront acres overlooking the harbor and Pacific Ocean. The setting is instantly relaxing, whether you gaze at the luxury yachts and sailboats bobbing in the calm waters or jog along the Promenade, part of a 21 mile coastal path that runs from Malibu to Manhattan Beach. Yacht charters, deep-sea fishing excursions or sailing may be arranged at the hotel's private dock.

Ritz-Carlton caring, personal service.

The Ritz-Carlton is home to some of the best restaurants in the marina. The Dining Room's menu focuses on fresh seafood, while The Terrace introduces guests to California cuisine. The Lobby Lounge serves traditional afternoon tea, and is also a relaxing spot for cocktails or a nightcap. The poolside bar refreshes while you enjoy the outdoors.

Sail away to The Ritz-Carlton, Marina del Rey.

All 294 rooms and 12 suites have French doors opening on to private balconies for enjoyment of spectacular water views. A chic, sophisticated California décor, sprinkled with art and antiques, creates a relaxed atmosphere. Of course, you will have every modern amenity and experience the traditional

**THE RITZ-CARLTON, MARINA DEL REY**
4375 Admiralty Way
Marina del Rey, CA 90292
USA

# Four Seasons Hotel Newport Beach

Newport Beach, located on a stretch of land between Los Angeles and San Diego, is often referred to as the California Riviera because of its temperate climate, glorious sunshine and beautiful beaches.

Minutes from the majestic Pacific and its golden beaches, the Four Seasons Hotel Newport Beach is the perfect definition of a city resort. The shimmering swimming pool and tropical garden views make it easy to forget your worries.

Private balconies in all 192 rooms and 93 suites make it easy to drink in the panoramic views. The rooms blend west coast style, contemporary furnishings and Continental flair for an unpretentious elegance. If you must work, take advantage

of the extensive meeting space and complete business center.

Total relaxation is paramount at the Four Seasons Hotel. The swimming pool even includes telephones and dataports at each set of lounge chairs to ensure all guests never miss an important call or email! A wonderful 17 foot fireplace has recently been added to the pool area to chase away the evening chill or warm early-risers as they read the morning paper.

Overlooking lush tropical gardens,

Pavilion creates the perfect backdrop for a memorable dining experience. Flavors from Italy and the Mediterranean enhance the delicious California cuisine. More informal dining is available at the Café.

Considered one of the best golf courses in the country, the Tom Fazio designed Pelican Hill Golf Club extends exclusive rates and preferred tee times for guests at the Four Seasons. Managed by the Four Seasons, the Pelican Grill overlooks the 18th hole and provides a nice spot for lunch and dinner.

Relax California style at the Four Seasons Hotel Newport Beach.

**FOUR SEASONS HOTEL NEWPORT BEACH**
690 Newport Center Drive
Newport Beach, CA 92660 USA

# The Ritz-Carlton, Huntington Hotel & Spa

The historic Ritz-Carlton, Huntington Hotel & Spa occupies 23 acres in the San Gabriel Mountain foothills. Its fresh air and open space make it hard to believe it is only a short distance from downtown Los Angeles.

The Huntington Hotel opened its doors in 1907, originally catering to wealthy East Coast residents escaping cold winters. Acquired by Ritz-Carlton in 1991, the hotel's original turn-of-the-century glamour remains intact. Oriental carpets and crystal chandeliers revive the romance of bygone days. The 367 rooms, 25 suites and 8 cottages are comfortably elegant. Though

historic, the hotel features all modern conveniences expected of a five-star resort.

Housed in the charming Carriage House, the hotel's fitness center and spa are a dynamic duo. The fitness club helps you set new, or achieve current, fitness goals. The spa eases tensions with its cleansing body treatments and therapeutic massages. Facials, manicures, hair services and other beauty treatments may also be scheduled.

Four restaurants keep guests enthralled during their stay. The Terrace, open all day, features California-Mediterranean cuisine, including a sensational Sunday brunch. As its name

suggests, The Grill specializes in grilled meats and fresh fish in a casual setting with views of Horseshoe Garden and the San Gabriel Valley. The lounge and pool bar are entertaining spots by day or night.

Everything's coming up roses at the legendary Ritz-Carlton, Huntington Hotel & Spa.

THE RITZ-CARLTON, HUNTINGTON HOTEL & SPA
1401 South Oak Knoll Avenue
Pasadena, CA 91106 USA

# The Ritz-Carlton, Rancho Mirage

The Ritz-Carlton, Rancho Mirage brings comfort and elegance to the California desert.

The resort rests atop a 650-foot-high plateau in the foothills of the Santa Rosa Mountains near Palm Springs. The Coachella Valley and the distant San Jacinto Mountains can be seen from all 219 rooms and 21 suites. The décor follows the traditional Ritz-Carlton style, though distinctive touches reflect the desert environment and a more casual atmosphere.

The Ritz-Carlton, Rancho Mirage is a playground for both adults and children. The Ritz Kids program is offered at no cost and entertains children with daily

themes, including cooking skills and rules of etiquette. The children are content, and parents are free to play a round of golf, enjoy the pool or hit the tennis courts. This "golf capital" offers 18 championship courses within a 30-minute drive from the resort.

The spa takes advantage of the desert's beauty and incorporates its serenity into programs customized to your needs. The spa's menu, with over 30 treatments, will intrigue you, and many of the products used here include indigenous ingredients.

The resort is home to four fine dining establishments. The Dining Room's French and Mediterranean cuisine is served

in a sophisticated setting - perfect for those evenings when you want to take a little more time at dinner. The Café, with views of the pool and valley below, prepares California-style food. Like all Ritz-Carltons, the Lobby Lounge serves traditional afternoon tea each day. For a really spectacular environment, visit Mirada at the resort. It is the desert's only cliffside restaurant.

The Ritz-Carlton, Rancho Mirage is a desert paradise.

**THE RITZ-CARLTON, RANCHO MIRAGE**
68-900 Frank Sinatra Drive
Rancho Mirage, CA 92270 USA

# Rancho Valencia

Rancho Valencia revives the romance of southern California.

Just 25 miles north of downtown San Diego, Rancho Valencia is set within 40 acres of rolling hills in the canyon of Rancho Santa Fe. Though the community of La Jolla is minutes away, Rancho Valencia enjoys a rural setting of green lawns lined with impatiens, hibiscus and geraniums as well as abundant wildflowers. Citrus groves produce the famous Valencia oranges, known for their superior quality, and guests greet each day with a fresh-squeezed glass of orange juice.

Spanish-Colonial architecture and details from the Mediterranean come together in

Rancho Valencia's 20 casitas with 43 suites. The suites showcase regional touches and authentic décor with whitewashed beams, cathedral ceilings, tile-bordered fireplaces and shuttered windows. All suites have private patios. The Hacienda is perfect for a special occasion or a family. This adobe home features three suites and a private patio with a swimming pool and whirlpool.

Enjoy California and Mediterranean cuisine at Rancho Valencia's signature restaurant. The indoor dining room is charming and alfresco dining is a pleasure on the tiered terrace.

Rancho Valencia's tennis facilities are top notch, prompting it to be named among the top ten

tennis resorts in the United States. It has 18 courts set among the gardens. A full range of lessons and activities is offered. Golf privileges at two prestigious local courses are extended to all guests of the resort. European traditions and California innovations in spa treatments can be enjoyed at Rancho Valencia's spa. Aromatherapy and specialty massages, like Jin Shin Jitzu, are favorites.

Relax at Rancho Valencia.

**RANCHO VALENCIA**
5921 Valencia Circle
Rancho Santa Fe, CA 92067
USA

# Campton Place Hotel

San Francisco, the city by the Bay, is a cultural sensation. It enjoys a lively arts scene, boasts some of the best restaurants in the United States and thrives with booming businesses. In short, it is one of the country's most exciting destinations.

Just off Union Square, Campton Place Hotel offers a unique character. This small, deluxe hotel has only 101 rooms and 9 suites. The rooms share a clean, contemporary look while imparting comfort with warm tones. Sophisticated and welcoming, many guests grow to look toward their accommodations as private apartments rather than hotel

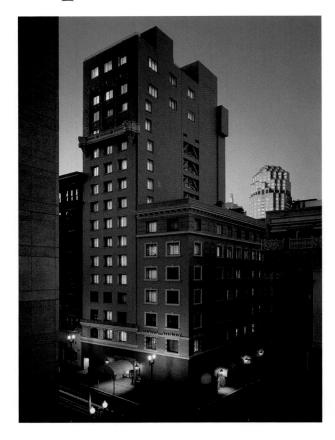

rooms, and the caring staff encourages this feeling. Window seats, featured in some rooms, are perfect for observing the city's beat from the comfort of your own room. Modem and data connections are provided in every room for those guests needing an office away from home.

Offering a destination of its own, the Campton Place Restaurant is consistently listed as one of San Francisco's top restaurants. Chef Laurent Manrique shares his family roots with cuisine from Gascony and the nearby Basque region of France. Noted for his foie gras, Manrique's food is delicious without being pretentious. A favorite on the menu is poule au pot, a delicious combination of chicken and broth. It is the essence of French comfort food. The serene, contemporary setting of the restaurant matches the kitchen's mood and style.

Make Campton Place your home away from home in San Francisco.

CAMPTON PLACE
HOTEL
340 Stockton Street
San Francisco, CA 94108 USA

# Four Seasons Hotel San Francisco

The Four Seasons returned to San Francisco with its legendary style in the fall of 2001.

The Four Seasons Hotel enjoys a central location in the middle of one of the city's most exhilarating neighborhoods, Yerba Buena. This area is known for its lively arts and entertainment scene as well as historic landmarks, such as the Phelan Flatiron building; practically next door to the hotel. The trendy restaurants, nightclubs and dot-com businesses of the South of Market area, as well as the attractions of Union Square are within a five minute walk from the hotel. Chinatown, home to the largest Chinese population in the United States, is just ten minutes away by foot.

The hotel's light-filled 231 guest rooms and 46 suites showcase views of the San Francisco skyline. Handsome furnishings in classic Four Seasons style complete the inviting look.

Located on the lobby level, Seasons Restaurant presents California cuisine in a stylishly informal atmosphere. Dramatic dark blue Norwegian granite floors and hardwood finishes add to the contemporary look. Carefully selected California wines complement delicious meals.

Guests at the Four Seasons are granted special access to the impressive Sports Club/LA, located directly below the hotel. This extensive fitness center is considered one of the best in the country because of its expert staff of personal trainers, nutritionists, spa technicians, the newest equipment and wide variety of classes, including martial arts, pilates and boxing. You will leave feeling in tip-top shape.

The Four Seasons, San Francisco's newest property, is one of the city's shining stars.

**FOUR SEASONS HOTEL SAN FRANCISCO**
735 Market Street
San Francisco, CA 94103 USA

# The Huntington Hotel

The Huntington Hotel & Nob Hill Spa reigns over San Francisco from its lofty position atop one of the city's highest hills.

Overlooking Grace Cathedral and the historic Flood Mansion, the intimate Huntington Hotel is located in the exclusive Nob Hill neighborhood. Built in 1924, the Huntington was the first steel and brick high rise west of the Mississippi.

Graceful and classic, the hotel's 100 guest rooms and 35 suites have always been favored by notable visitors. The rooms are the last word in luxury, from the exquisite furnishings to the enchanting views of the city's

charms. San Francisco is easily explored from here; a cable car stops just outside the hotel's front door.

The Big 4 Restaurant, named for the top four railroad tycoons, is a celebration of classic American cuisine. An outstanding collection of Western memorabilia is proudly displayed in this clubby setting. The splendid wine list is widely recognized for its excellence.

The Huntington Hotel is also home to the newly opened Nob Hill Spa. This urban escape is unlike anything else in the city, with celadon mosaic tiles inlaid with floor-to-ceiling windows and 24-karat gold with staggering views. A feng shui expert was consulted to ensure harmony in the space. Ten treatment rooms reflect San Francisco's different cultures. Fireplaces and hand-stenciled walls add to the luxurious ambience. Whether you partake in the champagne facial or the soothing ginseng milk bath, you will leave feeling refreshed.

Leave your heart in San Francisco at the wonderful Huntington Hotel.

**THE HUNTINGTON HOTEL & NOB HILL SPA**
1075 California Street
San Francisco, CA 94108 USA

# Mandarin Oriental, San Francisco

Occupying the top eleven floors of the city's third-tallest building, the Mandarin Oriental graciously towers above San Francisco.

The hotel's sophisticated 154 rooms and 4 suites blend Asian decorative touches with continental elegance. European duvets and silk headboards are incredibly inviting, and rich tones are used throughout all rooms. The four spacious suites are individually decorated with one-of-a-kind artwork. Picture windows in all rooms make for postcard-like views. Two of the suites feature terraces; don't forget to pack your camera! Some deluxe rooms have bathrooms that capture scenic San Francisco from the bathtub. Soak in luxury with one of the Mandarin Oriental's bathtub menu selections, like the Oceanic Minerals Bath with extracts from the Dead Sea or the Zen Blend Bath with energy, dream and tranquility bath teas.

Served daily, afternoon tea service honors its Asian heritage at the Mandarin Oriental. Six gourmet teas are served, including Rainforest Mint, Silver Jasmine or Chrysanthemint teas. A traditional cast iron teapot arrives with a bento box filled with Thai curried beef, shiitake triangles, unagi and a variety of sweets. Chopsticks and silk embroidered napkins complete the beautiful presentation.

Silks Restaurant is one of the city's premier dining establishments. European style carpeting, fabulous wall treatments and handpainted silk chandeliers reflect the restaurant's theme of Marco Polo's discovery of silk. Cinnamon, nutmeg and persimmon hues contribute to the inspirational décor. The menu is centered on California cuisine punctuated by Asian influences.

The Mandarin Oriental's location in the heart of the city makes it picture-perfect for all visitors, whether you are traveling on business, or simply want to enjoy the pleasures of San Francisco.

**MANDARIN ORIENTAL, SAN FRANCISCO**
222 Sansome Street
San Francisco, CA 94104 USA

# The Pan Pacific

Modern, yet comfortable, the Pan Pacific is one of San Francisco's architectural wonders.

Located on fashionable Post Street near Union Square, the Pan Pacific was designed a decade ago by acclaimed architect John Portman. Its Italian Renaissance façade is just a hint of the glories inside, with Oriental rugs, inlaid marble floors and a breathtaking 17 story atrium lobby.

The Far East meets the West in the Pan Pacific's 330 guest rooms and suites with lamps inspired by ancient Chinese ceramics, Chinoiserie patterned bed quilts and one-of-a-kind Asian prints. Deep soaking bathtubs and rare

In need of a quick breakfast before you dash off for a busy day? The hotel offers "flying pantry" room service, guaranteed to arrive within fifteen minutes of your call. A fleet of Rolls Royces and BMWs is available at all times to whisk you off to an important business meeting, and the hotel even provides business cards and stationery during your visit. Repeat visitors are encouraged to take advantage of the "luxury locker." This service ensures that you always have a change of business clothes pressed and ready for your next visit.

The Pan Pacific brings Asian standards of excellence to San Francisco.

Portuguese marble complete the spacious bathrooms.

The Pan Pacific's attention to detail is extraordinary. A pillow fluffing machine is on hand to fluff your pillows to your exact specifications. All guests are granted personalized butler service. Whether you need a button mended or require assistance with a project, your butler is at your service.

Business travelers are cosseted at the Pan Pacific.

THE PAN PACIFIC
500 Post Street
San Francisco, CA 94102 USA

# Park Hyatt San Francisco

Mirroring San Francisco's multicultural heritage, the Park Hyatt has international panache.

The Park Hyatt's location in the heart of the Financial District makes it an obvious choice for business travelers, but with the Waterfront, Chinatown and Fisherman's Wharf not far away, leisure visitors will not be disappointed. Also the Park Hyatt is adjacent to Embarcadero Center, a series of landscaped promenades with over 100 sidewalk cafés, shops and galleries.

goes the extra mile with chauffeured Mercedes service within the local downtown area. International guests may exchange over 40 different currencies directly at the hotel, and the business center assists business travelers from around the world.

The Park Grill showcases international grilled specialties in a club-like atmosphere, but for lighter meals, afternoon tea or cocktails, visit the Lobby Lounge.

The Park Hyatt shares San Francisco's delights with you.

Australian lace wood millwork, Italian polished granite, custom Chinese carpets and Spanish alabaster chandeliers comprise the eclectic,

international style that comes alive at the Park Hyatt. The hotel is also home to an impressive art collection, including a three-story bronze sculpture by Italian sculptor Arnaldo Pomodoro and a nine-foot gold-leaf tapestry woven by Colombian artist Olga de Amaral. Contemporary Bay Area artists are also represented in the Park Hyatt's collection.

The 360 rooms and 37 suites are equally dazzling with richly paneled foyers and granite-lined bathrooms. Personalized service is a hallmark of the Park Hyatt, and all guests treasure the special attention. The Park Hyatt

**PARK HYATT SAN FRANCISCO**
333 Battery Street
San Francisco, CA 94111 USA

# The Ritz-Carlton, San Francisco

The Ritz-Carlton breathed new life into one of San Francisco's landmarks. Bordering the financial district, this impressive Neo-Classical building was the former home of Metropolitan Life Insurance. When it opened in 1909, it caused controversy for not being in the heart of the business center. Left in ruins for years, the building was revitalized and recreated as a luxury hotel by Ritz-Carlton Hotels. It opened in 1991 as The Ritz-Carlton, San Francisco.

The Ritz-Carlton's unique atmosphere, exquisite décor and impeccable service make it one of the city's finest properties. The hotel boasts a museum quality collection of European and American artwork

and antiques. Two Louis XVI French blue marble covered urns with gilt mounts and a pair of 19th century Waterford crystal chandeliers are two of the highlights. Aubusson tapestries, Persian carpets, Georgian and Regency antiques and shining silver lend an aristocratic air to the hotel. The hotel even offers guided tours to see the collection.

The 294 rooms and 42 suites evoke turn-of-the-century elegance while featuring modern conveniences. A fitness center with indoor lap pool, whirlpool, exercise equipment and spa treatments is provided for guests' enjoyment.

The Ritz-Carlton's Dining Room is commended for its modern French cuisine and

complemented by attentive service. atmosphere and service. Contemporary Mediterranean food may be enjoyed at the Terrace Restaurant, while the bar features the largest single malt scotch collection in the United States. Of course, the famous Ritz-Carlton tea is served daily. The former cigar bar has been transformed into a paradise for sweet tooths. The pastry chef showcases his heavenly confections in one, two and three-course dessert menus.

The Ritz-Carlton, San Francisco is a classic.

**THE RITZ-CARLTON, SAN FRANCISCO**
600 Stockton at
California Street
San Francisco, CA 94108
USA

# Four Seasons Resort Santa Barbara

Known as the "American Riviera" because of its beaches and temperate climate, Santa Barbara rests between the Santa Ynez Mountains and the Pacific Ocean.

Opened in late 1927, The Biltmore, now known as the Four Seasons, became legendary as an exclusive enclave for the well-heeled. Though the Depression struck shortly after its opening, this grande dame graciously smiled through the tough times and refused to close its doors. When times turned better, the hotel began to thrive once again, particularly as a winter residence for wealthy women.

The Four Seasons Resort is nestled on 20 acres facing the sparkling Pacific Ocean. The landscaped

grounds are blessed with bountiful flowers, trees and plants, creating a garden setting for guests.

The Four Seasons shares the region's adoration of Spanish Colonial architecture in its hacienda-style main building and twelve cottages. Located in the main building and throughout the cottages, the 201 guest rooms establish a sense of place with regional style while incorporating international influences.

Capitalizing on the graceful arches that dominate this architectural style, La Marina is a casually elegant space for dining. Arched windows highlight unobstructed views of the Pacific. The Patio has a dreamy setting with its décor, oceanfront location and retractable roof.

The social center of the hotel is the exclusive beach club with a larger than Olympic size swimming pool and a lovely stretch of private beach. A health club, tennis courts, a second swimming pool in the garden, putting green, croquet and shuffleboard courts will keep you active, while the recently opened spa will satisfy all your sybaritic needs.

Live it up at the Four Seasons Resort Santa Barbara.

**FOUR SEASONS RESORT SANTA BARBARA**
1260 Channel Drive
Santa Barbara, CA 93108 USA

# Sonoma Mission Inn & Spa

Drink in the beauty of California's wine country at the Sonoma Mission Inn & Spa.

Sonoma Valley's rolling hills, balmy days and cool nights are ideal for the production of wine, and California's wines are among the most highly regarded in the world. For centuries, the region has also attracted visitors seeking the therapeutic benefits of its natural thermal mineral springs.

The Sonoma Mission Inn & Spa is the region's most luxurious resort. Steeped in history, the grounds were first discovered by Native Americans. The Mission-style inn dates to the late 1920's, and though it has undergone several

renovations, the original inn exists today.

The 170 rooms and 30 suites are romantic with country antiques and special touches. The historic inn houses 100 rooms, while across a wooden footbridge you will find additional rooms and suites in several buildings. Many accommodations feature fireplaces and terraces.

Considered one of the best in the United States, the spa at the Sonoma Mission Inn is heavenly. The spa focuses on the healing properties of the mineral springs with Roman bathing rituals, Watsu treatment pools and mineral baths. More than 50 treatments are available here, including the signature grape seed body polish. The resort's two swimming pools and various whirlpools are filled with natural artesian mineral water pumped from 1,100 feet below the inn.

A local favorite for over 50 years, the Big 3 Diner serves hearty country breakfasts and an eclectic American menu for lunch and dinner. The main restaurant expertly pairs its California and spa cuisine with an award-winning wine list.

Cheers to the Sonoma Mission Inn & Spa.

**SONOMA MISSION INN & SPA**
100 Boyes Boulevard
Sonoma, CA 95476 USA

# Four Seasons Hotel Washington, D.C.

Washington's tony and fun Georgetown neighborhood is home to the Four Seasons Hotel. Close to the business of the nation's capital, the Four Seasons introduces you to the quiet charms of the city's first residential district.

The 204 rooms and 55 suites are elegantly and tastefully appointed. A diverse selection of artwork adorns the walls of the private rooms. Collected for over 30 years, the collection includes works by Rackstraw Dounes, Red Grooms, Thornton Dial and Leonardo Cremonini.

The Four Seasons offers a comprehensive

fitness and spa facility. The indoor lap pool is a highlight, and you won't even need to worry about packing a swimsuit; the hotel provides all exercise wear free of charge! The Quiet Room, a soundproof facility that provides uninterrupted privacy and relaxation, is an intriguing addition. The spa offers a wide variety of treatments that may be enjoyed in the club or in the private spa room.

The Four Seasons is ideal for families visiting Washington. All guests, even the little ones, are pampered in the finest style. Children are welcomed with special in-room snacks, and video games are available upon request.

Even afternoon tea at the Four Seasons makes concessions for children with peanut butter and jelly finger sandwiches and hot fudge sundaes.

Fresh ingredients and dazzling flavors make the continental cuisine at Seasons Restaurant a delight, and private dining rooms overlook Washington's historic C & O Canal. Casual dining is available at the Garden Terrace and the Sunday jazz brunch is one of the city's best.

See a different side of Washington at the Four Seasons Hotel.

**FOUR SEASONS HOTEL WASHINGTON, D.C.**
2800 Pennsylvania Avenue N.W.
Washington, D.C. 20007 USA

# The Ritz-Carlton, Washington, D.C.

After a three year wait, The Ritz-Carlton is back in town.

Ideally located in downtown Washington's West End neighborhood, The Ritz-Carlton offers elegance and convenience. Washington's historical and cultural attractions like the White House, Capitol Hill and Embassy Row, are within a short distance from the hotel, and it is just three blocks from Georgetown.

The 265 rooms and 35 deluxe suites are beautifully appointed with European furnishings and equipped with modern amenities. Views of the city can be enjoyed from some rooms, while others overlook the tranquil Japanese garden. The private garden is multi-tiered and features a reflecting pool, bamboo plants and even a 30 foot cascading waterfall.

The Ritz-Carlton's service exceeds your expectations. Instead of the usual mint on your pillow, the Ritz-Carlton brings brownies, still warm from the oven, to your room. The recipe was inspired by one favored by legendary hotelier Cesar Ritz. Securing tickets to the Kennedy Center is just one of the services that the excellent concierge can perform for you. Whatever you may need during your visit, the caring and gracious staff is at your service.

The Sports Club/LA, one of the country's premier fitness facility chains, is located within the hotel. Hotel guests are granted access to this private club where you may play on one of the championship squash courts, swim laps in the pool or simply relax your mind. Keeping fit was never so much fun before! For a different kind of exercise, visit the boutiques located within the hotel, or walk the five minutes to Georgetown Park, a well-known local shopping area.

Live well at The Ritz-Carlton, Washington, D.C.

**THE RITZ-CARLTON, WASHINGTON, D.C.**
22nd and M Street, N.W.
Washington, D.C. 20037 USA

# The St. Regis Washington, D.C.

Regal and refined, The St. Regis Washington, D.C. is the preferred choice for many discerning travelers.

Opened in 1926 after President Calvin Coolidge cut the ceremonial ribbon, the property was known as The Carlton. Designed by Turkish architect Mihran Mesrobian to resemble an Italian palazzo, this grand hotel is a Washington, D.C. landmark and a National Historic Place. Throughout the years, the hotel has hosted many of the world's luminaries. During White House renovations, President Truman did most of the official entertaining here,

and it was the one and only choice for Queen Elizabeth's private reception during her visit to the United States. Charlie Chaplin, Princess Grace, The Duke of Windsor and Elizabeth Taylor all chose the hotel as their home in Washington, D.C.

After Starwood Hotels' restoration and renaming, The St. Regis' original gilded lobby and coffered ceiling again gleam with perfection. Marvel at the Louis XV Versailles chandeliers and relax to the gentle strains of a harp as you enjoy traditional afternoon tea here. The regal 179 rooms and 14 suites are traditionally designed with

furnishings in rich tones. Every detail is luxurious, from the beautiful fabrics and the gilded mirrors in the bathrooms to the satin hangers in the closets.

Even the most discriminating palates will be entranced by the creative dishes at Timothy Dean Restaurant and Bar. Inspired by the bounty of the Chesapeake, the menu features American cuisine with French accents.

The White House is just two blocks away, but I'd rather stay at The St. Regis.

**THE ST. REGIS WASHINGTON, D.C.**
923 16th Street, N.W.
Washington, D.C. 20006 USA

# The Ritz-Carlton, Amelia Island

Named by British loyalists for the daughter of King George II, Amelia Island is a barrier island off the northeast coast of Florida. Its protected harbor and high bluffs made it a favorite of soldiers, and the island has been under the rule of eight different flags throughout its history. The romantic South is alive here, with huge oaks draped in Spanish moss and windswept dunes.

The Ritz-Carlton is Amelia Island's premier resort. Nestled in the wild dunes along the Atlantic Ocean, the resort boasts 449 rooms, including 49 suites. All rooms have private terraces and feature coastal or ocean views. The décor is traditional Floridian, with flowered fabrics in gentle

village of Fernandina Beach retains its Victorian charm with cobblestone streets and ornately painted houses and has enticing restaurants, eclectic boutiques and art galleries.

Dining is an integral part of the Ritz-Carlton, Amelia Island experience with three mouthwatering restaurants and three lounges. Fresh seafood, meats and wild game are enhanced by Southern accents, like fresh Georgia peaches or pecans. The "seat in the kitchen" program gives diners a front-row seat, while the two day cooking school delves deeper into gourmet meal preparation.

Go south to the relaxing Ritz-Carlton, Amelia Island.

colors. The service is unbeatable, with a combination of Southern hospitality and Ritz-Carlton standards.

The Ritz-Carlton is a gracious world of its own, with an 18 hole PGA championship golf course, nine oceanfront tennis courts, exceptional spa and fitness facility plus indoor and outdoor swimming pools. A replica of a 19th century sailing schooner is available for day sails. Young children will thoroughly enjoy the Ritz Kids program. The nearby

## THE RITZ-CARLTON, AMELIA ISLAND
4750 Amelia Island Parkway
Amelia Island, FL 32034 USA

# Turnberry Isle Resort & Club

Set on 300 tropical acres in southern Florida, Turnberry Isle Resort & Club offers a well-rounded Florida experience.

Two golf courses, designed by Robert Trent Jones, Sr., lure you with their challenge and enchant you with their beauty. Surrounded by tropical foliage, the courses enjoy gentle bay breezes. Sharpen your game with one of the terrific clinics or private lessons given by the exceptional golf staff.

Turnberry's two tennis facilities are considered among the best in the country. Featuring Har-Tru and traditional hard courts, the tennis centers are also lit for evening play. Former Wimbledon champion Fred Stolle heads the professional teaching staff, and his private lessons are sensational. A three mile scenic jogging path complements the fitness facility which offers a tantalizing array of beauty and relaxation treatments. Windsurfing and Hobie cats are available at the private beach, and lessons are offered to beginners or those needing to brush up on their skills.

After a day of play, retire to one of Turnberry's 395 guest rooms. The cool, Mediterranean architecture is accentuated by a soft, pastel color scheme typical of southern Florida. The European trained staff attends to your every need, and with a ratio of three staff to one guest, you are guaranteed to feel pampered.

Five restaurants and six lounges create a wealth of dining and leisure opportunities. The restaurants suit your many moods, whether you choose to dine at The Veranda, known for its gourmet cuisine, or at the Ocean Club & Grill, a casual beach club with sandwiches and grilled specialties.

Turnberry Isle Resort & Club has something for everyone.

**TURNBERRY ISLE RESORT & CLUB**
19999 West Country Club Drive
Aventura, FL 33180 USA

# Boca Raton Resort & Club

Situated on Florida's Gold Coast, south of Palm Beach, is a magical resort known as the Boca Raton Resort & Club.

The Boca Raton Resort was the vision of Addison Mizner, an architect praised for his imaginative designs. Now representing a portion of the resort, the Cloister was the original structure. Its blend of Spanish-Mediterranean, Moorish and Gothic architectural styles is incredibly romantic. Hidden gardens, intricate mosaics and ornate columns add to the mystique. At the time of its opening in 1926, the Cloister was the most expensive 100-room hotel ever built. It soon attracted the likes of Harold Vanderbilt,

Elizabeth Arden and George Whitney, and its reputation as the playground of the rich and famous was cemented.

Today, the Boca Raton Resort & Club provides a total of 963 accommodations including 115 suites in several buildings throughout the 356 acre property, plus 60 one bedroom Golf Villas. A distinct Mediterranean style dominates the rooms in the Cloister, while the Tower is contemporary and the Boca Beach Club is casually elegant. All rooms are stylishly appointed and enjoy private terraces.

Mizner's wish was to build "the world's most architecturally beautiful playground" and with 5 swimming pools, 30 tennis courts, 2 golf courses, a basketball court, 25 slip marina and a private stretch of beach with a water sports center, his wish has been fulfilled. The excellent children's program makes this vacation spot ideal for families.

Whether you seek the old-world elegance of the Cloister or panoramic coastal views, you will be treated to a different ambience at each of the resort's many restaurants, lounges and clubs.

Live the good life at Boca Raton Resort & Club.

**BOCA RATON RESORT & CLUB**
501 E. Camino Real
Boca Raton, FL 33431 USA

# Cheeca Lodge

Cheeca Lodge is a family friendly resort for sports enthusiasts in the Florida Keys.

Seventy-five miles south of Miami in Islamorada, Cheeca Lodge occupies 27 acres of lush landscape fronting the Atlantic Ocean. Islamorada is considered the sport fishing capital of the world, and anglers who stay at Cheeca Lodge will not be disappointed. Every autumn, Cheeca hosts the George Bush Bonefish Tournament.

Cheeca's 139 rooms and 64 suites with full kitchens are a comforting blend of Florida and the Caribbean with tropical prints and ceiling fans.

Guests at Cheeca Lodge are never at a loss

for something to do, with six tennis courts, a 9 hole golf course designed by Jack Nicklaus' firm and a complete water sports facility that includes a dive center. Take the resort's sleek 42 foot catamaran to visit this country's only living coral reef. Of course, lounging by one of the three pools is always an option.

Cheeca Lodge is fully committed to preserving the fragile environment of the Florida Keys. Children visiting the resort will benefit from Camp Cheeca, a program that teaches them about the environment through swimming, fishing and snorkeling activities. Cheeca Lodge goes beyond recycling efforts to enforce bans on jet skis, which destroy the natural habitats of fish and other

marine life, and during turtle nesting season, beach lights are dimmed to avoid distracting the mothers and their young.

Even dining at Cheeca Lodge is environmentally conscious. Conch and swordfish, both endangered species, are no longer served in the resort's three restaurants. Priding themselves on fresh, indigenous products, the menus are full of tantalizing choices.

Get back to nature while living well at Cheeca Lodge.

**CHEECA LODGE**
Mile Marker 82
U.S. Highway One
Islamorada, FL 33036 USA

# Little Palm Island

Secluded and seductive, Little Palm Island is a fabulous hideaway in the Florida Keys.

Resting in the Atlantic Ocean three miles offshore, Little Palm is a five acre island with an exotic flavor. Resembling the South Pacific, the island was selected by Warner Brothers for the filming of *PT-109*, the story of John F. Kennedy's war experiences.

Established in 1986, Little Palm Island has 28 sumptuous suites housed in thatched-roof bungalows. Tucked among flowering hibiscus plants, dense tropical foliage and Jamaican coconut palms, the suites offer unparalleled privacy. Two additional suites are located on the ocean's edge and are nearly twice the size of the bungalow suites.

The suites are elegantly appointed with British Colonial furnishings and Caribbean decorative influences. Distractions from the outside world never interfere at Little Palm, where telephones, televisions and alarm clocks are pleasantly absent. Those who simply must connect to the outside world will be pleased to know that all suites do provide internet connections.

If resting on a hammock while being cosseted by tropical breezes or swimming in the lagoon like fresh water pool with waterfall are not enough to satisfy, Little Palm offers an array of physical activities as well as a spa with massages and beauty treatments.

Snorkeling and scuba diving at the nearby Looe Key National Marine Sanctuary are unbeatable, and several nearby shipwrecks make for fascinating diving.

Little Palm's dining room, once a rustic fishing lodge, is one of Florida's most highly regarded restaurants. The imaginative "Floribbean" menu with Asian and French accents even attracts off-island guests. The airy dining room with ocean views and the outdoor terrace are ideal spots for catching one of Florida's famous sunsets.

For a romantic and exotic escape, visit Little Palm Island.

**LITTLE PALM ISLAND**
28500 Overseas Highway
Little Torch Key, FL 33042
USA

# Mandarin Oriental, Miami

One of Miami's newest hotels, the Mandarin Oriental is also one of its most dramatic.

Tucked away on Brickell Key, a 44 acre residential community on Biscayne Bay, the Mandarin Oriental remains close to South Beach, Coconut Grove and Miami's financial district. Resembling a fan, the hotel company's logo, the 20 story glass building affords fantastic views of the bay and the city skyline.

The hotel's interiors draw on Miami's multicultural and Art Deco heritage. The lobby is sensational, with floor-to-ceiling windows overlooking the bay and eclectic furnishings. Dark wood furniture, vivid artwork and beige and white linens enhance the 298 rooms and 31 suites. Bamboo hardwood floors lend an Asian ambience to the suites. Balconies and terraces invite you to enjoy the views of the Atlantic Ocean, Biscayne Bay and the cityscape. High-speed internet connections, fax and data ports and two-line telephones ensure convenience for business travelers.

Indoor and outdoor dining are available at the Mandarin Oriental. Café Sambal, overlooking the infinity-edge pool, provides dining all day in a relaxed environment. Azul, the hotel's signature restaurant, is a fashionable place to dine, with a white marble-clad kitchen and floor-to-ceiling windows. The chef turns out delicious Latin influenced meals with Caribbean, Asian and classic French hints. Choose from over 800 different martinis at M Bar, or relax in the lobby lounge.

Stay in shape at the fitness center or pamper yourself with one of the Asian or European treatments offered at the spa.

The Mandarin Oriental makes a big splash in Miami.

**MANDARIN ORIENTAL, MIAMI**
500 Brickell Key Drive
Miami, FL 33131 USA

# The Tides

Only 90 miles from Havana, sizzling South Beach dances to a Latin beat. Pastel colored Art Deco buildings wink at the ocean, while residents and visitors frolic on the glorious beaches. South Beach's passion and energy are infectious, and before long, you will find yourself swaying to the salsa beat.

The Tides, located in the heart of the Art Deco district, is the sophisticated choice in South Beach. The tallest building on Ocean Drive, the hotel enjoys unobstructed views of the Atlantic Ocean.

Contemporary and hip, The Tides presents a serene setting in this spirited place.

The 42 rooms and 3 suites are decorated with clean, simple lines in a palette of beige, white, sand and taupe. Overstuffed chairs and soft fabrics create comfort in the cool interiors. All rooms overlook the glittering ocean, and telescopes provide an intriguing decorative touch while giving you a close-up of the action. State-of-the-art communications are available in all rooms, from multi-line telephones to high-speed internet access.

Fine dining is available at 1220, the hotel's signature restaurant. Setting new standards in Miami, 1220 features progressive American cuisine in a stylish setting. Grab a front-row seat to the Ocean Drive scene at the Terrace at The Tides, located on the hotel's front porch. Casual all-day dining and sensational people-watching are on the menu here. The poolside bar and grill pampers bikini-clad guests.

Stylish, yet relaxed, visit the ultra-hip Tides.

**THE TIDES**
1220 Ocean Drive
Miami, FL 33139 USA

# The Ritz-Carlton, Naples

Relax in style at The Ritz-Carlton, Naples.

Situated on Florida's southwest coast, Naples is an ideal holiday destination. Its balance of cosmopolitan shopping and gourmet restaurants, along with natural attractions like the nearby Everglades, Big Cypress Swamp and the Ten Thousand Islands, is delightful. Occupying 20 beach front acres, The Ritz-Carlton is the shining star of Naples.

The hotel recalls the grandeur of bygone days with manicured lawns and impressive architecture. Opened in 1985, The Ritz-Carlton is often credited with putting Naples on the map. A multi-million dollar collection of 18th and 19th century British and American art

is housed in the hotel, and Persian carpets and Austrian crystal chandeliers add elegance to the public areas.

The resort's 431 rooms and 32 suites are graciously appointed with a blend of European and Mediterranean inspired comfortable furnishings. The luxurious rooms offer a variety of views, many of the Gulf of Mexico, and almost all rooms feature private balconies.

Tucked away in the luscious rose garden, The Ritz-Carlton Spa shares 21st century innovations. A four-pronged approach to well being is practiced here, with relaxation, body treatments, nutrition

counseling and physical fitness. Ritz Kids have fun learning about ecological marine life or just playing in the sun.

A wealth of dining opportunities exists at The Ritz-Carlton with eight restaurants and lounges. Gourmet French cuisine with regional accents is available at The Dining Room, while the Grill is modeled on a traditional steak house featuring rare vintages. Southern and Caribbean flavors blend at The Terrace and Gumbo Limbo is a beach boardwalk restaurant with Caribbean cuisine.

Unwind in style at The Ritz-Carlton, Naples.

**THE RITZ-CARLTON, NAPLES**
280 Vanderbilt Road
Naples, FL 34108 USA

# The Breakers

Reflecting America's gilded age, The Breakers has a timeless elegance.

Having attained a considerable fortune as Rockefeller's partner in Standard Oil, Henry Morrison Flagler established a legacy of grand living when he built The Breakers in 1896. Originally named the Palm Beach Inn, it was renamed after guests repeatedly asked for rooms "down by the breakers." The grand Italian Renaissance exterior is resplendent inside, with Venetian chandeliers, oil paintings of Renaissance rulers, gold leaf ceilings and handpainted ceilings by Florentine artists.

Despite its grandeur, The Breakers is a family friendly resort. The Kids Advisory Board, comprised of eight children ranging in age from 5-12, meets once a month to discuss new programming and activities for young guests. Camps are offered year-round.

The Breakers' 524 rooms and 45 suites are elegant with European style furnishings and soft colors indicative of Florida. The resort's beautiful 140 oceanfront acres will likely convince you to leave the comforts of your room, however. Two 18 hole golf courses, including one of the state's oldest courses, ten tennis courts, a spa and fitness center, a heated swimming pool and a variety of water sports will keep you entertained during your visit.

Seven exciting restaurants and four bars guarantee something for everyone at The Breakers. From casual atmospheres to formal dining in The Florentine room, your many moods will be accommodated here.

Grand traditions are alive at the legendary Breakers.

**THE BREAKERS**
One South County Road
Palm Beach, FL 33480 USA

# Four Seasons Resort Palm Beach

The Four Seasons Resort is an elegant choice in Palm Beach. The hotel's dramatic architecture and manicured grounds invite you to unwind in elegance. Calling a gorgeous stretch of beach its own, the Four Seasons overlooks the Atlantic Ocean while remaining minutes away from Palm Beach's alluring Worth Avenue.

The 197 rooms and 13 suites are a refined interpretation of Floridian décor with gentle colors and fine furnishings. Private terraces or balconies provide breathtaking views of the ocean or the beautiful gardens.

on the patio, where Asian cuisine, favorites from the barbecue and tropical drinks are on the menu.

The lovely swimming pool is the heart of the resort. Set above the Atlantic, the pool terrace is a wonderful spot to bask in the glory of the South Florida sun. Three tennis courts create an athletic diversion, and the pro will help you perfect your serve. Children are tickled pink by the Kids for All Seasons program with its full range of activities.

The entire family will treasure a stay at the inviting Four Seasons Resort Palm Beach.

Three restaurants present a variety of dining options for guests of the Four Seasons. The formal setting of the signature restaurant is perfect for lingering on special evenings. Its award-winning menu changes seasonally to include the freshest local ingredients. The Ocean Bistro is a lovely canopied terrace looking out over the pool and the ocean. Wicker chairs, floral prints and an open-air setting create a garden ambience for informal dining. Casual oceanside dining is available

**FOUR SEASONS
RESORT PALM BEACH**
2800 South Ocean Boulevard
Palm Beach, FL 33480 USA

# The Ritz-Carlton, Palm Beach

The Ritz-Carlton is a haven in Florida's glorious Palm Beach. The resort rests on more than seven acres of prime oceanfront property in exclusive Manalapan. A little off-the-beaten path, The Ritz-Carlton remains close to major attractions. Just eight miles from Palm Beach's legendary shopping and fantastic restaurants, guests feel tucked away in a special paradise while visiting the resort.

The 214 rooms and 56 suites welcome guests to a privileged world of beautiful furnishings, state-of-the-art enhancements and attentive service. European-influenced, the rooms also reflect Florida's individual style.

Florida's great outdoors may be enjoyed at The Ritz-Carlton in one of the private cabanas on the

golden beach or on one of the lounges by the oceanfront pool. A highly-trained team of experts helps you master the finer arts of snorkeling and scuba diving. Hobie cats, ocean kayaks and waverunners may also be rented from the hotel's water sports center. Seven tennis courts, including Har-Tru and Supreme Courts, will entice you to pick up a racquet, while golfers have their choice of the area's championship golf courses. Soothing body treatments and nourishing facials are offered at the spa. A special skin care line, designed exclusively by European skin care leader Babor, provides the basis for many of the resort's treatments.

Recently transformed to suit guests' requests, The Restaurant is a tropical bistro suitable for lingering over the morning paper, enjoying lunch with the family or having a quiet dinner. The Grill focuses on beef and seafood, while the Ocean Café and Bar is a relaxed setting for lighter fare.

The Ritz-Carlton, Palm Beach is a perfect setting for a memorable vacation.

**THE RITZ-CARLTON, PALM BEACH**
100 South Ocean Boulevard
Manalapan, FL 33462 USA

# Four Seasons Hotel Atlanta

Atlanta is the capital of the New South, a place where traditions are duly honored and modern times are embraced. It is a thriving business capital, with the headquarters of internationally recognized companies based here, like CNN, Delta Airlines and UPS.

Five minutes from busy downtown, the Four Seasons Hotel is in the heart of midtown's cultural district. The hotel is just a stone's throw from the Woodruff Arts Center, home of the Atlanta Symphony Orchestra, the Alliance Theatre and the High Museum of Art.

Committed to providing personalized service, the hotel

ingredients. The warm glow from the iron candelabras and the commissioned watercolors give the interior a comforting ambience, though the ficus tree-lined terrace is another nice dining alternative. The Chef's table allows a behind-the-scenes look at the kitchen. Featuring primarily American wines, the wine list offers wonderful selections.

The Neo-Classical setting of the indoor pool gives the Four Seasons a resort-in-the-city atmosphere. Enjoy the panoramic views while lounging on the sun terrace.

Experience Southern hospitality at the Four Seasons Hotel Atlanta.

has just 226 rooms and 18 suites. Large windows look out over midtown or downtown Atlanta. The elegant décor of all rooms is classically Four Seasons, and pampering amenities abound.

Lauded for its New American cuisine, Park 75 is one of Atlanta's premier dining establishments. The chef, an avid gardener, bases many of the menus around the freshest and finest

**FOUR SEASONS HOTEL ATLANTA**
75 Fourteenth Street
Atlanta, GA 30309 USA

# The Ritz-Carlton, Buckhead

The Ritz-Carlton has a fashionable address in Buckhead, Atlanta's exclusive uptown neighborhood.

Not far from the city's attractions, The Ritz-Carlton enjoys a residential ambience. The 524 rooms and 29 suites are individually appointed with beautiful, traditional European furniture and unique decorative objects. Chinoiserie side tables add an exotic touch, while marble topped writing desks and plush carpeting add luxury. Four-poster beds lend romance to some rooms.

Guests will be pleased to discover the full-service fitness center with sauna and

steam facilities, fitness machines and aerobics instruction. Spa services and massages are also provided. The 60 foot indoor heated pool also has a whirlpool and a sun deck.

Afternoon tea at The Ritz-Carlton has become a local tradition. Even children enjoy partaking in this ritual; the decision to choose tea or hot chocolate is left to them. The award-winning Dining Room, Georgia's only Mobil

Five-Star, AAA Five-Diamond restaurant, has a grand setting for memorable dinners. The French chef creates distinctive menus daily for your dining pleasure. The casual Café is perfect for all-day dining, while the Deli is ideal for breakfast or lunch. The Wine Bar, featuring wines from Argentina, South Africa and Australia, presents an opportunity to try new wines or savor favorites. Some tables are adjacent to high-speed Internet ports for those guests who want to peruse the web while sampling the wines.

The Ritz-Carlton, Buckhead is a peach of a hotel.

**THE RITZ-CARLTON, BUCKHEAD**
3434 Peachtree Rd., NE
Atlanta, GA 30326 USA

# Four Seasons Resort Hualalai

Hawaii's culture comes alive at the exclusive Four Seasons Resort Hualalai.

The resort is located on the North Kona coast of Hawaii's Big Island, an astonishingly beautiful place with 4,000 square miles of rain forest, tropical orchards and rugged coastline. Carved from landscape formed by 19th century eruptions of the Hualalai volcano, the Four Seasons Resort gently blends with its surroundings. Exotic flora and rare birds are at home on the resort's lush grounds, where remnants of ancient lava flows can be discovered.

The Four Seasons' bungalow-style 212 rooms and 31 suites are organized around shimmering pools

and connected by landscaped walkways. The lanais, or porches, are spacious and ideal for enjoying the ocean views from almost all of the accommodations. The Pacific Rim décor is enhanced by rich, local wood, rattan furniture and upholstery based on ancient petroglyphs found in nearby lava. An extensive art collection focusing solely on art and artifacts created in Hawaii is shared with guests in the accommodations.

In addition to the three oceanfront swimming pools, the resort features a one-of-a-kind pond sculpted out of lava rock. This unique swimming hole is home to over 3,500 tropical fish, including green parrotfish and white puffers. Snorkelers and scuba divers will love this alternative to the Pacific Ocean.

Rooted in a tradition that brought the first Polynesian voyagers here, the four-person sailing canoe known as the Wa'a Hau'oli is the latest sport at the Four Seasons. Land sharks will be delighted with the non-aquatic opportunities at the Hualalai Sports Club, including eight tennis courts, a lap pool and a Jack Nicklaus golf course sculpted out of rugged terrain and black lava.

Say aloha to the Four Seasons Resort Hualalai.

**FOUR SEASONS RESORT HUALALAI**
100 Ka'upulehu Drive
Ka'upulehu-Kona, HI 96740

# The Mauna Lani Bay Hotel & Bungalows

Rising from a 16th century black lava flow, The Mauna Lani Bay Hotel & Bungalows is one of Hawaii's best resorts.

Resting along the Kona Kohala Coast, The Mauna Lani is a 3,200 acre resort rich in Hawaiian history and surrounded by ancient ponds, sheltered caves and petroglyphs. Three miles of stunning coastline bless the resort with powdery beaches, perfect for enjoying the year-round sunshine and temperate climate.

A breezy lobby with waterfalls welcomes you to this culturally and ecologically sensitive resort. Lauded for their commitment to conservation efforts, the resort celebrates each

July 4th with Turtle Independence Day, when endangered green sea turtles cared for in the resort's saltwater ponds are released back into the ocean. A Hawaiian historian hosts "talk story" evenings, where guests are invited to learn more about the island's history and folklore. Even the spa honors the island's culture with its volcanic hot rock therapy.

The 335 rooms, 10 suites and 5 bungalows remain true to their Hawaiian heritage while incorporating luxurious amenities. Local woods and soft colors create soothing enclaves for guests.

Activities are plentiful at The Mauna Lani, where you can try your hand at lei making or hula dancing, or sail or dive to one of Hawaii's few coral reefs.

Two championship "Gold Award" golf courses keep your golf game in shape with fantastic views.

The Mauna Lani's four restaurants offer stunning settings and terrific cuisine. Whether you fancy delicious seafood or California-style pizzas, there is something for everyone.

Mauna Lani, meaning "mountain reaching heaven," offers a slice of Hawaiian paradise in a picturesque setting.

**THE MAUNA LANI BAY HOTEL & BUNGALOWS**
68-1400 Mauna Lani Drive
Kohala Coast, HI 96743 USA

# Four Seasons Resort Maui at Wailea

Formed by two volcanoes that erupted long ago, Maui is Hawaii's most sophisticated island, with world-class shopping, luxurious resorts and spectacular golf courses.

One of the island's most exclusive resorts is the Four Seasons. Occupying 15 oceanfront acres, the Four Seasons is a marvelous mosaic of pools, terraces and exotic gardens set against a beautiful white sand beach. The resort, a softly colored eight story building, retains an intimate ambience. Open air spaces, showcasing the dramatic views and inviting the fragrant breezes, are integral to the resort's design. Reproductions of early Hawaiian furniture, paintings, screens, sculptures and crafts displayed throughout the resort capture the essence of Maui.

The 305 rooms and mostly 75 ocean view suites are decorated in soft pastels indicative of the tropical region. A carefree elegance is established with rattan and wicker furnishings with overstuffed cushions. Oversized marble bathrooms and thoughtful touches like whole bean coffee with mills and coffee makers speak of the Four Seasons tradition.

The swimming pool is a focal point of the resort. The large pool is topped off by a tall fountain in the center and a whirlpool at each end. A separate free-form pool with a waterfall connects by a slide to the children's pool.

Hawaii's abundant fresh fish and produce are highlighted at the three restaurants. Pacific Rim cuisine is tops at the Pacific Grill, a relaxed setting with ocean views, while Seasons features an American menu. Ferraro's at Seaside, the only restaurant on Wailea Beach, serves casual fare for lunch. At night, it transforms into a terrific Italian restaurant with unparalleled sunsets.

The Four Seasons Resort Maui at Wailea is perfection.

**FOUR SEASONS
RESORT MAUI
AT WAILEA**
3900 Wailea Alanui
Wailea, HI 96753 USA

# The Ritz-Carlton, Kapalua

The Ritz-Carlton, Kapalua shares the treasures of Maui with you.

Set amidst a 23,000 acre pineapple plantation, the resort enjoys a prime location in an unspoiled region of Maui. Just ten miles north of Lahaine, a century-old whaling village, The Ritz-Carlton enjoys a rugged, natural setting overlooking the island of Moloka'i.

The plantation style building is comprised of two six-story buildings that are contoured to the rolling terrain. Original paintings and ceramics by local Maui artists blend with 18th and 19th century artwork to create a distinctive Ritz-Carlton décor throughout the public rooms, 490 guest rooms and 58 suites.

The Ritz-Carlton is a golf and tennis paradise.

Three championship golf courses are nestled between the green West Maui Mountains and the Pacific. Certified as the world's only Audubon Heritage resort, the golf courses limit pesticides and conserve water to help provide food for wildlife. Home of the annual Mercedes Championships, you will walk in the footsteps of some of golf's greatest players at The Ritz-Carlton. Putt like Tiger Woods after a few lessons from the prestigious golf academy. Poised above the beach, the tennis facilities are widely considered the finest in Hawaii. After playing golf or tennis, escape to the three-tiered cascading swimming pool for some relief, or walk the unspoiled beach.

Savor the flavors of the islands at the resort's eight restaurants and bars. Comfortable settings, scenic views and fantastic food make dining a joy. Hawaiian hospitality and Ritz-Carlton service are combined to ensure an exceptional experience.

Nourish and refresh your spirit at The Ritz-Carlton, Kapalua.

THE RITZ-CARLTON, KAPALUA
One Ritz-Carlton Drive
Kapalua, HI 96761 USA

# Four Seasons Hotel Chicago

The capital of America's Midwest, Chicago is internationally recognized for its innovative architecture, thriving businesses and creative arts scene. The world comes to Chicago, and when they do, they love staying at the Four Seasons Hotel.

The Four Seasons enjoys close proximity to Chicago's business and financial centers while occupying a skytop location above glittering Michigan Avenue. Exuding the refinement of a private mansion, the Four Seasons' 191 rooms and 152 suites are an elegant place to call home while visiting the city. The atmosphere is old world, with Italian marble,

away with its opulent setting complete with rich wood paneling, brocade armchairs and handwoven carpet. The relaxing sounds of the piano are the perfect complement to the tasting menus or the seasonal lamb, beef and seafood menus. The Café is a more informal setting with three-course lunches and dinners.

The Four Seasons has one of the most spectacular indoor swimming pools in Chicago. A domed glass ceiling and Roman columns give your exercise routine a refined touch.

Let the excellence of the Four Seasons Hotel Chicago warm your soul.

handcrafted woodwork and botanical prints in all rooms. Classic Four Seasons touches, like the exceptionally comfortable beds and 21st century advances, are appreciated by discerning travelers.

The Four Seasons is home to one of Chicago's finest dining establishments, Seasons Restaurant. Rated the top American restaurant by *Zagat's*, it has also been called the most romantic restaurant in Chicago. Seasons chases the winter chill

**FOUR SEASONS
HOTEL CHICAGO**
120 East Delaware Place
Chicago, IL USA 60611

# The Ritz-Carlton Chicago

The Ritz-Carlton reigns over Chicago from its lofty position atop Water Tower Place.

The Ritz-Carlton Chicago, a Four Seasons Hotel, is just two blocks from Lake Michigan, five minutes from the financial center, but best of all, adjacent to world-renowned shopping on Michigan Avenue. The hotel is the crowning glory of the city's much-loved Water Tower, a vertical shopping mall filled with some of the city's finest stores and boutiques.

Tasteful, elegant style defines the Ritz-Carlton Chicago. Jewel tones and traditional décor set a rich mood in the Four Seasons' 344

rooms and 91 suites. Renowned for their impeccable levels of service, you are ensured a smooth and pleasant visit. Large windows share dazzling views of Chicago, whether you look out over Michigan Avenue, the Chicago skyline or even toward Lake Michigan. The luxurious bathrooms in the corner Anniversary Suites have oversized bathtubs that let you admire the city through floor-to-ceiling windows while soaking your tensions away. The State Suite is especially dramatic with its split-level design, gracious style and large windows.

Delightful contemporary French dishes are served in the exquisite Dining Room. The exceptional wine list consistently wins top awards from Wine Spectator and emphasizes Bordeaux, Burgundy and California wines. Potted plants and light wood furniture set a casual ease in the Café, famous for its chicken club sandwich. Relax in the airy ambience of the Greenhouse throughout the day or for afternoon tea.

Get swept away by the Ritz-Carlton Chicago.

**THE RITZ-CARLTON CHICAGO**
160 East Pearson Street at Water Tower Place
Chicago, IL 60611 USA

# The Ritz-Carlton, New Orleans

Known for being the birthplace of jazz and for its annual rollicking Mardi Gras celebrations, New Orleans is a fun-filled place. Though relatively small, the French Quarter is the best known neighborhood. Its wrought-iron balconies, outdoor cafés and lively spirit make it the place to be in New Orleans.

Bordering the French Quarter and within a one minute walk from Bourbon Street, The Ritz-Carlton brings new levels of excellence to New Orleans. Converted from the historic Maison Blanche department store, the hotel echoes the old-world while incorporating modern amenities.

The Ritz-Carlton's

and was the elite meeting place for almost a century. Now restyled and located in the hotel, Victor's shares some of the best Creole and Continental dishes in New Orleans with its diners.

Borrowing influences from the Court of Louis XIV, a day at the Ritz-Carlton's spa is a regal experience. Eau de Cologne, Napoleon's preferred scent, is used in many of the treatments, including manicures and massages. Another sumptuous treatment is the Four Hands Massage, reputedly a favorite of Marie Antoinette's.

The Ritz-Carlton, New Orleans brings you "all that jazz" like no one else.

415 rooms and 37 suites are gracious reminders of antebellum mansions. French heritage colors of purple, green and gold are used throughout all rooms, while local antiques and Southern hospitality provide a sense of place. Showcasing views of the city, some rooms offer unique vantage points for viewing the Mardi Gras festivities.

Even the main restaurant is a nod to history. Victor's originally opened in the 1830's

**THE RITZ-CARLTON, NEW ORLEANS**
921 Canal Street
New Orleans, LA 70112 USA

# Windsor Court Hotel

The Windsor Court Hotel offers an elegant slice of New Orleans.

In the center of the business district, the Windsor Court Hotel is conveniently located between the Riverwalk development and the French Quarter.

The elegant, European interiors are in striking contrast to the contemporary facade completed in rose colored granite. The hotel's impressive art collection spans the 17th to 20th centuries and includes many renowned artists, including Van Dyk, Reynolds, Gainsborough and Huysman. Special attention is paid to works of British origin or those that depict Windsor

sauna, steamroom and advanced fitness machines, is a favorite spot for active-minded travelers. Massages can be arranged upon request.

The Grill, one of only 14 restaurants in the United States with a Mobil Five-Star rating, serves haute cuisine in a stylish, formal setting. The less formal Le Salon is a delightful place to enjoy light meals and snacks, and the chamber music played here is a true pleasure. The Polo Club Lounge serves Louisiana specialties to the sounds of jazz in an English club-like setting.

The Windsor Court Hotel is an Anglophile's dream in New Orleans.

Castle or the Royal Family.

The Windsor Court's 322 deluxe rooms and suites are beautifully appointed with tasteful English-style furnishings and spacious Italian marble bathrooms. All rooms have a bay window or a private balcony, and many overlook the Mississippi River or the city of New Orleans.

Bask in the Louisiana sunshine on the Windsor Court's sundeck, take a dip in the outdoor swimming pool or relax in the whirlpool. The fitness center, with

**WINDSOR COURT HOTEL**
300 Gravier Street
New Orleans, LA 70130 USA

# Fifteen Beacon

Boston's Beacon Hill seems to be scripted straight from a Henry James novel. Home to the city's wealthiest residents for many years, Beacon Hill's turn-of-the-century elegance is reflected in its antique shops and glorious Brahmin mansions.

Chic and sophisticated, Fifteen Beacon is an elegant juxtaposition of old and new Boston. The 1903 Beaux Arts building belies the modernist interiors. The original cage elevator and cast brass-lit railing with brass newel speak of old Boston, while sleek furnishings, state-of-the-art technology and contemporary works by renowned artists ring of the new.

The 56 rooms and 3 suites are dramatic and stylish in a palette of taupe, cream, black or chocolate brown. Individually designed, all rooms feature built-in mahogany wall units and gas fireplaces that are easily controlled by the bedside panel. Four-poster beds are dressed with crisp, tailored linen. The striking décor is further enhanced by the outstanding service, where catching a taxi won't be necessary since guests are treated to in-town chauffeured Mercedes service.

The Federalist, or The Fed as it is affectionately known, is one of the city's most exciting dining spots. Tease your palate with one of the sensational dishes served in an artful manner. Everything from a traditional New England Clambake to Beef Wellington can be sampled here. The chef takes freshness seriously; a rooftop herb garden and in-kitchen fish tanks ensure the availability of fresh products. The wine cellar stocks a fine selection of rare wines, ports, cognacs and rare vintages. You will even find bottles of 1907 Heidsieck Monopole Champagne, preserved for most of this century at the bottom of the Baltic Sea in a schooner sunk by a German U-boat.

Fifteen Beacon is the cosmopolitan choice in Boston.

**FIFTEEN BEACON**
15 Beacon Street
Boston, MA 02108 USA

# Four Seasons Hotel Boston

America's independent spirit began in Boston. Ideally located near the city's historic attractions, the Four Seasons Hotel, built in 1985, reflects Boston's heritage in a refined setting. Across from the Public Garden, the hotel enjoys views of the tranquil lagoon and its swan boats. The gold dome of the State House glistens in the distance, and the theater district is just a short walk.

Period artwork and furniture, European style reproductions, handmade carpets and gleaming marble, evoke the glamour of the grand mansions of the Back Bay and Beacon Hill. Many of the 203 rooms and 71 suites offer

charming glimpses of the Public Garden and Boston Common.

The Four Seasons is graced with one of the city's finest restaurants, Aujourd'hui. Lauded for its superb New American cuisine, the restaurant also boasts one of the most romantic views in Boston with large windows showcasing the greenery of the Public Garden. More than half the diners are Boston residents – a testament to the restaurant's talents. Every Tuesday, Aujourd'hui hosts a Fashionable Luncheon,

where fashions from celebrated designers are presented alongside delicious culinary creations. Located at the base of the hotel's grand staircase, The Bristol offers all-day dining in a quaint spot with a crackling fireplace. You just might be lucky enough to catch a piano performance by one of the members of the Boston Pops – he plays regularly here.

The eighth-floor indoor pool, with greenhouse-like windows looking out to the park, is an oasis in the city. The hotel's signature Alternative Cuisine, served in all dining establishments, is also available here.

Experience New England's charms at the Four Seasons Hotel Boston.

**FOUR SEASONS
HOTEL BOSTON**
200 Boylston Street
Boston, MA 02116 USA

# The Ritz-Carlton, Boston

In a city of landmarks, The Ritz-Carlton, Boston is an aristocratic landmark of its own.

Overlooking Boston Common, The Ritz-Carlton opened in 1927 and in 1981 became the first hotel in the prestigious Ritz-Carlton Hotel Company group. The style and standards that were established here quickly became the benchmark for all future Ritz-Carlton properties.

Adhering to Boston's strict social traditions, the hotel mimicked an exclusive club in its early years. Guests were regularly checked to see if they were in the Social Register, and when guests wrote letters requesting reservations, the stationery was checked to determine its quality. The instantly recognizable Ritz-Carlton blue goblets, seen in

every property throughout the world, originated here. Imported European glass experienced a chemical reaction to the cold Boston air by turning blue, making it a status symbol in 1920's Boston.

A strong literary tradition lives at The Ritz-Carlton as well. Tennessee Williams wrote part of *A Streetcar Named Desire* here, and Oscar Hammerstein composed the lyrics to *Edelweiss* in his room's shower. Richard Rodgers composed *Ten Cents a Dance* on a piano in his Ritz-Carlton suite.

It is easy to see why artists were inspired once you are inside the hotel's 241 rooms and 34 suites. Antique furniture, fine paintings, rich fabrics and decorative accessories make the sumptuous rooms feel like regal residences.

Cherished dining memories are to be made at The Ritz-Carlton's distinctly elegant restaurants. The Roof Restaurant has reestablished itself as the place to swing. Once host to musical talents Benny Goodman and Tommy Dorsey, a big band plays every Friday and Saturday. Of course, no visit would be complete without having your own Ritz-Carlton "tea party" in the exquisite lounge.

Experience the legacy of The Ritz-Carlton, Boston.

**THE RITZ-CARLTON, BOSTON**
15 Arlington Street
Boston, MA 02117 USA

# Blantyre

Set in the foothills of the Berkshires, stately Blantyre brings a bit of Britain to the Massachusetts countryside.

Built at the turn of the century by wealthy businessman Robert Patterson, Blantyre was modeled after his wife's ancestral castle in Scotland. No matter the season, this 100 acre estate is glorious. The deliciously rich colors of autumn appear like spun gold, while luxuriant greenery harkens spring's arrival. However, it is summer that brings music to your ears with nearby Tanglewood and the Berkshire Theatre Festival.

Blantyre is the sort of place where Edith Wharton would feel right at home, and indeed she was a guest

here in the early 1900's for a lavish garden party. This baronial estate's formal gardens and croquet lawns make it easy to imagine the scene.

Four-poster beds, charming fabrics, floral wall coverings and period antiques set a romantic tone in the 12 rooms and 11 suites. Blantyre reflects its illustrious heritage with an elegant country décor.

Dining at Blantyre is rather like an intimate dinner party. The kitchen turns out splendid dishes, often taking their inspiration from Scottish cuisine. These elegant feasts are served grandly on tables laid with damask and set with delicate bone china and antique crystal. The gentle strains of a harp often accompany dinner. The scrumptious breakfast with

favorites like fluffy eggs and freshly baked muffins will convince you to rise early. The verdant pastures and rolling hills of the Berkshires are ideal for toting one of the chef's special picnic baskets, available by request.

As if Blantyre didn't already seem suspended in time, a lovely antique surrey drawn by a Morgan horse takes guests for rides around the grounds.

Reserve early to relive the gilded age at Blantyre.

BLANTYRE
16 Blantyre Road
Lenox, MA 01240 USA

# Four Seasons Hotel Las Vegas

Rather like an adult version of Disney World, Las Vegas is an eye-popping place of glittering lights and endless energy. Founded by gold miners, Las Vegas attracts contemporary gold seekers from all over the world.

In a place best known for its outrageous, over-the-top architectural designs, the Four Seasons Hotel offers refined, serene accommodations. It is quite simply the most luxurious hotel in Las Vegas, bringing you the best of Four Seasons and the best of Las Vegas together in one place. It is the only non-gaming hotel on the Strip - a welcome change from the frenetic pace of the rest of the town.

Try the Jamu massage, an intoxicating blend of Hindu, Chinese and European massage techniques.

The swimming pool is an oasis in the Las Vegas desert. Its lushly landscaped pool deck is a perfect escape for the afternoon, and attendants with Evian spritz, fresh fruit and chilled water ensure your comfort.

Leave the hustle and bustle of Las Vegas behind and retreat to the Four Seasons Hotel.

The 338 guest rooms and 86 suites enjoy fabulous views of the famous strip or the surrounding desert and mountains. Serene color schemes are used in all rooms, while rich fabrics and antiques lend an aristocratic flair.

Relax at the Four Seasons spa, where you will be pampered with Jamu Asian spa rituals. Exotic ingredients and ancient traditions are blended to optimize internal and external health. An image of Kuan Yin, the goddess of compassion, greets all guests upon arrival and serves as the spa's guiding force.

**FOUR SEASONS HOTEL LAS VEGAS**
3960 Las Vegas Boulevard South
Las Vegas, NV 89119 USA

# La Posada de Santa Fe Resort & Spa

Santa Fe is the spiritual and cultural capital of the American Southwest. Pueblo Revival-style houses serve as reminders of the city's Spanish and Mexican rule. Known for its striking sunsets and light that has served as inspiration for artists, including Georgia O'Keefe, Santa Fe is a triumph of Native American, Hispanic and Anglo cultures.

La Posada de Santa Fe Resort & Spa is a fine example of Southwestern adobe architecture. The walled compound with adobe cottages is built around the remnants of a Victorian mansion of the late 1800's. Built by wealthy German immigrant Abraham

Staab, the mansion was the center of Santa Fe's society.

La Posada's 159 rooms and suites are defined by a dazzling Southwestern style. Handmade Native American rugs, colorful stucco walls, wrought-iron beds and beamed ceilings create enticing environments. The traditional kiva fireplaces, available in many rooms, extend a warm invitation to relax with a book.

Located in the Staab House, Fuego Restaurant teases your tastebuds with its unusual and delicious creations. Spacious patio dining allows you to enjoy the lovely outdoors, though the interior's Spanish Colonial charm with leather banquettes and wood

tables is equally charming. Meals like macadamia pancakes with shredded coconut and cinnamon marinated spitfire quail will surely not be forgotten. Once the Staab's living room, the lounge provides a cozy spot to enjoy live music or a cocktail.

Guided by regional influences, the Aranyu Spa offers unique treatments like the adobe mud wrap and the corn dance purification treatment.

Once you are ensconced at La Posada, you will never want to leave. Julia Staab, the resort's longtime resident ghost, completely agrees.

**LA POSADA DE SANTA FE RESORT & SPA**
330 East Palace Avenue
Santa Fe, NM 87501 USA

# The Emerson Inn & Spa

The Emerson Inn & Spa brings country sophistication just a little over two hours from New York City.

Only minutes from the famed artist community of Woodstock, The Emerson Inn & Spa is located within the Catskills Forest Preserve. The inn is named in honor of Ralph Waldo Emerson who championed environmental preservation, and copies of his famous "Nature" lectures can be found within all rooms.

The inn's 21 guest rooms and 3 suites are an eclectic collection of Persian, Victorian, African,

Oriental and West Indian decorative styles. Handpicked objects d'art create individuality, while Frette linens and Hermes amenities bring European elegance.

The Emerson's Spa captures the essence of the Orient with Tibetan thanka paintings and bamboo screening. In addition to the resistance pool, whirlpool and fitness equipment, the spa features 40 spa treatments tailored to your individual needs.

Cuisine is an integral part of the experience at the Emerson Inn. European-trained chefs turn out wonderful French food accented with regional ingredients. The dining room, resembling an elegant country home, is set with the finest crystal, china and silver. Hemingway would feel right at home in the African Bar. This exotic atmosphere is filled with animal print fabrics and unique objects. The 4,000 bottle Wine Room with a floor-to-ceiling humidor and 30 cigar brands is a special spot.

The luscious interiors, elegant dining and soothing spa at The Emerson Inn & Spa make for a wonderful country retreat.

**THE EMERSON INN & SPA**
146 Mount Pleasant Road
Mt. Tremper, NY 12457 USA

# The Carlyle

The Carlyle is an intimate hotel on a grand scale.

Since 1930, The Carlyle has held a special place in the hearts of many world travelers. Inviting you to escape to its genteel world, The Carlyle is positioned uptown on Madison Avenue, where chic boutiques and elegant residences are de rigueur. The hotel's original character remains intact, and unique touches can be found throughout the hotel. Just off the main lobby, an intricately carved fireplace stands guard and a beautiful postal box reminds you of the days when letter writing was an art. Recently acquired by

Rosewood Hotels & Resorts, The Carlyle will remain a prestigious landmark.

The Carlyle has 180 rooms and suites, as well as 65 permanent residences. Each room has an individualized style, though chintz fabrics, vibrant colors and celadon greens are often used. Audubon prints, architectural renderings by Piranesi or scenes of the English countryside by Kips enhance the walls. Baby grand pianos, tuned twice a week, can be found in 25 of the suites.

My, what secrets The Carlyle could tell. Blue-blooded royals, queens of the silver screen, leaders of industry and nations have all graced the hotel. John F. Kennedy considered The Carlyle his private hideaway in New York.

No visit to The Carlyle is complete without a night at Café Carlyle. Nightly performances by the inimitable Bobby Short who has performed in this room for 34 years. Decorated with murals of his most famous character, Madeline, Bemelmans Bar celebrates Ludwig Bemelmans' creativity. Fine dining is topped off with the restaurant's gracious English drawing room style décor.

Open your heart to The Carlyle.

**THE CARLYLE**
35 East 76th Street
New York, NY 10021 USA

# Four Seasons Hotel New York

Bustling 57th Street, the nerve center of midtown Manhattan, seems like an unlikely place for a soothing haven, yet the Four Seasons Hotel is just that.

World-renowned architect I.M. Pei designed the Four Seasons to be a temple of peace in an otherwise harried city. Inspired in part by the skyscrapers that define New York's skyline, the Four Seasons is New York's tallest hotel. Once you glide past the doors, the 33 foot ceiling and impressive French limestone columns of the lobby will leave you awe-struck.

The Four Seasons Hotel capitalizes on its jaw-dropping, unparalleled

views with large windows in each of the 307 rooms and 61 suites. Triple-paned windows ensure that only the sights of the city, and not the sounds, fill your room. The décor is sleek and contemporary, and the rooms are among the most spacious in Manhattan. Simple lines and soothing honey tones of English sycamore wood are used in the custom-designed furniture, and fine leathers and fabrics are used throughout the rooms. The large marble bathrooms are fitted to perfection.

Fifty Seven Fifty Seven, playing off the hotel's address, has a bistro feel with a polished appearance. Maple floors with walnut inlays, coffered ceilings and bronze chandeliers with onyx inlays add to the elegance, while the contemporary American cuisine draws locals as well as hotel guests. The adjacent bar is one of New York's hottest places to be seen, especially noted for its menu with 15 varieties of martinis.

The Four Seasons is the chic, urbane choice in New York.

**FOUR SEASONS
HOTEL NEW YORK**
57 East 57th Street
New York, NY 10022 USA

# The Lowell

The Lowell is a gracious hideaway nestled on a quiet street between Park and Madison Avenues.

This Art Deco landmark building originally opened in 1928 as an apartment and hotel building. Some of this century's most interesting celebrities lived here, including Noel Coward, F. Scott and Zelda Fitzgerald and Dorothy Parker.

A distinct residential ambience defines The Lowell. The rich, jewel-toned lobby is a tiny gem, from its elegant furnishings to its bountiful floral displays. The Lowell's smaller size ensures that all guests are treated to very personalized service.

The 47 suites and 21 rooms are havens from the hectic city just outside. Rather like your own pied-a-terre, the rooms and suites are elegantly decorated with soft green or taupe tones or flowered fabrics. Fully-equipped kitchens and wood-burning fireplaces, a rarity in New York, create inviting personal spaces. Three suites feature special designs. The Garden Suite takes its cue from the beautiful outdoors with a garden inspired décor and beautiful terrace. The Gym Suite, originally built for Madonna, is ideal for fitness fanatics who seek the ultimate in privacy and luxury. For a more whimsical décor, try the Hollywood Suite with its celebration of 1930's Hollywood. Attention to detail, marvelous amenities and exquisite flowers are a hallmark of The Lowell.

The Pembroke Room is a nice spot to linger over breakfast or afternoon tea, though the Post House is the hotel's signature restaurant, with its delicious array of steaks and seafood. Reminiscent of a dinner club with its leather armchairs and large paintings, the Post House is considered one of America's top steakhouses.

Live graciously while staying at The Lowell.

**THE LOWELL**
28 East 63rd Street
New York, NY 10021 USA

# The Mark

The Mark's understated elegance brings serenity to New York. This 16 story hotel is located just off Madison Avenue on the Upper East Side. Close to New York's acclaimed museums, world-class shopping and business districts, The Mark retains a residential style, more like a large townhouse. Area residents regularly visit The Mark's bar and restaurant, and in turn, guests feel like part of this exclusive New York City neighborhood.

The 120 rooms and 60 suites share a contemporary blend of Italian, English or Biedermeier decorative styles. Overstuffed chairs and exceedingly comfortable beds encourage

you to linger for just a moment longer. Asian accents, like traditional blue porcelain lamps and black lacquer cabinets, can be found throughout the accommodations. Solariums and terraces accompany several rooms, providing charming views of Central Park or Madison Avenue.

Mark's Bar is a tiny jewel. The dark green walls and black wood trim give it an English club ambience, but its informal ease is undeniably American. Mark's Restaurant has a comfortable Edwardian décor and serves wonderful French and American cuisine.

Afternoon tea at The Mark takes on a different twist with guidance from Tea Master, Ringo Lo. Lo advises guests on the proper tea selection, as well as providing insight into the history and culture of drinking tea.

Though informal, The Mark's service is superb. There is always someone ready to help a guest, from to the general manager, to the doorman for the complimentary Wall Street shuttle service, to the concierge for securing difficult dinner reservations.

The hotel's elegantly relaxed style and quiet location are right on "The Mark."

THE MARK
25 East 77th Street
New York, NY 10021 USA

# The Peninsula New York

The Peninsula, housed in a stunning Beaux Arts building, reigns over New York's celebrated Fifth Avenue.

The facade of The Peninsula New York is glorious with Doric columns and limestone carvings. Completed in 1905, the building was designed to complement the neighboring University Club. The grand world of Fifth Avenue, with its glittering and world famous stores, is just outside the Peninsula's door.

The 186 rooms and 55 suites are handsomely appointed with polished woods and furnishings typical of the Art Nouveau period. Known worldwide for its advanced technology, The Peninsula does

not disappoint. A bedside panel controls the entertainment system, the room's temperature, as well as three different levels of mood lighting. Many suites have decorative fireplaces and bathrooms with "his and hers" vanity areas. My favorite rooms look down Fifth Avenue, while upper level corner rooms enjoy views of Central Park in the distance.

Adrienne Restaurant's French-Asian cuisine is served in a classically elegant, yet informal dining room that overlooks Fifth Avenue. More casual meals may be enjoyed in the Bistro, while guests looking for a place to unwind will find a welcoming seat in the Gotham Bar. For a quintessential New York experience, visit the Pen-top Bar, the hotel's rooftop bar. Resembling a garden in the sky, only The Peninsula can share the city's skyline with you like this.

Shake up your fitness routine at the hotel's exceptional rooftop fitness center and spa. The panoramic city views will inspire you to run just a little bit longer or swim that extra lap.

The Peninsula New York is a cosmopolitan choice.

**THE PENINSULA NEW YORK**
700 Fifth Avenue
at 55th Street
New York, NY 10019 USA

# The Pierre

New York is constantly changing. Overnight sensations wake up to learn they are yesterday's news, and something new emerges before you have had a moment to realize that something else has disappeared. Luckily, some things remain the same. The Pierre, with its spectacular location on Fifth Avenue and across from Central Park, has always been one of New York's grandest hotels.

Traditional and dignified, The Pierre opened to great fanfare in 1930. Inspired by a French château, the beautiful 41 story building soon became the favorite of the crème de la crème of American society. Throughout

its history, The Pierre has hosted countless glamorous balls and society weddings. Four Seasons Hotels and Resorts has managed the hotel for ten years, making it that much more special. The Pierre's distinct character and original splendor endure, even to the magnificent floral arrangements gracing the sumptuous public areas.

The resplendent lobby is large, yet maintains an intimacy. The 149 guest rooms and 53 suites are classically elegant. Twelve one-of-a-kind Grand Suites are exceedingly luxurious and spacious, and maintain an apartment-like style. Many

accommodations enjoy stunning views of Central Park, while others showcase the neighborhood's charms. Private apartments are interspersed among the hotel rooms, lending a residential air to The Pierre.

Afternoon tea at The Pierre is an institution. The gleaming, white marble staircase and trompe l'oeil murals of the Rotunda create a dreamy setting for the scrumptious and elegant tea. Enjoy a cocktail or a light meal in the Rotunda, as I often do. Café Pierre's classic and contemporary French food is delightful.

The Pierre shines as one of New York's brightest stars.

## THE PIERRE
Fifth Avenue at 61st Street
New York, NY 10021 USA

# Hôtel Plaza Athénée

Hôtel Plaza Athénée, located on a pretty tree-lined residential street on New York's prominent Upper East Side, is one of the city's gems.

This enchanting hotel is blessed with the services and conveniences of a large hotel, yet its decidedly private manner makes it a favorite of visitors seeking a residential atmosphere. Indeed, with Central Park, the alluring stores of Madison and Fifth Avenues just a few blocks away and the palatial residences of Park Avenue just a few doors down, you will feel like a native New Yorker while staying at the Hôtel Plaza Athénée.

to enjoy the finer things in life. Rich fabrics and furnishings reflect the hotel's French panache. Eight of the suites feature dining rooms or solarium terraces with charming views of the city.

The newly opened Arabelle is sure to be a big success featuring inventive French cuisine with an Asian twist. Earth tones have replaced the gilded furniture, giving it a more soothing and modern appearance. The lounge, perfect for cocktails or light meals, captures the essence of British Colonial Asia.

For a bit of Paris in the heart of New York, stay at the Hôtel Plaza Athénée.

Even the lobby feels like a private residence. Glide past the brass doors to this intimate space with gleaming marble floors, tapestries and French antique furniture. Personalized service is a hallmark of the Hôtel Plaza Athénée. The European tradition of seated check-in is a particularly appreciated touch.

The Plaza Athénée's 117 rooms and 36 suites are havens from the bustle of Manhattan. The hushed interiors inspire you to take a few moments

HÔTEL PLAZA
ATHÉNÉE
37 East 64th Street
New York, NY 10021 USA

# The St. Regis New York

When it was built in 1904, The St. Regis on 55th Street and Fifth Avenue was New York's tallest building. Today other buildings reach higher for the sky, yet this dignified hotel has never lost its impressive and legendary stature.

Enter through the polished revolving doors to the rarefied world of The St. Regis. Seeking a princely home for his wealthy colleagues and friends, John Jacob Astor commissioned The St. Regis and spared no expense in its construction. Gleaming marble floors, 22 karat gold leafing, glittering chandeliers and Louis XVI furniture complete the European, elegant décor.

to the expectations of the St. Regis' guests.

The King Cole Bar, dominated by the famous mural of King Cole by Maxfield Parrish, is itself a New York institution. The Red Snapper, or Bloody Mary as it is known throughout the world, was introduced here in 1934. The Astor Court looks out to 55th Street and is a lovely spot for lunch or afternoon tea. Of course, no visit to The St. Regis is complete without an evening at Lespinasse. Its haute cuisine and special setting are sublime.

Return to the age of elegance at The St. Regis New York.

Though Astor went down with the Titanic, the legacy he created lives on today.

The 222 guest rooms and 93 suites are magnificent, with glorious furnishings, gilded mirrors, exquisite antiques, and silk wall coverings. An English style butler is assigned to each floor to service guests' needs. The service is exemplary, so much so, that Starwood Hotels has created a brand for a few, select hotels which can live up

THE ST. REGIS
NEW YORK
Two East 55th Street
at Fifth Avenue
New York, NY 10022 USA

# The Waldorf Towers

The Waldorf Towers, an elegant boutique hotel within the Waldorf-Astoria, is a New York City landmark.

The legend of the Waldorf-Astoria began in the late 1800's, when two adjacent hotels shared a fine reputation for providing the city's most luxurious lodging. When the buildings were demolished to make room for the Empire State Building, the Art Deco masterpiece at Park Avenue and 50th Street was built. Finished in 1931, the Waldorf-Astoria and its Towers took the world by storm.

The Waldorf Towers was the first of its kind – a hotel within a hotel. Tucked inside the Waldorf-Astoria,

the Towers occupy floors 27 to 42. The Towers function as a separate hotel with a different entrance, separate elevators and a dedicated staff, yet access is provided to all Waldorf-Astoria facilities. The 101 guest rooms and 118 suites have a regal presence. Each one is entirely different from the next, though French Provincial and Old English themes prevail.

The history that has unfolded here is incomparable. Every United States President since Herbert Hoover has selected the Waldorf Towers as his New York White House. Traditionally, the First Lady handpicks the fabrics used in the suite's bedroom and many past presidents have left rare pieces for

others to enjoy. The Duke and Duchess of Windsor resided in the Royal Suite for many years, and her delicate dressing chair remains in use in the suite's bathroom.

Access to the Waldorf-Astoria's fitness center, restaurants and lounges is granted to all Towers guests. Peacock Alley's "power breakfast" is particularly notable for the business deals brokered here daily. You'll be inspired to tickle the ivories on Cole Porter's piano in the cocktail balcony in the lobby.

For a taste of yesterday's New York, stay at the gracious Waldorf Towers.

**THE WALDORF TOWERS**
100 East 50th Street
New York, NY 10022 USA

# The Point

There are no signs that lead you to The Point, but you will most certainly know when you have arrived at this rustic Eden.

The Point rekindles the spirit of the grand Adirondack camps of the early 19th century, when the Vanderbilts and Posts came to the Adirondacks to live out their sylvan fantasies. The original home of William Avery Rockefeller, The Point is gloriously situated on a ten-acre peninsula on Upper Saranac Lake.

Do not let the native materials used in the exteriors fool you; The Point's stylish guest suites will delight all discerning travelers. Eleven guest accommodations, spread throughout four buildings, are uniquely decorated with a rustic elegance.

Massive stone fireplaces and custom-made beds with hand-sewn mattresses add comforting touches, while antiques and Adirondack furniture provide a sense of place. Set away from the Main Lodge on the lake, the Boathouse is a distinctive suite resembling a magnificent houseboat.

The Point's grand style extends to its fine dining. Reviving the style of the Rockefellers, The Point encourages dressing for dinner, and black tie is suggested for Wednesday and Saturday evenings. The tantalizing flavors of the kitchen are enhanced by the enlightening dinner conversation with your fellow guests.

As the seasons change, so does all at The Point. Fishing, boating and hiking are favorite pastimes in the spring, summer and fall months, while the winter brings cross-country skiing and ice skating on the lake. Of course, The Point is also the sort of place that begs to be enjoyed while turning the pages of a literary classic.

Far from roughing it, The Point is a refined and romantic country retreat.

THE POINT
HCR #1, Box 65
Saranac Lake, NY 12983
USA

# The Castle at Tarrytown

Just thirty minutes north of Manhattan, the unique Castle at Tarrytown is a world away in spirit.

Majestically perched on ten hilltop acres overlooking the Hudson River, this luxury inn rests within the walls of an authentic castle built between 1897 and 1910. Gothic windows and Romanesque archways hint of Norman fortifications in Ireland, Scotland and Wales. The castle's main tower is the highest point for miles in the Hudson River Valley.

The Castle was a private residence for the family of General Howard Carroll, a prominent man who served his country in the Spanish-American War. Purchased in 1992 by Hanspeter and Steffi Walder, The Castle was lovingly transformed and opened as a hotel in 1996.

The Castle at Tarrytown is a rare blend of magnificence and coziness. The entrance hall's oriental carpets and period tapestries are inviting, not imposing, and many public rooms are warmed by the glow of a fire. The 31 guest rooms and suites are romantically furnished, some with four-poster or canopied beds. Wake up to beautiful views of the Hudson River Valley just outside your window. Befitting a castle, the grounds are luscious and complete with swimming pool and tennis courts for leisure pursuits.

The innovative cuisine at Equus is highly regarded among gourmets and is served in three unique settings. The Garden Room provides an airy setting with stunning views of the river and twinkling skyline lights, while the Tapestry Room is a more formal alternative. The Oak Room is a favorite for its Tudor-style iron chandeliers, tapestry-covered chairs and wainscoting brought from General Carroll's house outside of Paris.

Live regally at The Castle at Tarrytown.

**THE CASTLE AT TARRYTOWN**
400 Benedict Avenue
Tarrytown, NY 10591 USA

# Four Seasons Hotel Philadelphia

Philadelphia, the city of brotherly love, has much to offer. From its impressive collection at the art museum to its museums dedicated to American independence, Philadelphia is a delight.

Close to everything, the Four Seasons Hotel is one of the city's top hotels. The Four Seasons offers a gracious world of its own with acclaimed service, luxurious accommodations and attention to detail.

The contemporary building is superbly situated at Logan Square. The plush 261 rooms and 103 suites are stylishly decorated with beautiful fabrics and soft tones. Philadelphia's traditional style and American heritage are represented throughout the hotel.

The Benjamin Franklin Suite has specially commissioned reproductions from the Federal period.

Fine dining is synonymous with the Four Seasons, especially in Philadelphia. The Fountain Restaurant is an elegant dining room, handsomely furnished with rich wood and subdued lighting. The cuisine is renowned for its quality and presentation, and the restaurant is continually honored with top culinary awards. Be sure to ask for a table with a view of Swann Fountain! The Swann Lounge has fantastic views of its namesake along with a cozy fireplace.

A fitness center and indoor swimming pool keep healthy-minded guests happy. Spa services pamper sybaritic guests with treatments like La Stone therapy, a treatment that places hot or cold volcanic stones in a pattern to alleviate tension.

As with all Four Seasons, the Four Seasons Hotel Philadelphia welcomes children with special menus, bedtime milk and cookies, and other special amenities like child-size bathrobes and no-tear shampoo.

In the city of brotherly love, you'll certainly love the Four Seasons Hotel.

FOUR SEASONS HOTEL
PHILADELPHIA
One Logan Square
Philadelphia, PA 19103 USA

# The Ritz-Carlton, Philadelphia

Located within a historic landmark building, The Ritz-Carlton celebrates Philadelphia's past while enlightening its future.

Built in the early 1900's as the Girard Trust Company and onetime home to Girard and Mellon banks, this splendid building now houses a premier hotel. Designed by the famous architectural firm of McKim, Mead & White, the building was inspired by the Pantheon in Rome. Its grand rotunda is made entirely of marble.

Opened in June 2000, The Ritz-Carlton, Philadelphia is the centerpiece of Ten Avenue of the Arts, in the heart of Philadelphia's arts community. The hotel lobby is in the impressive and magnificent grand

Some of Philadelphia's most inventive restaurants are located within The Ritz-Carlton. The Rotunda, an enormous space anchored by large white marble pillars, is an unusual setting for breakfast, lunch, afternoon snacks and cocktails. Pantheon is a terrific Italian restaurant and the Paris Bar & Grill serves French bistro food in a casual space. Inspired by the elegance of the 1920's, The Vault is a seductive lounge for enjoying cigars, cognac, armagnac, single malt Scotch and handmade truffles.

Enjoy America's heritage at the historical Ritz-Carlton, Philadelphia.

rotunda structure. Appropriately so, the entire hotel and all 303 rooms and 27 suites reflect the 18th and 19th century design philosophy of The Ritz-Carlton Hotels and Philadelphia's history. The rooms are formal, yet very comfortable, and cutting-edge technology for the business and leisure traveler is available in all rooms. Technology butlers are on call for any technical problems that may arise, while butler-drawn baths will relax you after a long day of meetings or museum hopping.

THE RITZ-CARLTON,
PHILADELPHIA
Ten Avenue of the Arts
Philadelphia, PA 19102 USA

# Charleston Place

Charleston is at once historic and cosmopolitan. Its antebellum mansions, horse drawn carriages and cobblestone streets smelling of fragrant honeysuckle and jasmine remind one of the Old South. It is here, at Fort Sumter, that the first shots of the Civil War were fired. However, chic restaurants, exclusive boutiques and a thriving cultural scene prove that Charleston is as much a contemporary destination as a historical attraction.

Southern hospitality meets European elegance at Charleston Place. Graciously reflecting its city's historic and modern charms, Charleston Place is best known for its Italian marble lobby with a magnificent 12 foot crystal chandelier and sweeping staircase. The hotel is ideally located at the corners of King, Meeting and Market Streets, in the heart of the historic district. Whether you choose to admire the sweetgrass baskets in the Market or take a tour of the city's houses and gardens, Charleston Place is in the center of it all.

The 400 guest rooms and 42 suites are decorated with traditional furnishings and Southern style armoires. Baths are sumptuous with Botticino marble and brass fixtures, while business travelers will take comfort in finding direct dial telephones and the latest data port capabilities.

A rooftop tennis court and an indoor-outdoor swimming pool with retractable roof lend a resort ambience to this city hotel. Check your worries at the door of the European-style day spa, where fitness and spa services are available.

Charleston Place's two restaurants are locally influenced in design and cuisine. Charleston Grill, one of the city's finest dining establishments, focuses on delicious lowcountry cuisine, while the Palmetto Café is reminiscent of a plantation with its airy ambience and rattan furnishings.

Charleston Place is a Southern delight.

CHARLESTON PLACE
205 Meeting Street
Charleston, SC 29401 USA

# Four Seasons Hotel Austin

Austin is a big city with a small town charm. Nicknamed the "live music capital of the world," Austin is also Texas' version of California's Silicon Valley. Its rolling hills, clear lakes and friendly people make it a pleasure to visit.

Close to downtown and the entertainment district, yet located in a tranquil spot, the Four Seasons Hotel presents the best of Austin. Situated on rolling hills overlooking Town Lake, the hotel has the ambience of a resort even though it is located in one of the state's major cities.

The Four Seasons has a dynamic décor that combines Southwestern flavor and unique

cuisine, a delicious blend of American, Southwestern, Continental and Asian cooking styles using local foods and herbs. The Four Seasons' alternative cuisine, available in all hotels, is ideal for diners who seek meals lower in sodium, cholesterol and calories. The Lobby Lounge, decorated with a regional flair, is a comfortable and casual gathering place. Enjoy the Four Seasons' outdoor grounds while sampling one of their picnic hampers out on the lawn. Pick a favorite tree, have the hamper delivered and relax by the lake.

Experience the best of Texas' capital at the Four Seasons Hotel Austin.

Texan touches with the traditional style of Four Seasons hotels. Wildflowers and fabrics indicative of Texas, like cow prints, decorate the warm lobby. The 263 rooms and 28 suites enjoy expansive views of Town Lake or Austin's cityscape and are fitted with 21st century advances, like high speed internet connections and two-line telephones.

Adjacent to the wildflower gardens, the Café exudes a park-like atmosphere. The Café serves acclaimed "hill country"

**FOUR SEASONS HOTEL AUSTIN**
98 San Jacinto Boulevard
Austin, TX 78701 USA

# Hotel Crescent Court

Designed by renowned architect Philip Johnson, the Hotel Crescent Court is a classic design of timeless style.

Opened in 1985, the Hotel Crescent Court is part of a complex that includes upscale boutiques and trendy restaurants in Dallas' fashionable uptown area. Built from the same quarry as the Empire State Building, the Crescent Court complex is the world's largest assemblage of limestone.

The hotel's gleaming exterior only hints at the gracious design to be discovered once inside. Marble floors and columns complement vaulted ceilings, while French windows add elegance. The seven story hotel has 178 guest rooms and 42 suites, all defined by fine furnishings, distinctive artwork and wrought iron balconies.

Restore your spirit while enjoying the soothing environment of the Hotel Crescent Court's spa. Lady Primrose products, created by Caroline Hunt, founder of the exclusive Rosewood Hotels & Resorts, are used in many of the beauty treatments. With more than 77 different beauty and relaxation treatments, the spa has something for everyone. Nutritious and refreshing fruit and vegetable juices are available at the juice bar along with healthy, satisfying snacks and meals. Guests seeking retail therapy will delight in the shops and boutiques of the Crescent Court complex.

Hotel Crescent Court's Beau Nash Restaurant is one of Dallas' preferred dining spots. The brasserie-style restaurant specializes in New American cuisine and has a lively atmosphere with live music on the weekends. Beau Nash's wine collection is highly esteemed; it has been named top American wine cellar by *Wine Spectator* twice. Visit the swanky Crescent Club located 18 stories up, where the people-watching and the views of Dallas are dazzling.

Hotel Crescent Court greets you with a Texas-size warm welcome.

**HOTEL CRESCENT COURT**
400 Crescent Court
Dallas, TX 75201 USA

# The Mansion on Turtle Creek

The Mansion on Turtle Creek is a Dallas landmark. Blending the Old World elegance of the 1920's mansion with an expertly designed hotel tower, The Mansion on Turtle Creek brings you the best of both worlds in Dallas' most fashionable area. The Sheppard King Mansion is a former private residence built during the 1920's by a wealthy cotton baron. Inspired by the Italian Renaissance, the mansion is gloriously decorated with intricately carved ceilings, marble fireplaces and a 32 foot high rotunda. Today, the mansion is home to the hotel's highly acclaimed restaurant, bar and private dining rooms.

Constructed in the early 1980's after the mansion's sale to

helmeted faces stand guard at the entrance to the Mansion Restaurant, richly decorated with original carvings and museum quality works of art. Credited with inventing Southwestern cuisine, Chef Dean Fearing oversees this restaurant, widely recognized for its creative concoctions. Plan ahead for reservations, as the Mansion Restaurant is number one in Dallas. The bar provides a casual alternative for lunch and dinner in a setting reminiscent of a hunting lodge.

Guests are rewarded with superior levels of service, guaranteeing a memorable stay.

Escape the everyday at Dallas' extraordinary Mansion on Turtle Creek.

Rosewood Hotels, the adjacent nine-story hotel tower perfectly complements the architecture of the original mansion. The Mansion on Turtle Creek set the standards for all future Rosewood Hotels with its philosophy of superior service in unique properties. The 126 guest rooms and 15 suites exude Southern charm and grace. French doors open out to private balconies, while the suites have marble fireplaces and original works of art.

Two pairs of 19th century Spanish cathedral doors with carved

**THE MANSION ON TURTLE CREEK**
2821 Turtle Creek Boulevard
Dallas, TX 75219 USA

# Four Seasons Resort and Club Dallas at Las Colinas

The Four Seasons Resort and Club offers a different slice of Dallas.

Resting on 400 acres just outside of Dallas, the resort provides a myriad of leisure opportunities in one of the country's most sprawling metropolitan areas.

The main, nine-story building is home to 301 rooms and 6 suites, while the golf villas have 44 rooms and 6 suites. The golf villas overlook the 18th green of the Tournament Players course or the landscaped pool garden. The luxurious accommodations with all modern conveniences are a welcome sight after a challenging round of golf or tennis match.

Two championship golf courses make the Four Seasons one of the top golf resorts in the United States. Home of the annual Byron Nelson Classic, the Tournament Players course's third hole was counted among the toughest holes on the PGA tour in 1994. The Cottonwood Valley course, designed by Robert Trent Jones, Jr., is a scenic course that shares its state pride with all golfers; the number one green is shaped like Texas. The Byron Nelson Golf School pays homage to one of the game's legendary players with its dedication to improving players' games through private instruction and clinics.

The tennis facility includes eight outdoor courts, including a stadium court with seating for up to 3,000, and four indoor, climate controlled courts. Three outdoor pools, a heated indoor pool and a children's pool keep swimmers satisfied. The spa eases your tensions with its own brand of relaxation and beauty treatments.

You will sing *The Yellow Rose of Texas* after a stay at the Four Seasons Resort and Club Dallas at Las Colinas.

FOUR SEASONS RESORT
AND CLUB DALLAS
AT LAS COLINAS
4150 North MacArthur Boulevard
Irving, TX 75038 USA

# Four Seasons Hotel Houston

Houston is the fourth largest city in the United States and the country's energy capital, though it is probably best known as the home base of NASA. The first words spoken from the moon blasted Houston's name throughout the world, sealing its reputation as the aerospace mission control center.

Bringing a bit of European flair to Houston, the Four Seasons is a luxurious hotel in this booming city. Located near the Convention Center, the theater and museum districts, the Four Seasons is perfect for business and leisure travelers. Shoppers will be thrilled to discover the Park Shops in Houston Center. This three-level shopping mall is connected to the hotel via a climate controlled skywalk.

The 387 spacious rooms and 12 suites are furnished with a cosmopolitan elegance. All accommodations are well equipped for business travelers; even exercise equipment is available by request in your room. Extra large windows show off Houston's downtown skyline. Southern hospitality is added to the famous Four Seasons service.

The Four Seasons' DeVille Restaurant is a marvelous place for dining on American cuisine with Continental influences. The art filled dining room is elegant. Try the chef's table for a unique and fun experience, where you will dine in the kitchen amidst the chef's preparations.

The full service spa, salon and 24 hour fitness center offers a total workout with a lap pool, sauna, whirlpool and fitness machines fitted with E-Zone personal entertainment systems. Shaded by palm trees and surrounded by cabanas, the outdoor pool goes beyond the typical city pool and creates a resort experience.

Tip your cowboy hat to the Four Seasons Hotel.

**FOUR SEASONS HOTEL HOUSTON**
1300 Lamar Street
Houston, TX 77010 USA

# The Equinox

Nestled on 2,300 acres in the Green Mountains of southern Vermont, The Equinox is a picture-perfect New England resort.

The Equinox's history stretches back to pre-Revolutionary War days. Though it was then called the Marsh Inn, The Equinox quickly earned a reputation as one of America's premier retreats. Attracted by its reputation, Mrs. Lincoln vacationed here in the summer of 1863 with her two sons. The family made plans to return the following year with President Lincoln, and the hotel even constructed a special suite in their honor. Sadly, they would never return. Today, the original structure houses the Marsh Tavern restaurant.

The Equinox's 183 guest rooms and suites exude a refined country elegance. Rooms are decorated with antique furniture, Audubon prints and country fabrics typical of the Vermont countryside. Adjacent to the main building, the Charles Orvis Inn, original home of fly-fishing entrepreneur, Charles Orvis, functions as part of the resort with nine one and two bedroom suites.

In keeping with its rugged setting, The Equinox offers a dazzling array of outdoor activities. The British School of Falconry, the first of its kind in America, offers truly fascinating insight into the world of hawks. Off-road driving techniques, from introductory to advanced, are taught at the Land Rover Driving School. Of course, cross-country skiing, snowmobiling, snowshoeing and ice skating are popular winter pastimes, while canoeing, hiking, fly fishing and tennis are favorites during the summer months. Discerning golfers will appreciate the 18 hole Gleneagles Golf Course. The Equinox offers full spa programs and Manchester Village's tempting brand name outlets are just a few paces away.

Share in Vermont's bucolic splendor at The Equinox.

**THE EQUINOX**
Route 7A
Manchester Village, VT 05254
USA

# Rosario

Off the coast of Washington in the scenic San Juan Islands lies a special place called Rosario, which breathes a new life into all who visit.

After being diagnosed with heart disease and given a year to live, shipping magnate and former Seattle mayor Robert Moran set about building his dream house on the shores of Cascade Bay on Orcas Island. The tranquility of this magical place strengthened Moran, who not only beat his doctor's predictions, but lived there for another 30 years!

Arrival at Rosario is an incredibly scenic trip, whether you choose to sit back on the ferry and

enjoy the ride, or opt for the thrilling seaplane trip, where you will land in the bay directly in front of the resort!

The Moran Mansion is the center of the resort and home to the two restaurants, spa, shipbuilding museum, lounge and music room. Beautiful mahogany paneling and hand-crafted furniture create an inviting atmosphere. The Orcas Room and Compass Room restaurants both feature local seafood and have stunning views of the bay.

The 127 guest rooms are located on a hill above the mansion. The rooms are a cheerful blend of colors with a relaxed elegance. Deep-soaking tubs with picturesque

bay views persuade you to linger longer.

Activities are plentiful at Rosario, where you can opt for sea kayaking, scuba diving, sailing or whale watching, and spot one of the island's namesake orcas in its natural habitat. Nature hikes in the forest, mountain biking in Moran State Park or relaxing by the bayside pool will calm your spirits. After an afternoon at the spa, you will feel energized.

Live the natural life to its fullest at Rosario.

**ROSARIO**
1400 Rosario Road
Orcas Island, WA 98245 USA

# Four Seasons Hotel Seattle

Seattle has its own brand of urban sophistication. Defined by its rivers, lakes and canals, Seattle is an incredibly cultured city. The city's per capita book purchases are among North America's highest, and it has a thriving arts and entertainment scene.

Sharing its home city's affection for the arts, the Four Seasons Hotel is Seattle's most deluxe hotel. This Renaissance Revival masterpiece took the world by storm when it opened in the early 1920's as the Olympic Hotel. Its grand architecture and interior design were unprecedented in this part of the country. Terrazzo marble floors, antique mirrors and Italian and Spanish statuary set a refined, formal tone that lingers today.

special occasions. The menu showcases creative Northwest cuisine with a French flair. The greenhouse-like Garden Court is an airy and delightful setting for finger sandwiches, specialty martinis and cocktails, along with an outstanding wine list. The oyster bar, Shuckers, is a popular spot with locals who wash down the fresh seafood with local microbrews.

A well-equipped fitness center and indoor swimming pool help you maintain your fitness schedule while visiting Seattle.

When in Seattle, stay at the sophisticated Four Seasons Hotel.

The Four Seasons is perfectly situated in downtown Seattle's Rainier neighborhood. Located near the financial and retail districts, the Four Seasons is within walking distance to the waterfront and the city's museums.

The hotel's 241 rooms and 209 suites are lavishly decorated with antiques, fine furnishings, plush carpeting and the signature Four Seasons beds. All rooms have city views, while some offer glimpses of Elliot Bay.

The Four Seasons is renowned for its restaurants. The Georgian is one of the city's finest restaurants and its romantic setting makes it ideal for

**FOUR SEASONS
HOTEL SEATTLE**
411 University Street
Seattle, WA 98101 USA

# Salish Lodge & Spa

Renew both body and soul at the rejuvenating Salish Lodge & Spa. Located 30 minutes from downtown Seattle, the lodge is perched atop the 268 foot Snoqualmie Falls in the foothills of the Cascade Mountains. In the local language, Snoqualmie, means "valley of the moon." It is a true paradise in the unspoiled, natural Pacific Northwest.

All of the lodge's 87 rooms and 4 suites have wood-burning fireplaces to chase away the evening chill, soothing whirlpool tubs and cozy feather beds with down comforters. Natural tones are used in the décor, with neutral fabrics and light-colored woods playing off the colors of the outdoors. Savor the fantastic views of the valley from the comforts of your own room.

Salish Lodge & Spa features two fabulous dining selections. The Dining Room is a stylish place with breath-taking views of the Falls. Fresh, seasonal ingredients from the Pacific Northwest serve as the inspiration for the delicious meals. Sample regional wines from an award winning wine list. The five course country breakfast is a local favorite. The Attic, on the top floor, is an informal spot with casual dining and spectacular views.

The resort's spa perfectly captures the tranquility of the valley and the Falls. Therapeutic soaking pools and massages, like the heated stone massage, will work out the tension in your body, while specialized skin care and body treatments replenish your natural glow.

This picturesque place and its surroundings are ideal for exploration, whether you take in the unparalleled scenery, visit the nearby valley towns on the local railroads, tour a winery or fish the beautiful lakes and rivers.

Delight in the scenic and superb Salish Lodge & Spa.

**SALISH LODGE & SPA**
6501 Railroad Avenue SE
Snoqualmie, WA 98065 USA

# Spring Creek Ranch

Spring Creek Ranch invites you to experience America's last frontier.

Eagles soar, wildflowers blanket the meadows and elk run free in this blessed stretch of the American West. Spring Creek Ranch is nestled on 1,000 acres atop East Gros Ventre Butte, 1000 feet above the valley of Jackson Hole. Facing the Teton mountain range, the resort rests between cattle ranches, the National Elk Refuge and Grand Teton National Park.

Wildlife flourishes at Spring Creek Ranch, where you will share your experience with various animals. Each winter, the mule deer herd migrates to the resort, and 100 species of birds and 40 species of mammals call Spring Creek Ranch their home.

Comprised of lodges constructed of fir, spruce and pine, the ranch epitomizes Western chic. All 36 rooms, 32 suites, 32 studios, 21 condominiums and 6 luxury houses have handmade lodge pole pine furniture, stone fireplaces and sweeping views of the majestic outdoors.

The Granary tantalizes your palate with its American menu dotted with western specialties, like medallions of elk and antelope carpaccio. Its wine list is highly regarded, winning awards from *Wine Spectator*.

Spring Creek Ranch provides the perfect setting for enjoyment of the great outdoors. During winter, horse drawn sleigh rides – imagine one through a herd of thousands of elk – dog sledding, and snowmobile trip to Old Faithful in Yellowstone National Park are unique options. Nearby enjoy a myriad of skiing choices, including heli-skiing. In the summer, horseback riding, swimming, tennis and golf are available, along with the exciting experiences of hot air ballooning, hiking and mountain climbing, or whitewater rafting down the Snake River.

Go West to Spring Creek Ranch!

**SPRING CREEK RANCH**
1800 Spirit Dance Road
Jackson Hole, WY 83001 USA

# Las Ventanas al Paraiso

Mexico's Baja Peninsula is a stunning desert landscape dotted with flowering acacia and saguaro cacti. The warm waters of the Sea of Cortes and the wild waves of the Pacific Ocean meet here with a dazzling result. It is a playground for a wide variety of marine life, including dolphins, turtles and whales.

Las Ventanas al Paraiso, or "windows on Paradise," is the region's most glorious resort. Hugging the slopes above the sapphire ocean, Las Ventanas is a blend of Mediterranean and Mexican architecture. Grand, hacienda style buildings house 61 guest suites. The resort's dedication to Mexican handicraft is noticeable throughout, with colorful native paintings, intricately carved furnishings and traditional Conchuela limestone floors. Adobe or terracotta wood-burning fireplaces add a comforting touch. All rooms feature telescopes, excellent for stargazing or observing whales in the distance.

The dramatic setting and graceful curves of the infinity-edge swimming pools are the resort's signature. A swim-up bar with in-water stools completes the mood. Pool butlers attend to sunbathers with frosted Evian spray, cold towels and refreshing frozen chocolate sorbet cups. The adjacent Sea Grill's delicious specialties keep hunger at bay. Those who prefer to rest on the beach will be delighted to discover the same services along with special hammocks equipped with flags. The flags advise butlers of the guest's desired waking time, should they fall asleep in the afternoon sun.

Two restaurants with inventive cuisine garner high marks from discerning guests, and the tequila and ceviche bar is another popular spot.

At Las Ventanas, open the windows of your soul to paradise.

**LAS VENTANAS AL PARAISO**
Km. 19.5 Carretera Transpeninsular
Cabo San Lucas
San Jose Del Cabo, 23400 Mexico

# The Ritz-Carlton, Cancun

Toss your cares to the wind at The Ritz-Carlton, Cancun.

This exclusive resort rests along 1,200 feet of golden beach on the tip of Mexico's Yucatan Peninsula. The lively town of Cancun is just 20 minutes away, yet The Ritz-Carlton enjoys unprecedented peace and quiet.

Mexico's Spanish heritage is relived at The Ritz-Carlton with tiled roofs, wrought-iron railings, and a colorful stained glass ceiling crafted by a local artist. The 315 rooms and 50 suites are tastefully appointed in soft colors, and all are topped off with magnificent sea or pool views.

The resort's two beachfront swimming pools are stunning, and the beach is dotted with signature blue "cabana chairs." Special services provided by beach and pool concierges ensure that your afternoon is enjoyable and massages are even offered on the beach. I can think of no better way to spend an afternoon in Mexico than with a freshly blended tropical drink and a soothing beachfront massage!

Four restaurants with varied menus and two lounges keep your nights as exciting as your days. After a day in the sun, perhaps you will want to try the resort's unique Margarita bath. Taking its inspiration from the famous cocktail, your bathtub is transformed with fresh limes, colorful flowers and even salt lining the tub.

Outside of the resort, there is shopping in Cancun, Mayan archaeological sites and spectacular reef diving. The resort makes visiting Mexico's charms easy for all ages.

The Ritz-Carlton, Cancun glitters as one of Mexico's finest resorts.

**THE RITZ-CARLTON, CANCUN**
*Retorno Del Rey #36*
*Cancun 77500, Mexico*

# Four Seasons Hotel Mexico

Mexico City, the oldest capital city in the Western Hemisphere, is Mexico's cultural, political and economic capital. Its wide, tree-lined boulevards are home to modern glass structures and low-rise colonial buildings; and like most world capitals, the city pulsates with a frenetic pace.

Away from the whirlwind of activity, the Four Seasons Hotel is an oasis in Mexico City. The hotel has represented the best of the city since 1994. Its prime location on the Paseo de la Reforma places it near the major corporate, retail and residential districts. The National Museum of Anthropology and History, one of the world's most notable museums, is within ten minutes

of the hotel. Though you can get almost anywhere from the hotel, you may choose to simply relax within this sanctuary.

The eight story building celebrates Mexican colonial architecture while adding a European twist. The building surrounds a traditional courtyard with a trickling fountain. Most of the 240 guest rooms and suites overlook this tranquil setting. The accommodations tastefully blend European antiques and furniture with Mexican decorative objects.

Three restaurants present terrific dining options. Fine dining is available at El Restaurante, while the Café is ideal for informal occasions. El Sálon, a library-styled bar, also offers light dining. A swim in the rooftop pool is a great way to work off a decadent meal or busy day.

The Four Seasons has a terrific cultural program for guests. Guided tours by art historians give visitors insight into Mexican history and culture. Tours extend beyond the city to explore Mexico's glories.

The Four Seasons Hotel Mexico is a dynamic hotel in a vibrant city.

**FOUR SEASONS HOTEL MEXICO, D.F.**
06600 Paseo de la Reforma #500
Colonia Juárez, Mexico, D.F.

# Four Seasons Resort Punta Mita

The Four Seasons Resort Punta Mita is a slice of paradise on Mexico's western coast overlooking the Pacific Ocean.

Punta Mita, northwest of Puerto Vallarta, is an enviable stretch of unspoiled landscape that is on the northern tip of Bahia de Banderas, one of the world's largest bays. Offering distant views of the rugged Sierra Madre Mountains, Punta Mita has abundant marine life and some of the finest beaches in Mexico. Each winter, the gray whales come to Banderas Bay to raise their young.

Designed to live in harmony with the spectacular setting, the Four Seasons Resort resembles a small village. The main building is open-sided and

features a palapa roof, handwoven from palm fronds. The building overlooks the breathtaking infinity-edge pool that curves along a hill above the beach. It is indistinguishable where the pool ends and the ocean begins.

Thirteen traditional tile roofed casitas house 113 guest rooms and 27 suites. All guest accommodations open out to terraces facing the ocean, and the suites feature private plunge pools. Textiles hand embroidered by native

Huichol Indians complement the serene interiors, and native wood is used in custom made closets and furnishings.

Some of the best surfing beaches in Mexico are located to the north and south of the resort, and just ten minutes offshore are the Marietas Islands, known for fantastic snorkeling and scuba diving. The 18 hole Jack Nicklaus designed golf course is marvelous. It features the only natural island hole in the world - 199 yards out into the ocean. The Punta Mita massage, featuring sage and tequila, is a must-try at the resort's spa.

The Four Seasons Resort Punta Mita brings you Mexico like you have never seen it before.

**FOUR SEASONS RESORT PUNTA MITA**
Bahia de Banderas
Nayarit 63734, Mexico

# Alvear Palace Hotel

Its very wide boulevards and French-influenced architecture prompt many to call Buenos Aires the "Paris of South America." The city's distinctly European flavor is due in large part to its residents, or porteños as they are known, who often hail from abroad. Its distinct blend of European grandeur and Latin sizzle makes Buenos Aires an exciting and sophisticated city.

The Recoleta district glitters with palatial mansions, chic cafés and exclusive shopping, not to mention the city's best hotel, the Alvear Palace. Established in 1932, the hotel shares the best of Buenos Aires with its guests. Step through the revolving doors to the exclusive world of the Alvear Palace where the intimate lobby with rich furnishings and gleaming brass is reminiscent of Paris. Tea at the Alvear's Jardin d'Hiver has become a local classic, and the city's most fashionable women don their very best jewels and fashions to take tea here.

The Alvear Palace's 85 rooms and 125 suites are classically European, with Louis XV and Empire furnishings. Objets d'art and fresh flower arrangements add a personal touch to the elegant rooms, and 24 hour personal butler service guarantees contentment. A health club with an indoor swimming pool and an efficient business center are also located within the hotel and are at your disposal.

Dining is of the highest caliber at the Alvear Palace. La Bourgogne is the only Relais Gourmand restaurant in Argentina and it is an epicurean's delight. Exquisite French cuisine is served in a soothing atmosphere, and a few tables are reserved in the wine cellar for a truly unique experience.

The Alvear Palace Hotel proves that elegance and first-rate service never go out of style.

### ALVEAR PALACE HOTEL
Avenida Alvear 1891
1129 Buenos Aires, Argentina

# Copacabana Palace

Brazil's Rio de Janeiro needs no introduction. Its playful, fun-loving spirit is renowned and perhaps best expressed in the yearly festival of Carnaval, where the cariocas, or residents of Rio, take to the streets to dance until the wee hours.

Rio's infectious enthusiasm is closely tied to its beautiful beaches, and Copacabana Beach stands out as one of the finest. Reigning over this popular spot since the early 1920's, the Copacabana Palace is the most glamorous hotel in all of Brazil. It is the darling of Rio society and the international jet set. The pulse of the city is just outside its refined doors.

Designed by a French architect who was inspired

two very distinct atmospheres. Cipriani Restaurant serves the sophisticated cuisine of the famous Venetian hotel. The Pergula, poolside and casual, is popular with Rio's residents, as is the lively Copa Bar.

Whether you choose to sun on its beaches or visit Sugar Loaf Mountain, Copacabana Palace provides the ideal location for experiencing Rio, though the private swimming pool with sun deck, rooftop tennis courts and array of other activities may convince you to remain here!

Adopt the carefree spirit of Rio at the fun-loving Copacabana Palace.

by the grand architecture of the French Riviera, Copacabana Palace has 91 guest rooms and 135 suites. The international décor is stylish, and the penthouse suites take full advantage of the ocean views with carefully positioned bathtubs and large terraces.

Copacabana Palace has two restaurants with

### COPACABANA PALACE
Avenida Atlantica 1702
Rio de Janeiro, 22021-001,
Brazil

# Hotel Monasterio

Hotel Monasterio offers a unique perspective on Peruvian culture on a corner of an idyllic square in Cusco. A rare blend of museum and five-star hotel, the hotel occupies the converted San Antonio Abad Seminary, originally built in 1592.

The colonial city of Cusco, with its terracotta roofs and blend of Incan and Spanish architecture, is a marvelous destination. Its cobblestone streets lead you to fascinating ruins and bustling markets where you will find colorful crafts and traditional festivals. The town's main square is a short walk from the hotel, and though the mysterious ruins of Machu Picchu are seventy-five miles from Cusco, they are an essential stop for all visitors to Peru. The ruins can be reached by a scenic train journey, or opt for the thrilling helicopter ride which affords spectacular vistas.

Hotel Monasterio's 105 rooms and 17 suites combine colonial and modern styles and incorporate many decorative objects from the Incas. While all rooms have luxurious amenities and services, the monastery's building has been carefully preserved. It is easy to imagine the monks that resided here when you glance out your window to the cloistered courtyard. Whether you are in your room, or enjoying the stone courtyard or gardens, a great sense of peace pervades. Hotel Monasterio's 18th century chapel is glorious with intricate carvings, frescoes and paintings that date from the Inquisition. The hotel is even complete with its own resident ghost; an old woman in white is said to roam the roof late at night.

Tupay, the monastery's original refectory, serves Peruvian and international dishes, while the Illariy Café offers a continental menu. The seminary's ancient paintings line the walls of the café. Or, dine in the outdoor cloistered courtyard.

Blessing you with its serenity, Hotel Monasterio is the perfect base for exploring the wonders of Peru.

## HOTEL MONASTERIO
Calle Palacios 136
Plazoleta Nazarenas, Cusco, Peru

# Four Seasons Hotel Caracas

Built at an altitude of almost 3,000 feet along Avila Mountain, Caracas enjoys a temperate climate and a breathtaking natural setting. This dynamic and thriving city is one of South America's leading business and culture capitals and its modern skyline proves it.

Four Seasons Hotel Caracas, the first South American hotel in the group, opened in the early part of 2001. Its impressive tower with twenty-one levels is situated within a complex that includes condominiums, offices and stores. Located in the exclusive residential area of Altamira, the hotel has

free-form pool has a waterfall, fountain and whirlpools, and its terrific views of the city are unparalleled. Exotic drinks and specialties are served poolside, reminding you of Caracas' tropical spirit.

Two main restaurants are located within the hotel and are appropriate for both business dinners and friendly gatherings. L'Azur offers French specialties, while Vivaldi is open all day for casual Italian fare. In addition to the poolside bar, there is a piano lounge for nightly entertainment.

Experience Venezuela's lively spirit at the modern Four Seasons Hotel Caracas.

sensational views of the hills of Bello Monte and Avila Mountain.

The 178 rooms and 34 suites are among the most spacious in the city. Locally crafted furnishings that echo the energetic spirit of Caracas are blended with Four Seasons amenities, like the exceptionally comfortable, trademark beds.

The superb ninth floor rooftop pool is a highlight of the hotel. The gorgeous

**FOUR SEASONS HOTEL CARACAS**
Av. Francisco de Miranda con
Av. Luis Roche
Altamira, Caracas, Venezuela

# Bahamas
# Bermuda
# Caribbean

| | |
|---|---|
| ANGUILLA | PUERTO RICO |
| ANTIGUA | SAINT-BARTHÉLEMY |
| BAHAMAS | ST. JOHN |
| BERMUDA | ST. MARTIN |
| JAMAICA | ST. THOMAS |
| NEVIS | TURKS & CAICOS |
| PETER ISLAND | VIRGIN GORDA |

# Cap Juluca

Resting between the Atlantic Ocean and the Caribbean Sea, Anguilla is a tranquil island only 16 miles long and 3 miles wide. The most northerly of the Leeward Islands, Anguilla enjoys British influences with a decidedly tropical flair.

Though it was 1972, it seems like just yesterday that I sailed into Maundays Bay on a Chinese junk. At the time, this pristine, crescent-shaped beach was an undiscovered slice of paradise, and I thought to myself, "what a fabulous spot for a resort." The 179 secluded acres are now home to Cap Juluca, one of the world's most exclusive resorts.

Cap Juluca brings a little bit of Morocco to Anguilla with its inspired, whitewashed architecture of turrets, domes and parapets. The cool interiors of the 58 rooms, 7 suites and 6 villas provide a relaxing atmosphere. Panoramic views of the turquoise Caribbean may be enjoyed from your room.

If the beach isn't enough, the swimming pool at the Beach Pavilion will entice and George's Restaurant, named for its award-winning chef, will tempt you with its delicious, casual menu. The brilliant white arches and billowing tented interiors of Pimm's Restaurant make it a feast for the eyes and the palate.

Cap Juluca's newest addition is a lively and fun tapas bar with a wide international selection.

Cap Juluca's spa facility utilizes the island's tropical flowers, herbs and intoxicating scents to create a menu of unique rituals. Treatments may be enjoyed in the privacy of your own room, in the Main House or in a gazebo against the backdrop of the azure Caribbean.

With its seductive architecture and truly magnificent beach, Cap Juluca is a perfect romantic retreat.

**CAP JULUCA**
Maundays Bay
Anguilla, BWI

# CuisinArt Resort & Spa

Located on secluded Rendezvous Bay on the southern shore of Anguilla, CuisinArt is a refreshing resort with contemporary ideals.

CuisinArt's whitewashed buildings with distinctive arches and blue domes are reminiscent of the seductive Greek Isles. The Mediterranean influences extend indoors, where the 80 suites, 11 guest rooms and 2 penthouses are accented with Italian fabrics and imported furnishings. Many of the suites feature private solariums. The resort's relaxed ease is perfect for children, who will feel very much at home here.

A philosophy of healthy living and enjoyment of the outdoors prevails at CuisinArt. An exciting array of water sports may be enjoyed and a one-mile fitness course with exercise stations provides a great way to stay in shape while enjoying the fresh air. A well-equipped fitness center is also on the property. Anguilla's premier spa pampers you with its wide array of treatments and highly professional staff. CuisinArt nurtures the intellect as well, with an impressive art gallery on the third floor. The gallery features exhibitions from around the world, and they are rotated on a monthly basis.

Three restaurants are supplied by the resort's own hydroponic farm, the first in the Caribbean. Vegetables, fruit, edible flowers and herbs are grown here, using this unique process that eliminates soil and utilizes only water and special nutrients. The plants harvested are fresh, pesticide-free and known for their superior taste and appearance.

Cuisine is a large part of the CuisinArt experience, whether you are visiting the demonstration kitchen, enrolling in the cooking school or simply enjoying a homegrown salad.

CuisinArt is addictive to all ages.

**CUISINART RESORT & SPA**
Rendezvous Bay
Anguilla, BWI

# Malliouhana Hotel

Surrounded by beaches and secluded coves, Malliouhana Hotel offers a little bit of the French Riviera on Anguilla.

Malliouhana overlooks Meads Bay and Turtle Cove on the northwest coast of Anguilla. Whitewashed villas dot Malliouhana's 25 acres of tropical gardens. The villas provide 36 guest rooms and 19 suites, all graciously furnished with rattan furnishings and Brazilian walnut wardrobes. Whether you are atop the bluff, beachside, near the pool or in the gardens, the resort's aristocratic grace captures your attention.

Guests at Malliouhana dine in the finest style. The terrace restaurant is inviting, with panoramic views and flowering vines. Michel Rostang, a top French restaurateur, creates gourmet French cuisine with hints of the Caribbean. The wine cellar is considered one of the best in the Caribbean, with 25,000 bottles showcasing 800 different vineyards. Le Bistro provides a more casual alternative to the main restaurant.

Malliouhana makes your little ones feel right at home with their own beach-view playground. The playground even has a 26-foot pirate ship with water cannons and a water slide. Childcare counselors ensure safe recreation. A diving pool, suitable for older children, is adjacent to the playground.

Adults are equally well taken care of, with sailing snorkeling, and windsurfing just outside your door. Championship tennis courts, fitness center, massage facilities and two freshwater swimming pools are also located on the property.

With splendid service and its own brand of panache, Malliouhana is one of the Caribbean's best resorts.

**MALLIOUHANA HOTEL**
Meads Bay
Anguilla, BWI

# Jumby Bay Resort

Escape to Jumby Bay Resort, a private 300 acre island two miles north of Antigua.

First discovered by Christopher Columbus, Jumby Bay has been on the map for savvy travelers since its opening in 1983. Accessible from the mainland by private boat service, Jumby Bay is a sophisticated retreat. Its 39 suites and 11 villas are spread throughout the island and are connected by charming stone pathways. All accommodations are near the beach and feature ocean views. The décor is a stylish blend of West-Indian influences and English plantation manor style, with louvered doors, mahogany furniture and four-poster beds.

Jumby Bay is a naturalist's haven. Pasture Bay Beach, one of the island's three powdery, white sand beaches, is home to the endangered Hawksbill turtle. A variety of rare birds and even sheep, whose ancestors were brought here over 300 years ago, also share this lovely spot.

Windsurfing, snorkeling and other water sports are popular at Jumby Bay, and scuba instruction on Antigua can be arranged. Tennis courts, a croquet lawn and putting green are also provided for your enjoyment.

Jumby means "friendly spirit" in Arawak, and the resort takes its name seriously with a caring staff and pleasant attitude. Jumby Bay offers relaxed dining in two beautiful settings. The Estate House, a 230-year old English plantation manor, provides a charming setting, while the Verandah Restaurant is beachside for your convenience.

Indulge your fantasies of a private tropical island at Jumby Bay Resort.

**JUMBY BAY RESORT**
St. Johns
Antigua

# Ocean Club

It is called Paradise Island for a reason, and the island's Ocean Club is a tropical nirvana.

The Ocean Club, once a grand private estate, is a stylish resort with delightful accommodations, spectacular gardens and impeccable service. The intricately landscaped gardens are unlike any in the Caribbean. Based on Versailles, the gardens have seven terraced levels. Each plateau features rock ridges and stone steps and magnificent European marble and bronze statues can be found within the grounds. The majestic gardens are topped off by a 12th century stone Augustinian cloister.

The resort's 98 rooms, 14 suites and 5 villas are decorated in either contemporary tropical or British Colonial décor. Thoughtful services and amenities are included and all rooms have private balconies or terraces. The private bathrooms are incredibly spacious and have sumptuous bathtubs.

Critically acclaimed chef Jean Georges Vongerichten has created a stir with his fabulous Dune restaurant at the Ocean Club. The chic interior, designed by Christian Liaigre, perfectly complements his inventive cuisine. The historic Courtyard Terrace restaurant is a nice alternative with fresh seafood and classic French cuisine. In addition to the two main dining rooms, two grills quell your hunger throughout the day.

Indulge yourself at the Mandara Spa, just opened in 2001. Unique beauty treatments are created from fresh local spices, fruits and minerals. The experiences offered here are truly uplifting.

In addition to water sports, tennis and fitness facilities, the Ocean Club welcomed an 18-hole golf course in late 2000. This championship course was designed by Tom Weiskopf and is both challenging and awe-inspiring.

Heaven waits for you at the Ocean Club.

## OCEAN CLUB
Nassau, Bahamas

# Pink Sands

Settled by Loyalists fleeing the American Revolution more than 300 years ago, Harbour Island is a quaint spot on the rim of the Bahamas Island chain. This tiny place, known for its fabulous pink beaches, enjoys colonial charm and a playful Bahamian spirit. Reachable by a short ferry ride from nearby Eleuthera, Harbour Island is home to one of the Caribbean's most unusual resorts, Pink Sands.

Pink Sands occupies 18 acres overlooking the most beautiful stretch of pink sand beach in the Bahamas. Bicycles and golf carts are the preferred mode of transportation at this peaceful

and sophisticated resort. There are 25 one and two bedroom cottages with garden or ocean views. All cottages feature private terraces with sleek furniture and private Jacuzzis. The décor is eclectic and has great pizzazz, with unusual patterns and objects.

This secluded hideaway's three-mile private beach sheltered by a coral reef and the freshwater pool provide perfect settings for relaxing. Guests at Pink Sands seek peace and quiet, and that is exactly what they get

in this tranquil place.

Casual lunch is served at the beachside Blue Bar. Be sure to try the Bahamian Conch Chowder spiked with dark rum – it is a specialty! The Garden Restaurant is a seductive setting for intimate dinners. Its colorful spirit and private candlelit corners provide a romantic spot for the restaurant's Caribbean and International fusion cuisine. Additionally, some of the Bahamas' most exciting restaurants are within walking distance from the resort.

Look at the world through rose-colored glasses at Pink Sands.

**PINK SANDS**
Harbour Island
Bahamas

# Cobblers Cove

Barbados is absolutely charming. Its rolling hills and perfect white beaches make it a popular Caribbean island, and its own brand of British dash gives it an inimitable character. Afternoon tea is an honored ritual and cricket is a national passion. In fact, many of the world's top cricketers hail from Barbados.

Located on Barbados' Gold Coast, Cobblers Cove is a particularly intimate resort. Reflecting the island's heritage, the original steel in the buildings came from the old island railway and the coral rock used to build the stone walls was cut on the island. Like the island itself, Cobblers Cove harmoniously blends the best

English country house and Caribbean cultures and styles together.

Pink and white cottages comprise this all-suite resort that rests within flourishing tropical gardens and overlooks a crescent shaped fine sand beach. Ten two story cottages house four suites each, and the Great House features the Camelot and Colleton suites, two very special accommodations. Vibrant cottons and rattan furnishings of the Caribbean are at home with English patterns in the 38 standard suites. The Camelot Suite is darling, with blue and white fabrics, canopied bed, marble

floor and hand-painted furnishings. The Colleton Suite is romantic with an airy white and red theme featuring botanical prints and his and hers showers. Both suites feature spiral staircases that lead to rooftop terraces with private plunge pools and fabulous sea views.

Located at the beach's edge, the Terrace Restaurant serves you in the finest style. The delicious cuisine of the French-trained chefs will inspire you to dress for dinner.

Offering a quaint slice of life, Cobblers Cove is a perennial favorite.

**COBBLERS COVE**
St. Peter, Barbados
West Indies

# Sandy Lane

Barbados has a warm, friendly spirit blended with the traditions of Britain. In fact, polo is regularly played here. The glittering turquoise Caribbean Sea, gentle hills and perfect beaches make for a glorious tropical setting.

The west coast of Barbados has earned the sobriquet as the "platinum coast" because of its stunning setting and posh resorts, though it is Sandy Lane that stands out as one of the world's most revered resorts. Committed to providing the highest levels of service in the most luxurious setting, Sandy Lane closed its doors in 1998 for a multi-multi-million dollar total rebuild that completely redeveloped its accommodations and facilities while retaining its original

character. Reopened in March 2001, Sandy Lane is once again dressed to the nines.

The 96 rooms, 14 suites and two penthouses are a testament to understated elegance with elements of British Colonial design. The accommodations reflect the latest developments, including plasma flat-screen televisions, DVD players, advanced stereos and Internet access. All guest rooms feature large verandas with ceiling fans, extending the guest room experience while highlighting the garden or ocean views.

Tom Fazio has designed Sandy Lane's 45 holes of championship golf. Two courses

have been built into the hillside, while the other provides a tropical garden setting. Nine championship tennis courts, supervised by professionally recognized tennis management, provide guests with the best possible facilities for a rewarding match. Designed by ESPA, the spa is a true nirvana with twelve treatment rooms and a variety of sensational treatments.

Haute cuisine and refined Caribbean food are served at the two seaside restaurants, where you may dine formally or informally on the terrace or at beach level.

Renew the legend at the alluring Sandy Lane.

SANDY LANE
St. James, Barbados

# Cambridge Beaches

Bermuda is an enchanted island with pastel houses, manicured lawns and pink beaches. One of the wealthiest countries in the world, Bermuda enjoys British traditions while retaining its individuality.

Cambridge Beaches is Bermuda's best resort. Situated on a 25 acre private peninsula on the western tip of the island in Somerset, it is nearly surrounded by ocean and bay waters. Opened in 1928, Cambridge Beaches is a distinguished pink cottage colony with five private beaches and numerous coves. Impeccable service and a spectacular setting make a holiday at Cambridge Beaches unforgettable.

Evoking Bermuda's seagoing heritage, several of the resort's cottages date back over 200 years, such as Windswept and Pegem. Multi-million dollar renovations and new facilities have elevated Cambridge Beaches to one of the world's premier resorts. All 66 rooms and 25 suites have private terraces, exquisite antiques, cheerful, flowered fabrics and a charming décor.

The world-class Aquarian Baths & Ocean Spa is spectacular, providing the ultimate in relaxation, rejuvenation and fitness. Enjoy the European-influenced massage and beauty treatments, or relax in the indoor Aquarian Baths overlooking the Atlantic Ocean. Three tennis courts, natural ocean pool and a full-service marina with a variety of water sports keep active-minded guests content.

The Tamarisk Room wins top marks from guests for its haute cuisine served in a formal setting indoors or on the elegant Mangrove Bay Terrace, where Somerset Maugham and James Thurber once sipped rum punches. Enjoy lunch casually poolside or at the beach. Traditional afternoon tea, with freshly baked scones and finger sandwiches, is a time-honored tradition here.

Live graciously at Cambridge Beaches.

**CAMBRIDGE BEACHES**
30 Kings Point
Somerset MA 02, Bermuda

# Half Moon Golf, Tennis & Beach Club

The spirited island of Jamaica, the third largest in the Caribbean, is a wondrous place of jungle mountain tops, waterfalls and sandy beaches.

Overlooking a crescent-shaped portion of Montego Bay, Half Moon Golf, Tennis & Beach Club is one of the island's most deluxe resorts. Occupying 400 acres of lush property, the resort encompasses 253 accommodations, including a shopping village and a conference center. Half Moon is renowned for its dedication to the environment, and a 26 acre natural preserve harvests fruit, vegetables and herbs for the resort's restaurants.

Half Moon's 32 villas, 47 rooms and 174 suites are located within white plantation-style buildings. All accommodations feature traditional Queen Anne and Chippendale-style furnishings with Jamaican paintings and vibrant carpets. The villas have five, six or seven bedrooms and are located along Sunrise Beach. Well-staffed, the villas have private housekeepers, butlers and chefs.

Half Moon's 18 hole Robert Trent Jones golf course, sculpted from the western Jamaican foothills, is consistently ranked among the best courses in the world. The David Leadbetter Golf Academy provides excellent instruction for players of all levels. Half Moon has over 52 swimming pools located on the property, including an Olympic-size pool. Tennis and squash facilities, water sports and an equestrian center provide additional opportunities. Hydro therapy, reflexology and massages are offered at the spa.

Several restaurants feature delicious, local Caribbean cuisine. In addition, fashionable boutiques and gift shops will certainly catch your eye.

Half Moon Golf, Tennis & Beach Club is a world of its own on Jamaica.

**HALF MOON GOLF, TENNIS & BEACH CLUB**
Rose Hall
St. James, Jamaica

# Jamaica Inn

Just outside of Ocho Rios, Jamaica Inn is a genteel hideaway steeped in tradition, yet bearing a young spirit.

Winston Churchill stayed at Jamaica Inn for the light, declaring it was the best for his watercolors, and Noel Coward, Errol Flynn and Ian Fleming were also regular guests. With its lovely stretch of private beach, charming accommodations and timeless elegance, it is certainly no wonder!

The 42 rooms, 3 suites and 1 cottage are decorated with period pieces and Jamaican antiques. All rooms enjoy terrific views of the sea, gardens or mountains from their spacious balconies. Private beachfront verandas create an old-world feel.

Grand traditions are revived at Jamaica Inn. Waiters dressed in refined red jackets serve tropical drinks on silver trays to parched sunbathers, while guests dress up in the evenings to enjoy Caribbean-influenced European cuisine. Elegant without ever being stuffy, Jamaica Inn makes guests feel as if they are at home. Indeed, this is one of the many reasons the resort attracts a loyal clientele that visits annually.

Though water sports are available, and golf or tennis is nearby, the favorite pastime here is relaxation. The thatched umbrellas that dot the pristine beach are perfect for reading a book, enjoying the view or even taking a leisurely nap.

Civilized and aristocratic, Jamaica Inn is a gem in the Caribbean.

JAMAICA INN
Ocho Rios, Jamaica

293

# The Ritz-Carlton Rose Hall, Jamaica

The Ritz-Carlton Rose Hall, Jamaica's newest resort, is also one of the island's most luxurious.

The Ritz-Carlton Rose Hall, Jamaica is nestled on 25 acres fronting the Caribbean Sea and framed by the mountains of Montego Bay in the distance. Lush and tropical, the Ritz-Carlton also enjoys a historic location near the Rose Hall plantation, a National Trust Commission monument.

The Ritz-Carlton resembles a grand plantation house, best expressed by its elegant British Colonial décor. Arched doorways and beautiful staircases add a romantic touch, while vibrant color schemes remind you of the resort's tropical location. Floral prints, rattan furniture and Jamaican artwork define the 377 guest rooms and 51 suites. All rooms have private, covered balconies overlooking the golf course, grounds and countryside or the pristine beach.

Carved from 4,000 acres of foothills and countryside, the White Witch golf course is a sheer delight where 16 of the 18 holes face the Caribbean. Spa aficionados will be thrilled with the Ritz-Carlton's spa. The full-service spa borrows from the tropical flair of the Caribbean for many of its treatments, including inventive favorites like hibiscus facials and herbal tea and grasses body wraps.

The casual poolside restaurant, Mango's, brings a delicious selection of American, Continental and Caribbean cuisines, while Horizon's keeps your toes tapping with its nightly entertainment and your palate happy with its creative Asian and Jamaican dishes. Exclusive to the Ritz-Carlton Rose Hall, the West Indian "Bush" tea is not to be missed.

The Ritz-Carlton Rose Hall, Jamaica will cast a spell on you.

**THE RITZ-CARLTON ROSE HALL, JAMAICA**
One Ritz-Carlton Drive,
Rose Hall
Montego Bay, Jamaica

# Round Hill Hotel & Villas

A former pineapple plantation, Round Hill Hotel & Villas has epitomized chic since opening as a hotel in 1952.

John Pringle, a successful Jamaican businessman, envisioned Round Hill as a vacation destination for the international elite. He developed a hotel and divided the former plantation into 29 lots. Prominent Americans and Europeans soon built cottages on these lots, and Round Hill's reputation as one of the world's most exclusive resorts was sealed.

Today's visitors to Round Hill may reside in one of the 39 oceanfront rooms

owners, all reflect the relaxed elegance of Round Hill. Most have private swimming pools and all are staffed with a private housekeeper who prepares you a delicious breakfast daily.

Three settings for the main dining room include the seaside terrace, upper terrace or Georgian room. The cuisine uses fresh, local ingredients to enhance its Jamaican and international specialties.

Whether you are playing a set of tennis, reclining on the beach or wandering through the gardens, you will feel the magic of Round Hill Hotel & Villas.

in the Pineapple House or in one of the 27 private villas. The cathedral ceilings and louvered windows of the rooms are reminiscent of grand plantation manors. Rich woods are complemented by splashes of color in the various prints. The fabrics are influenced by designer Ralph Lauren, owner of one of Round Hill's private villas.

The 27 villas offer a very private way to experience Round Hill. While they are individually decorated by the

ROUND HILL HOTEL & VILLAS
Montego Bay, Jamaica

# The Tryall Club

The Tryall Club presents a well-rounded experience for relaxed or active-minded travelers.

The Tryall Club is nestled on 2,200 acres of rolling hills and manicured gardens on Jamaica's pristine northern coast. First developed as a coastal fort by the English against French and Spanish invaders, this beautiful site was also home to an important 18th century sugar plantation. The resort's water is still supplied by an ancient aqueduct that runs for two miles throughout the property.

This exclusive Caribbean destination is comprised of 69 privately owned villas. Thirteen of the villas are adjacent to the Great House, the heart of the resort where the restaurant, dining terrace, bar and shops are located. The Great House villas feature one or two bedrooms and are staffed with housekeepers.

The other 56 villas, located throughout the property, bear the distinctive style and tasteful designs of their private owners. Some villas evoke old-world charm, others reflect British Colonial influences, while several are Caribbean casual. The villas range in size from one to six bedrooms, and all are fully staffed with chefs, housekeepers and butlers. Most have private swimming pools to add to the luxurious lifestyle.

Jamaica is one of the Caribbean's top destinations for activities and The Tryall Club is no exception. It is a paradise for sports enthusiasts with an 18 hole PGA championship golf course and extensive tennis facilities, as well as horseback riding, sailing and deep sea fishing for blue and silver marlin. The children's program is filled with fun and educational activities, from dancing to reggae to learning to tie dye. The powdery, white sand of the beach and the shimmering swimming pool also beckon.

Join the club at The Tryall Club.

**THE TRYALL CLUB**
Montego Bay, Jamaica

# Four Seasons Resort Nevis

Nevis, in the West Indies archipelago of the Leeward Islands, enjoys a rich history. This verdant island of fertile volcanic soil was the birthplace of Alexander Hamilton and was once a playground for wealthy sugar cane plantation owners. Today, the island enjoys little development and with no traffic lights, it retains its quaint charm.

The luxurious Four Seasons Resort is the only full-service property on the island. Located on a four mile stretch of beautiful beach, the resort blends with its tropical setting. Twelve two-story gingerbread trimmed cottages house 181 rooms and 15 suites. All rooms are enhanced with Anglo-Indian mahogany furniture and combine the elegance of a bygone era with the convenience of the 21st century. All accommodations feature terraces or screened verandas and enjoy views of the beach or golf course. The Great House is the resort's heart, with dining and relaxation outlets, and interiors reminiscent of a West Indies plantation house.

The glorious Pinney's Beach is served up Four Seasons style with a Beach Concierge. The concierge pampers lounging guests with reading materials, music selections, books on tape and a selection of sunblocks. Those who want to keep sand out of their toes will be delighted with the two spectacular infinity swimming pools.

Activities offered at the Four Seasons are boundless. Ten tennis courts, health club and an amazing array of water sports are offered, along with a sensational 18 hole golf course that meanders up the hills toward Mt. Nevis and down to the beach. Exclusive to the resort, golfers will be thrilled with its challenge. After a busy day, three restaurants will satisfy your hunger with their appetizing selections.

Only the Four Seasons Resort Nevis shares the Caribbean like this.

**FOUR SEASONS RESORT NEVIS**
Pinney's Beach
Charlestown, Nevis, West Indies

# Peter Island Resort

Peter Island is the fifth-largest island in the more than 50 islands, cays and exposed reefs that comprise the British Virgin Islands. With five beaches and more than twenty secluded coves, Peter Island is a paradise of untouched beauty blessed with just one fetching resort.

Peter Island Resort is decidedly Caribbean in its flavors, style and spirit. Guests are treated like family by a staff of dedicated, friendly professionals with ebullient spirits. Privacy is ensured at Peter Island Resort, as there are only 32 rooms, 20 suites and 2 villas. There is never

more than one guest per ten acres.

At Peter Island, the question is never whether you will visit the beach; rather which one! Perhaps White Bay's Beach, where the fish will eat out of your hands, strikes your fancy or maybe you would prefer the honeymoon beach, with just two lounge chairs under one thatched hut. The crashing waves of Big Reef Bay are perfect for romantic walks, and Deadman's Bay is the largest beach with calm, protected waters and towering palm trees.

Little Deadman's Beach is a smaller extension and ideal for snorkeling.

All accommodations are distinctly Caribbean in their design and use of color. Mahogany chaises and Caribbean wicker dressers complete the island décor.

The cerulean waters of Sir Francis Drake Channel make a beautiful backdrop for Tradewinds Restaurant. Diners enjoy Caribbean-infused flavors while listening to lively calypso or reggae music. Other dining options include the beach bar and grill and the lounge.

Let the gentle trade winds and sunny spirit of Peter Island Resort wash over you.

**PETER ISLAND RESORT**
Road Town, Tortola, BVI

# The Ritz-Carlton, San Juan Hotel, Spa & Casino

Puerto Rico is a dynamic tropical destination with beautiful beaches, turquoise water and a lively spirit.

The Ritz-Carlton, in the exclusive area of Isla Verde, brings the best of Puerto Rico together in one spectacular beachfront setting. Minutes from the attractions of Old San Juan, The Ritz-Carlton has many attractions of it own, including Puerto Rico's largest casino.

The 403 rooms and 11 suites are decorated with a Caribbean and Hispanic influence. Rattan furniture, vibrant colors and contemporary artwork by Puerto Rican

and fitness facilities. The passion fruit massages and rainforest facials at the innovative spa are a sybaritic and delightful choice.

The Ritz-Carlton is children-friendly and provides fabulous activities with its Ritz Kids program. Cooking classes, arts and crafts and water sports are just some of the opportunities. The spa even has a program that introduces children to "My First" manicures and pedicures.

Experience exciting Puerto Rico at its best at The Ritz-Carlton, San Juan Hotel, Spa & Casino.

artists complete the look.

The resort offers several dining options, including the Caribbean Grill, with local specialties and The Vineyard, with California and Mediterranean cuisine in a setting reminiscent of a Napa Valley winery. Casual fare and sushi are also available at the resort.

The sparkling blue swimming pool and pristine beach are all most people would want, but other recreational options exist, including tennis

THE RITZ-CARLTON, SAN JUAN HOTEL, SPA & CASINO
6961 Avenue of the Governors
Isla Verde, Puerto Rico 00979

# Eden Rock

Though just over eight square miles, Saint-Barthélemy, affectionately known as St. Barts, packs a stylish punch. This chic island is an alluring combination of stunning Caribbean landscape with French savoir-faire. Resembling the French Riviera, St. Barts has it own character.

Eden Rock, St. Barts' first hotel, was established in the 1950's by adventurer and famous aviator Remy De Haenen. Originally a private residence, Eden Rock enjoys a unique and favorable setting

carved out of a rocky promontory in Baie de Saint-Jean. Surrounded by delicately soft beaches and the turquoise waters of the bay, Eden Rock is a spectacular hideaway. Its stylish setting and incredible privacy made it a favorite of Robert Mitchum and Greta Garbo.

Eden Rock's fourteen accommodations at the water's edge comprise 8 suites, 2 deluxe rooms, 2 beach cottages and 2 cabins. The interiors are breezy and romantic, with rich wood and hand carved canopy beds swathed in mosquito netting. Original oil paintings and French provincial antiques from the owner's private

collection add sophistication.

St. Barts is known for its splendid cuisine and the four restaurants at Eden Rock are no exception. Next to the pool and right on the beach, Michael's Restaurant has something for everyone with its delicious menu, while The Rock Restaurant delights gourmands with its French cuisine. Two bars provide fun settings for all-day relaxation and fun.

Eden Rock lives up to its reputation as a true hideaway.

EDEN ROCK
Baie de Saint-Jean
97133 Saint-Barthélemy, FWI

# Guanahani

Guanahani has its own personality and brand of style.

All of the 44 rooms and 31 suites are housed in brightly painted cottages nestled among the fragrant bougainvillea, hibiscus and coconut groves. Ranging in vivid colors from yellow and purple to indigo and bright green, the cottages have a distinctive West Indian flavor with a dash of colonial charm. Each cottage has an individualized and vibrant personality. The accommodations have an eclectic décor, while rare woods and cotton fabrics remind you that you are in the luscious Caribbean. The suites, all with private terraces and gardens, are located on a bluff overlooking the beach

Guanahani's location at the end of Grand Cul de Sac Bay means that two gorgeous beaches are at your disposal during your visit. One beach faces the reef protected bay, while the other is located on the ocean side of Marigot Bay. Whether you fancy the waves or prefer a gentle swim, you will be pleased. Two fresh water swimming pools provide a scenic spot for a meal or a lazy afternoon.

Two restaurants live up to the island's culinary reputation. A tropical refreshing breakfast buffet at the Indigo Restaurant is a terrific way to begin your day. The grilled lobsters and refreshing salads at lunch are fresh and delicious. Dinner is served at Bartolomeo, which fuses Creole and French cuisine in a tropical garden setting.

Water sports, excursions and a Clarins spa will keep you both active and relaxed during your visit.

Let the spirit of the islands wash over you at Guanahani.

**GUANAHANI**
Anse de Grand Cul de Sac
97098 Saint-Barthélemy, FWI

# Le Toiny

One of St. Barts' best-kept secrets is Le Toiny. Tucked into the hills above Anse de Toiny on the southeastern coast of the island, Le Toiny is a charming cottage enclave. Its exclusivity stems from its size; only 13 villas comprise this seductive hideaway. The cottages resemble old West Indian plantation homes and are painted in pale lavender, peach and mint green. The interiors are luscious. French toile de jouy fabrics enhance the teak and mahogany furnishings, and four-poster beds set a romantic tone. Each villa has a private swimming pool and terrace with chaises that beg you to remain idle. With views of the lagoon framed by coconut palms, who would ever want to leave?

Le Toiny's Le Gaiac Restaurant is named for the rare gaiac tree that grows on the property. Located next to the main pool with terrific views of the sea, Le Gaiac has a wonderful French menu infused with Creole and Provencal flavors. The chef, Maxime Deschamps, was recently honored with the Gault-Millault award for his great culinary talents.

While most guests come to Le Toiny to seek refuge from the hustle and bustle, an array of activities can be arranged to fill your days. The island's capital, Gustavia, is a scenic harbor town with boutiques, duty-free shops and art galleries. Deep-sea fishing, snorkeling, scuba diving and sunfish rentals can be arranged through the hotel. Due to its location between Antigua and Virgin Gorda, both major sailing centers, yachting is popular on St. Barts. Excursions and full-day sails will give you a new perspective on the island.

Le Toiny is a French-Caribbean dream.

LE TOINY
Anse de Toiny
97133 Saint-Barthélemy, FWI

# Caneel Bay

Caneel Bay is a lush paradise on the island of St. John in the U.S. Virgin Islands.

First developed by Laurance Rockefeller in the 1950's, Caneel Bay lives in harmony with its natural setting and seven pristine beaches. Rockefeller's dedication to environmental conservation lives on today at Caneel Bay, where great care is taken to preserve natural habitats for plants and wildlife. This 171 acre resort is located within the Virgin Islands National Park.

The 166 guest rooms and cottages perfectly blend modern-day luxuries with the landscape of St. John. Natural woods and native stones have been used in the resort's

interiors, and all rooms feature expansive views of the island's hillsides, Caneel Bay's fragrant gardens or the sapphire sea. Pastel colors and handcrafted furniture complete the Caribbean décor. Once the Rockefeller family's home, Cottage 7 is one of the most requested accommodations at Caneel Bay. Five rooms feature individualized decoration, and many include Dutch four-poster beds.

Whether you are looking for a romantic retreat or seeking a spot where your family can unwind together, Caneel Bay is perfect for everyone. The Caneel Kids program offers special activities for children of all ages. Adults may set sail for a neighboring island, take a garden tour with the resident botanist or enjoy an underwater adventure. Caneel Bay's Self Centre focuses on personal well being with courses in meditation, yoga and breathing techniques. Three restaurants in a variety of settings ensure lively or romantic evenings.

Come back to nature at Caneel Bay.

CANEEL BAY
Cruz Bay
St. John, USVI 00831

303

# La Samanna

Divided between the French and the Dutch, St. Martin is a tropical paradise with a European flavor and sophistication. Its lush foliage, turquoise waters and pristine beaches attract savvy travelers from all over the world. Born out of an idea for a couple's private romantic retreat, La Samanna is the most elegant and luxurious destination on St. Martin.

Located on the French side of the island, La Samanna is on one end of Baie Longue, the largest and most beautiful beach on St. Martin. With its crescent shape and deep blue waters, it is considered one of the finest and most secluded beaches in the world.

Part of La Samanna's appeal is that it offers all of the amenities of a luxury beachfront resort while maintaining the privacy and personalization of a private villa.

The informal elegance is complemented by the variety of activities offered; wind-surfing, water-skiing, sailing, snorkeling, tennis, chartered cruises for sightseeing, diving and deep-sea fishing, along with the fitness center and new spa, are some of the options. La Samanna's 81 rooms, suites and villas are tastefully decorated with indigenous prints, Mexican tile, tropical colors and terra cotta. Caribbean wicker, bamboo and hardwood furniture set a casual tone.

The reception, lobby and dining areas, perched above the sea, have spectacular views and are bathed in sunlight and fresh sea air. The individual villas are scattered along the powdery beach. Palm trees and fragrant foliage abound at La Samanna.

French and Caribbean cuisines are the specialty at La Samanna. A main dining room and poolside grill keep you satiated, and private dining on your terrace is always a wonderful treat.

La Samanna will fulfill all of your tropical dreams.

**LA SAMANNA**
Baie Longue
97064 St. Martin, FWI

# The Ritz-Carlton, St. Thomas

The Ritz-Carlton graciously resides on the eastern tip of St. Thomas, in the U.S. Virgin Islands. Its combination of European sophistication and warm island spirit make it the island's best resort.

The resort is located on a private 15 acre waterfront estate where color just seems to explode. The magenta of the bougainvillea seems brighter, and the sapphire sea seems richer here. The Ritz-Carlton, St. Thomas is reminiscent of a Mediterranean villa with its peach stucco walls and coppertine roofs surrounded by trickling fountains and lush landscaping. The property exudes elegance, from its manicured grounds to its 148 rooms and 4 suites. All rooms open out to the sea and have a distinctly Caribbean atmosphere with rattan furnishings and rich colors.

Relax with a blended tropical drink by the free-form freshwater swimming pool, or enjoy a sail on the Lady Lynsey, the 53-foot luxury catamaran. Other recreational opportunities include tennis, fitness facilities and an aquatic center.

The Ritz-Carlton provides its guests with fine dining options. The lively café serves breakfast and dinner in an open-air setting, and local artists entertain diners on weekends. Iguana's is a full service restaurant with casual beach-front dining. The Dining Room is a wonderful venue with American and European specialties.

The Ritz-Carlton presents you with the very best of St. Thomas.

**THE RITZ-CARLTON, ST. THOMAS**
6900 Great Bay
St. Thomas, USVI 00802

305

# Grace Bay Club

Leave the world behind at Grace Bay Club in the Turks & Caicos Islands.

Halfway between Florida and Puerto Rico, the Turks & Caicos remain relatively undiscovered despite their turquoise water and white sand beaches. Comprised of more than 40 different islands and cays and ringed by a barrier reef, the Turks & Caicos is an underwater paradise, with pristine waters teeming with marine life.

Located on the peaceful island of Providenciales, Grace Bay Club is an intimate hideaway. Nestled above a twelve-mile stretch of powdery beach, Grace Bay Club shares just 21 suites with a lucky few. Secluded and luxurious, the resort resembles a Spanish hacienda with its red-tiled roofs and trickling fountains. Rattan and

wicker furniture, Colombian pottery and Haitian artwork set an informal elegance throughout. No two suites are alike, and the one and two bedroom suites are a celebration of international cultures, from the Guatemalan armoires to the Turkish rugs that cover the floors. Of course, the pièce de résistance of all suites is the magnificent terrace framing unforgettable views of the crystal clear water.

Rather than bombard guests with a menu of activities, Grace Bay encourages you to do as you please, whether you opt for snorkeling or scuba diving, partake in treatments at the spa or simply relax poolside. The island's 18 hole golf course is also minutes away. Ultimately, it is the blissful

quietude of Grace Bay Club that attracts its sophisticated clientele; children under 12 are not permitted.

The restaurant offers a special dining experience with its light and healthy Euro-Caribbean menu, clear views of the bay and romantic seating under thatched-roof palapas lit by flickering tiki torches.

Let the gentle trade winds of Grace Bay Club cosset you.

GRACE BAY CLUB
Providenciales
Turks & Caicos Islands

# Parrot Cay

Situated on an otherwise uninhabited island in the Turks & Caicos, Parrot Cay introduces you to a world of serenity.

Opened in early 1999, Parrot Cay is a stylish Caribbean hideaway with more than three miles of powdery, white sand beaches and crystal clear water. The 58 room resort reflects a modern colonial sensibility. Parrot Cay's main buildings and beachfront villas were designed to blend with the natural environment and landscape, while avoiding disruption of the island's skyline.

Parrot Cay is comprised of 42 guest rooms, 4 suites and 12 beachfront villas. The villas feature private plunge or

swimming pools. The resort's serene décor is a study in minimalist luxury. Soft, polished woods complement romantic four-poster beds swathed in white muslin. Many rooms showcase inspiring ocean views.

This enlightened resort is dedicated to relaxation and personal well-being, whether you are taking a swim, practicing yoga or sipping a fresh juice from the juice bar. The Shambhala Spa, the centerpiece of the resort, is housed in three beachfront

pavilions. This Eastern inspired, holistic spa's mind and body treatments include meditation and contemplation, Chi balancing, Thai/Chinese massage and yoga.

In keeping with its principle of promoting healthy lifestyles, the cuisine at Parrot Cay is nutritious and delicious. The Spa features a juice and salad bar, while the poolside restaurant will also serve guests who want to dine alfresco on the beach. Special menus are designed for guests seeking to lose weight or adopt healthier eating habits. Blending spices, Asian and Caribbean cooking styles combine to create tantalizing selections at this gourmet restaurant.

Parrot Cay offers peaceful seclusion in the Turks & Caicos.

**PARROT CAY**
Providenciales, Turks & Caicos

# Little Dix Bay

Named by Christopher Columbus on his second world voyage, Virgin Gorda is a ruggedly beautiful island in the British Virgin Island chain.

Little Dix Bay, on the island's northwest corner, was developed by Laurance Rockefeller in the early 1960's. Little Dix was the realization of a dream for Rockefeller, who was noted for his conservation efforts and who wanted to create a resort where natural beauty and native vegetation could coexist with travelers.

Surrounded by sea grapes and bougainvillea, the 92 rooms and 4 suites are not visible from the sea. The essence of the islands is instilled in the rooms with bright, pastel colors and Pacific Rim furnishings. All rooms have balconies or terraces and enjoy splendid seascapes or garden views.

Little Dix Bay and Virgin Gorda's stunning scenery beg to be explored. For a little adventure, try seeing the island by horseback or Jeep safari. Nature hikes are a terrific way to appreciate the landscape while learning more about native plants and trees. Gorda Peak, at 1,500 feet, gives a birds-eye view of the island. Have the hotel take you and someone special by one of their Boston Whaler boats for the day to a secluded beach with a picnic lunch.

A fabulous children's program entertains young guests while their parents enjoy a little quiet time. Based on Rockefeller's founding principles, the children's program is located in a mahogany preserve and focuses on the island's natural and cultural richness. Programs highlighting Caribbean folk art, West Indian music and even shell collecting expose young minds to a fascinating ecological culture.

Little Dix Bay's three restaurants provide intimate settings and feature tastes of the Caribbean.

It may be hard to believe there is a world outside of Little Dix Bay!

LITTLE DIX BAY
Virgin Gorda, BVI

# HOTELS

**HOTEL ADLON**
Unter den Linden 77
10117 Berlin, Germany
Tel: 49 30 2261 0
Fax: 49 30 2261 2222
www.kempinski-hotels.com

**ALVEAR PALACE HOTEL**
Avenida Alvear 1891
1129 Buenos Aires, Argentina
Tel: 54 11 4808 2100
Fax: 54 11 4804 0034
www.alvearpalace.com

**AMARVILÄS**
Taj East Gate Road
Agra 282001, India
Tel: 91 562 231515
Fax: 91 562 231516
www.oberoihotels.com

**ANASSA**
P.O. Box 66006 at Latchi
8830 Polis, Cyprus
Tel: 357 6 888000
Fax: 357 6 322900
www.thanoshotels.com

**ARIZONA BILTMORE RESORT & SPA**
24th Street & Missouri
Phoenix, AZ 85016 USA
Tel: 602 955-6600
Fax: 602 381-7600
www.arizonabiltmore.com

**HOTEL ARTS BARCELONA**
Carrer de la Marina, 19-21
08005 Barcelona, Spain
Tel: 34 93 221 1000
Fax: 34 93 221 1070
www.ritzcarlton.com

**ASHFORD CASTLE**
Cong
County Mayo, Ireland
Tel: 353 92 46003
Fax: 353 92 46260
www.ashford.ie

**HOTEL ASTORIA**
39 Bolshaya Morskaya
190000 St. Petersburg, Russia
Tel: 7 812 313 5757
Fax: 7 812 313 5059
www.rfhotels.com

**ATHENAEUM HOTEL & APARTMENTS**
116 Piccadilly
London W1V OBJ, England
Tel: 44 207 499 3464
Fax: 44 207 493 1860
www.athenaeumhotel.com

**BADRUTT'S PALACE**
Via Serlas 27
7500 St. Moritz, Switzerland
Tel: 41 81 837-1000
Fax: 41 81 837 2999
www.rosewoodhotels.com

**THE BALMORAL**
1 Princes Street
Edinburgh EH2 2EQ, Scotland
Tel: 44 131 556 2414
Fax: 44 131 557 3747
www.rfhotels.com

**HOTEL BALTSCHUG KEMPINSKI MOSCOW**
Ulitsa Balchug, 1
113035 Moscow, Russia
Tel: 7 501 230 6500
Fax: 7 501 230 6502
www.kempinski-hotels.com

**HOTEL BAUR AU LAC**
Talstrasse 1
8022 Zurich, Switzerland
Tel: 41 1 220 5020
Fax: 41 1 220 5044
www.bauraulac.ch

**HOTEL BAYERISCHER HOF**
Promenadeplatz 2-6
80333 Munich, Germany
Tel: 49 89 2120 0
Fax: 49 89 2120 906
www.bayerischerhof.de

**BEAU-RIVAGE**
13 Quai du Mont-Blanc
1201 Geneva, Switzerland
Tel: 41 22 716 6666
Fax: 41 22 716 6060
www.beau-rivage.ch

**BEAU-RIVAGE PALACE**
Ch. du Beau-Rivage
1006 Lausanne, Switzerland
Tel: 41 21 613 3333
Fax: 41 21 613 3334
www.brp.ch

**HOTEL BEL-AIR**
701 Stone Canyon Road
Los Angeles, CA 90077 USA
Tel: 310 472 1211
Fax: 310 476 5890
www.hotelbelair.com

**THE BERKELEY**
Wilton Place, Knightsbridge
London SW1X 7RL, England
Tel: 44 20 7235 6000
Fax: 44 20 7235 4330
www.savoy-group.co.uk

**THE BEVERLY HILLS HOTEL & BUNGALOWS**
9641 Sunset Boulevard
Beverly Hills, CA 90210 USA
Tel: 310 276 2251
Fax: 310 281-2905
www.thebeverlyhillshotel.com

**BLANTYRE**
16 Blantyre Road
Lenox, MA 01240 USA
Tel: 413 637 3556
Fax: 413 637-4282
www.blantyre.com

**BOCA RATON RESORT & CLUB**
501 E. Camino Real
Boca Raton, FL 33432 USA
Tel: 561 447-3000
Fax: 561 447-3183
www.bocaresort.com

# HOTELS

**IL BORRO**
Loc. Borro, 1/A
52020 San Giustino
Valdarno, Italy
Tel: 39 055 977053
Fax: 39 055 977055
www.ilborro.it

**THE BREAKERS**
One South County Road
Palm Beach, FL 33480 USA
Tel: 561 655 6611
Fax: 561 659 8403
www.thebreakers.com

**BRENNER'S PARK-HOTEL & SPA**
Schillerstrasse 4-6
76530 Baden-Baden, Germany
Tel: 49 7221 9000
Fax: 49 7221 38772
www.brenners.com

**HOTEL LE BRISTOL**
112 rue du Faubourg St. Honoré
75008 Paris, France
Tel: 33 1 53 43 43 00
Fax: 33 1 53 43 43 01
www.hotel-bristol.com

**HOTEL BYBLOS**
Avenue Paul Signac
83990 Saint-Tropez, France
Tel: 33 4 94 56 68 00
Fax: 33 4 94 56 68 01
www.byblos.com

**CALA DI VOLPE**
Costa Smeralda
07020 Porto Cervo, Sardinia, Italy
Tel: 39 0789 976 111
Fax: 39 0789 976617
www.luxurycollection.com

**CAMBRIDGE BEACHES**
30 Kings Point
Somerset MA 02 Bermuda
Tel: 441 234-0331
Fax: 441 234-3352
www.cambridgebeaches.com

**CAMPTON PLACE HOTEL**
340 Stockton Street
San Francisco, CA 94108 USA
Tel: 415 781 5555
Fax: 415 955 5536
www.camptonplace.com

**CANEEL BAY**
P.O. Box 720 Cruz Bay
St. John, U.S.V.I. 00831
Tel: 340 776 6111
Fax: 340 693 8280
www.rosewoodhotels.com

**CAP JULUCA**
P.O. Box 240
Maunday's Bay, Anguilla
Tel: 264 497 6666
Fax: 264 497 6617
www.capjuluca.com

**THE CARLYLE**
35 East 76th Street
New York, NY 10021 USA
Tel: 212 744 1600
Fax: 212 717 4682
www.rosewoodhotels.com

**THE CASTLE AT TARRYTOWN**
400 Benedict Avenue
Tarrytown, NY 10591 USA
Tel: 914 631 1980
Fax: 914 631 4612
www.castleattarrytown.com

**CECIL**
Chaura Maidan
Shimla 171 001, India
Tel: 91 177 20 4848
Fax: 91 177 21 1024
www.oberoihotels.com

**CHARLESTON PLACE**
205 Meeting Street
Charleston, SC 29401 USA
Tel: 843 722 4900
Fax: 843 722 0728
www.orient-express.com

**CHÂTEAU DE LA CHÈVRE D'OR**
Rue du Barri
06360 Èze-Village, France
Tel: 33 492 10 66 66
Fax: 33 493 41 06 72
www.chevredor.com

**CHÂTEAU DU DOMAINE ST. MARTIN**
Avenue des Templiers
06140 Vence, France
Tel: 33 4 93 58 02 02
Fax: 33 4 93 24 08 91
www.chateau-st-martin.com

**CHEECA LODGE**
Mile Marker 82, U.S. Highway One
Islamorada, FL 33036 USA
Tel: 305 664 4651
Fax: 305 664 2893
www.rockresorts.com

**THE CHESTER GROSVENOR**
Eastgate
Chester CH1 1LT, England
Tel: 44 1244 324024
Fax: 44 1244 313246
www.chestergrosvenor.com.uk

**CHEWTON GLEN**
Christchurch Road
New Milton
Hampshire, BH25 6QS, England
Tel: 44 1425 275 341
Fax: 44 145 272 310
www.chewtonglen.com

**CHOBE CHILWERO CHIEF'S CAMP**
Abercrombie & Kent
1520 Kensington Road
Oak Brook, IL 60523
Tel: 800 323 7308
Fax: 630 954 3324
www.abercrombiekent.com

**HOTEL CIPRIANI & PALAZZO VENDRAMIN**
Giudecca 10
30133 Venice, Italy
Tel: 39 041 520 7744
Fax: 39 041 520 7745
www.orient-express.com

**CIRAGAN PALACE HOTEL KEMPINSKI ISTANBUL**
Ciragan Caddesi No. 84
Besiktas, 80700 Istanbul, Turkey
Tel: 90 212 258 3377
Fax: 90 212 259 6687
www.kempinski-hotels.com

# HOTELS

HÔTEL DE LA CITÉ
Place de l'Église
11000 Carcassonne, France
Tel: 33 468 71 98 71
Fax: 33 468 71 50 15
www.orient-express.com

CLARIDGE'S
Brook Street
London W1A 2JQ, England
Tel: 44 207 629 8860
Fax: 44 207 499 2210
www.savoy-group.co.uk

COBBLERS COVE
St. Peter, Barbados, West Indies
Tel: 246 422 2291
Fax: 246 422 1460
www.cobblerscove.com

THE CONNAUGHT
Carlos Place, Mayfair
London WIY 6AL, England
Tel: 44 207 499 7070
Fax: 44 207 495 3262
www.savoy-group.co.uk

COPACABANA PALACE
Avenida Atlântica, 1702
Rio de Janeiro, 22021-001 Brazil
Tel: 55 21 548 7070
Fax: 55 21 235 7330
www.orient-express.com

HOTEL CRESCENT COURT
400 Crescent Court
Dallas, TX 75201 USA
Tel: 214 871 3200
Fax: 214 871 3272
www.rosewoodhotels.com

HÔTEL DE CRILLON
10, Place de la Concorde
75008 Paris, France
Tel: 33 1 44 71 15 00
Fax: 33 1 44 71 15 02
www.crillon.com

CUISINART RESORT & SPA
Rendezvous Bay
Anguilla, British West Indies
Tel: 264 498 2000
Fax: 264 498 2010
www.cuisinartresort.com

HOTEL DANIELI
Riva degli Schiavoni 4196
30122 Venice, Italy
Tel: 39 041 522 6480
Fax: 39 041 520 0208
www.luxurycollection.com

DOLDER GRAND HOTEL
Kurhausstrasse 65
8032 Zurich, Switzerland
Tel: 41 1 269 3000
Fax: 41 1 269 3001
www.doldergrand.com

THE DORCHESTER
Park Lane
London W1A 2HJ, England
Tel: 44 20 7629 8888
Fax: 44 20 7317 6309
www.dorchesterhotel.com

HOTEL EDEN
Via Ludovisi 49
00187 Rome, Italy
Tel: 39 06 478 121
Fax: 39 06 482 1584
www.hotel-eden.it

EDEN ROCK
Baie de Saint-Jean
97133 Saint-Barthélemy
Tel: 011 590 29 79 99
Fax: 011 590 27 88 37
www.edenrockhotel.com

ELOUNDA BEACH HOTEL
& VILLAS
720 53 Elounda, Crete, Greece
Tel: 30 841 41412
Fax: 30 841 41373
www.eloundabeach.gr

THE EMERSON INN & SPA
146 Mount Pleasant Road
Mt. Tremper, NY 12457 USA
Tel: 845 688 7900
Fax: 845 688 2789
www.the-emerson.com

THE EQUINOX
Route 7A
Manchester Village, VT 05254 USA
Tel: 800 362 4700
Fax: 802 362 4861
www.equinoxresort.com

EUROPA & REGINA
A WESTIN HOTEL
San Marco 2159
30124 Venice, Italy
Tel: 39 041 240 0001
Fax: 39 041 52 33043
www.westin.com

HOTEL EXCELSIOR
A WESTIN HOTEL
Piazza Ognissanti, 3
50123 Florence, Italy
Tel: 39 055 264201
Fax: 39 055 210278
www.westin.com

HOTEL EXCELSIOR
A WESTIN HOTEL
Via Veneto, 125
00187 Rome, Italy
Tel: 39 064 7081
Fax: 39 0648 26205
www.westin.com

FIFTEEN BEACON
15 Beacon Street
Boston, MA 02108 USA
Tel: 617 670 1500
Fax: 617 670 2525
www.xvbeacon.com

47 PARK STREET
47 Park Street, Mayfair
London W1K 4EB, England
Tel: 44 207 491 7282
Fax: 44 207 491 7281
www.47parkstreet.com

FOUR SEASONS HOTEL
ATLANTA
75 Fourteenth Street
Atlanta, GA 30309 USA
Tel: 404 881 9898
Fax: 404 888 8610
www.fourseasons.com

# HOTELS

**FOUR SEASONS HOTEL AUSTIN**
98 San Jacinto Boulevard
Austin, TX 78701 USA
Tel: 512 478 4500
Fax: 512 478 3117
www.fourseasons.com

**FOUR SEASONS HOTEL BERLIN**
Charlottenstrasse 49
10117 Berlin, Germany
Tel: 49 30 20 33 8
Fax: 49 30 20 33 61 66
www.fourseasons.com

**FOUR SEASONS HOTEL BOSTON**
200 Boylston Street
Boston, MA 02116 USA
Tel: 617 338 4400
Fax: 617 423 0154
www.fourseasons.com

**FOUR SEASONS HOTEL CAIRO**
At The First Residence
35 Giza Street
Giza, Cairo, Egypt 12311
Tel: 202 573 1212
Fax: 202 568 1616
www.fourseasons.com

**FOUR SEASONS HOTEL CANARY WHARF**
46 Westferry Circus, Canary Wharf
London, E14 8RS England
Tel: 44 20 7510 1999
Fax: 44 20 7510 1998
www.fourseasons.com

**FOUR SEASONS HOTEL CARACAS**
Av. Francisco de Miranda
con Av. Luis Roche
Altamira, Caracas, Venezuela
Tel: 58 2 280 1000
Fax: 58 2 280 2000
www.fourseasons.com

**FOUR SEASONS HOTEL CHICAGO**
120 East Delaware Place
Chicago, IL 60611 USA
Tel: 312 280 8800
Fax: 312 280 1748
www.fourseasons.com

**FOUR SEASONS HOTEL DUBLIN**
Simmonscourt Road, Ballsbridge
Dublin 4, Ireland
Tel: 353 1 269 6446
Fax: 353 1 269 6453
www.fourseasons.com

**FOUR SEASONS HOTEL GEORGE V PARIS**
31, avenue George V
75008 Paris, France
Tel: 33 1 49 52 7000
Fax: 33 1 49 52 7010
www.fourseasons.com

**FOUR SEASONS HOTEL HOUSTON**
1300 Lamar Street
Houston, TX 77010 USA
Tel: 713 650 1300
Fax: 713 276 4787
www.fourseasons.com

**FOUR SEASONS HOTEL ISTANBUL**
Tevkifhane Sokak No.1
34490 Sultanahmet-Eminönü
Istanbul, Turkey
Tel: 90 212 638 82 00
Fax: 90 212 638 82 10
www.fourseasons.com

**FOUR SEASONS HOTEL LAS VEGAS**
3960 Las Vegas Boulevard South
Las Vegas, NV 89119 USA
Tel: 702 632 5000
Fax: 702 632 5195
www.fourseasons.com

**FOUR SEASONS HOTEL LONDON**
Hamilton Place, Park Lane
London W1A 1AZ, England
Tel: 44 20 7499 0888
Fax: 44 20 7493 1895
www.fourseasons.com

**FOUR SEASONS HOTEL LOS ANGELES AT BEVERLY HILLS**
300 South Doheny Drive at Burton Way
Los Angeles, CA 90048 USA
Tel: 310 273 2222
Fax: 310 859 3824
www.fourseasons.com

**FOUR SEASONS HOTEL MEXICO CITY**
06600 Paseo de la Reforma #500
Colonia Juarez, Mexico, D.F.
Tel: 52 5 230 1818
Fax: 52 5 286 5588
www.fourseasons.com

**FOUR SEASONS HOTEL MILAN**
via Gesù, 8
20121 Milan, Italy
Tel: 39 02 77088
Fax: 39 02 7708 5000
www.fourseasons.com

**FOUR SEASONS HOTEL NEWPORT BEACH**
690 Newport Center Drive
Newport Beach, CA 92660 USA
Tel: 949 759 0808
Fax: 949 720 1718
www.fourseasons.com

**FOUR SEASONS HOTEL NEW YORK**
57 East 57th Street
New York, NY 10022 USA
Tel: 212 758 5700
Fax: 212 758 5711
www.fourseasons.com

# Hotels

**FOUR SEASONS HOTEL PHILADELPHIA**
One Logan Square
Philadelphia, PA 19103 USA
Tel: 215 963 1500
Fax: 215 963 9506
www.fourseasons.com

**FOUR SEASONS HOTEL PRAGUE**
Veleslavinova 2a
110 00 Prague, Czech Republic
Tel: 420 2 2142 7000
Fax: 420 2 2142 6000
www.fourseasons.com

**FOUR SEASONS HOTEL SAN FRANCISCO**
735 Market Street
San Francisco, CA 94103 USA
Tel: 415 633 3000
Fax: 415 633 3009
www.fourseasons.com

**FOUR SEASONS HOTEL SEATTLE**
411 University Street
Seattle, WA 98101 USA
Tel: 206 621 1700
Fax: 206 623 2271
www.fourseasons.com

**FOUR SEASONS HOTEL SINGAPORE**
190 Orchard Boulevard
Singapore 248646
Tel: 65 733 8888
Fax: 65 738 9747
www.fourseasons.com

**FOUR SEASONS HOTEL THE RITZ LISBON**
Rua Rodrigo da Fonseca, 88
1099-039 Lisbon, Portugal
Tel: 351 21 383 2020
Fax: 351 21 383 1783
www.fourseasons.com

**FOUR SEASONS HOTEL TOKYO AT CHINZAN-SO**
10-8 Sekiguchi 2-Chome, Bunkyo-ku
Tokyo 112-8667, Japan
Tel: 81 3 3943 2222
Fax: 81 3 3943 0909
www.fourseasons.com

**FOUR SEASONS HOTEL TORONTO**
21 Avenue Road
Toronto, Ontario M5R 2G1, Canada
Tel: 416 964 0411
Fax: 416 964 2301
www.fourseasons.com

**FOUR SEASONS HOTEL VANCOUVER**
791 West Georgia Street
Vancouver, B.C., Canada V6C 2T4
Tel: 604 689 9333
Fax: 604 684 4555
www.fourseasons.com

**FOUR SEASONS HOTEL WASHINGTON, D.C.**
2800 Pennsylvania Avenue N.W.
Washington, DC 20007 USA
Tel: 202 342 0444
Fax: 202 944 2076
www.fourseasons.com

**FOUR SEASONS RESORT AND CLUB DALLAS AT LAS COLINAS**
4150 North MacArthur Boulevard
Irving, TX 75038 USA
Tel: 972 717 0700
Fax: 972 717 2486
www.fourseasons.com

**FOUR SEASONS RESORT AT TROON NORTH**
10600 Crescent Moon Drive
Scottsdale, AZ 85255 USA
Tel: 480 515-5700
Fax: 480 515-5599
www.fourseasons.com

**FOUR SEASONS RESORT AVIARA**
7100 Four Seasons Point
Carlsbad, CA 92009 USA
Tel: 760 603-6800
Fax: 760 603 6878
www.fourseasons.com

**FOUR SEASONS RESORT BALI AT JIMBARAN BAY**
Jimbaran, Denpasar
80361 Bali, Indonesia
Tel: 62 361 701010
Fax: 62 361 701020
www.fourseasons.com

**FOUR SEASONS RESORT BALI AT SAYAN**
Sayan, Ubud, Gianyar
80571 Bali, Indonesia
Tel: 62 361 977577
Fax: 62 361 977588
www.fourseasons.com

**FOUR SEASONS RESORT HUALALAI**
100 Ka'upulehu Drive
Ka'upulehu-Kona, HI 96740 USA
Tel: 808 325 8000
Fax: 808 325 8100
www.fourseasons.com

**FOUR SEASONS RESORT MALDIVES AT KUDA HURAA**
North Malé Atoll
Republic of the Maldives
Tel: 960 444 888
Fax: 960 441 188
www.fourseasons.com

**FOUR SEASONS RESORT MAUI AT WAILEA**
3900 Wailea Alanui
Wailea, Maui, HI 96753 USA
Tel: 808 874 8000
Fax: 808 874 2244
www.fourseasons.com

# HOTELS

**FOUR SEASONS RESORT NEVIS**
Pinney's Beach
Charlestown, Nevis, West Indies
Tel: 869 469 1111
Fax: 869 469 1040
www.fourseasons.com

**FOUR SEASONS RESORT PALM BEACH**
2800 South Ocean Boulevard
Palm Beach, FL 33480 USA
Tel: 561 582 2800
Fax: 561 547-1557
www.fourseasons.com

**FOUR SEASONS RESORT PUNTA MITA**
Bahia de Banderas
Nayarit 63734, Mexico
Tel: 52 3 291 6000
Fax: 52 3 291 6060
www.fourseasons.com

**FOUR SEASONS RESORT SANTA BARBARA**
1260 Channel Drive
Santa Barbara, CA 93108 USA
Tel: 805 969 2261
Fax: 805 565 8323
www.fourseasons.com

**FRÉGATE ISLAND PRIVATE**
Victoria Rahe
Seychelles
Tel: 49 69 83 83 76 35
Fax: 49 69 83 83 76 36
www.fregate.com

**GLENEAGLES**
Auchterarder
Perthshire PH3 INF, Scotland
Tel: 44 1764 662 231
Fax: 44 1764 662 134
www.gleneagles.com

**HOTEL GOLDENER HIRSCH**
Getreidegasse 37
5020 Salzburg, Austria
Tel: 43 662 80 84 0
Fax: 43 662 84 33 49
www.goldenerhirsch.com

**GRACE BAY CLUB**
Providenciales
Turks & Caicos, BWI
Tel: 649 946 5050
Fax: 649 946 5758
www.gracebayclub.com

**GRAND HOTEL**
Piazza Ognissanti 1
50123 Florence, Italy
Tel: 39 055 288 781
Fax: 39 055 217 400
www.luxurycollection.com

**GRAND-HOTEL DU CAP-FERRAT**
06230 Saint-Jean Cap-Ferrat, France
Tel: 33 4 9376 5050
Fax: 33 4 9376 0452
www.grand-hotel-cap-ferrat.com

**GRAND HOTEL EUROPE**
Mikhailovskaya 1/7
191011 St. Petersburg, Russia
Tel: 7 812 329 6000
Fax: 7 812 329 6001
www.kempinski-hotels.com

**GRAND HOTEL ZERMATTERHOF**
Bahnhofstrasse
3920 Zermatt, Switzerland
Tel: 41 27 966 6600
Fax: 41 27 966 6699
www.zermatt.ch/zermatterhof

**GRAND HYATT SHANGHAI**
Jin Mao Tower, 88 Century Boulevard
Pudong, Shanghai 200121
Tel: 86 21 5049 1234
Fax: 86 21 5049 1111
www.hyatt.com

**HOTEL GRITTI PALACE**
Campo Santa Maria del Giglio, 2467
30124 Venice, Italy
Tel: 39 041 794 611
Fax: 39 041 520 0942
www.luxurycollection.com

**GUANAHANI**
Grand Cul de Sac
97133 Saint-Barthélemy
Tel: 590 27 66 60
Fax: 590 27 70 70
www.leguanahani.com

**HALF MOON GOLF, TENNIS & BEACH RESORT**
Half Moon Post Office, Rose Hall
St. James, Jamaica, West Indies
Tel: 876 953 2211
Fax: 876 953 2731
www.halfmoon.com.jm

**HOTEL HASSLER**
Trinità dei Monti 6
00187 Rome, Italy
Tel: 39 06 699 340
Fax: 39 06 678 9991
www.hotelhasslerroma.com

**HAYMAN**
Great Barrier Reef
Queensland 4801, Australia
Tel: 61 7 4940 1234
Fax: 61 7 4940 1567
www.hayman.com.au

**HOTEL HELVETIA & BRISTOL**
Via dei Pescioni, 2
50123 Florence, Italy
Tel: 39 055 287814
Fax: 39 055 288353
www.charminghotels.it/helvetia

**HOLBECK GHYLL COUNTRY HOUSE HOTEL**
Holbeck Lane
Windermere LA23 1LU, England
Tel: 44 15394 32375
Fax: 44 15394 34743
www.holbeck-ghyll.co.uk

**THE HUNTINGTON HOTEL**
1075 California Street
San Francisco, CA 94108 USA
Tel: 415 474 5400
Fax: 415 474 6227
www.huntingtonhotel.com

**HUKA LODGE**
Huka Falls Road
Taupo, New Zealand
Tel: 64 7 378 5791
Fax: 64 7 378 0427
www.hukalodge.co.nz

# HOTELS

**HOTEL IMPERIAL**
Kärntner Ring 16
1015 Vienna, Austria
Tel: 43 1 50 110 0
Fax: 43 1 50 110 410
www.luxurycollection.com

**JAMAICA INN**
P.O. Box 1
Ocho Rios, Jamaica, West Indies
Tel: 876 974 2514
Fax: 876 974 2449
www.jamaicainn.com

**JUMBY BAY RESORT**
P.O. Box 243
St. Johns, Antigua
Tel: 268 462 6000
Fax: 268 462 6020
www.elegantresorts.com

**HOTEL KÄMP**
Pohjoisesplanadi 29
00100 Helsinki, Finland
Tel: 358 9 576 111
Fax: 358 9 576 1122
www.hotelkamp.fi

**KEMPINSKI HOTEL CORVINUS**
Erzsébet Tér 7-8
1051 Budapest, Hungary
Tel: 36 1 429 3777
Fax: 36 1 429 4777
www.kempinski-hotels.com

**KEMPINSKI HOTEL TASCHENBERGPALAIS**
Taschenberg 3
01067 Dresden, Germany
Tel: 49 351 49 12 0
Fax: 49 351 49 12 812
www.kempinski-hotels.com

**KEMPINSKI RESORT HOTEL**
Ctra. de Cadiz, km 159
29680 Estepona, Spain
Tel: 34 95 280 9500
Fax: 34 95 280 9550
www.kempinski-hotels.com

**LA MAMOUNIA**
Avenue Bab Jdid
40 000 Marrakech, Morocco
Tel: 212 4 44 44 409
Fax: 212 4 44 49 40
www.mamounia.com

**LA POSADA DE SANTA FE RESORT & SPA**
330 East Palace Avenue
Santa Fe, NM 87501 USA
Tel: 505 986 0000
Fax: 505 982 6850
www.rockresorts.com

**LA SAMANNA**
Baie Longue
St. Martin, FWI
Tel: 590 87 64 00
Fax: 590 87 87 86
www.orient-express.com

**LA VALENCIA HOTEL**
1132 Prospect Street
La Jolla, CA 92037 USA
Tel: 858 454 0771
Fax: 858 456 3921
www.lavalencia.com

**THE LANCASTER**
7, rue de Berri, Champs-Elysées
75008 Paris, France
Tel: 33 1 40 76 40 76
Fax: 33 1 40 76 40 00
www.hotel-lancaster.fr

**THE LANESBOROUGH**
1 Lanesborough Place, Hyde Park Corner
London SW1X 7TA, England
Tel: 44 20 7259 5599
Fax: 44 20 7259 5606
www.rosewoodhotels.com

**LAPA PALACE**
Rua do Pau de Bandeira, 4
1249-021 Lisbon, Portugal
Tel: 351 21 395 0005
Fax: 351 21 395 0665
www.orient-express.com

**LAS VENTANAS AL PARAISO**
Km. 19.5 Carretera Tranpeninsular
Cabo San Lucas 23400, Mexico
Tel: 52 114 40300
Fax: 52 114 40301
www.rosewoodhotels.com

**LILIANFELS BLUE MOUNTAINS**
Lilianfels Avenue, Echo Point
Katoomba NSW 2780, Australia
Tel: 61 2 4780 1200
Fax: 61 2 4780 1300
www.orient-express.com

**LITTLE DIX BAY**
P.O. Box 70
Virgin Gorda, BVI
Tel: 284 495 5555
Fax: 284 495 5661
www.rosewoodhotels.com

**LITTLE PALM ISLAND**
28500 Overseas Highway
Little Torch Key, FL 33042 USA
Tel: 305 872 2524
Fax: 305 872 4843
www.littlepalmisland.com

**HOTEL DU LOUVRE**
Place André Malraux
75001 Paris, France
Tel: 33 44 58 38 38
Fax: 33 01 44 58 38 01
www.hoteldelouvre.com

**THE LOWELL**
28 East 63rd Street
New York, NY 10021 USA
Tel: 212 838 1400
Fax: 212 319 4230
www.lhw.com

**THE LYGON ARMS**
Broadway, Worcestershire
WR12 7DU, England
Tel: 44 1386 852255
Fax: 44 1386 858611
www.savoy-group.co.uk

# HOTELS

MALLIOUHANA HOTEL
P.O. Box 173
Meads Bay, Anguilla
Tel: 264 497 6111
Fax: 264 497 6011
www.malliouhana.com

MANDARIN ORIENTAL,
HONG KONG
5 Connaught Road, Central
Hong Kong, China
Tel: 852 2522 0111
Fax: 852 2810 6190
www.mandarinoriental.com

MANDARIN ORIENTAL
HYDE PARK, LONDON
66 Knightsbridge
London SW1X 7LA, England
Tel: 44 20 7235 2000
Fax: 44 20 7235 4552
www.mandarinoriental.com

MANDARIN ORIENTAL,
MIAMI
500 Brickell Key Drive
Miami, FL 33131 USA
Tel: 305 373 0141
Fax: 305 373 0147
www.mandarinoriental.com

MANDARIN ORIENTAL,
MUNICH
Neuturmstrasse 1
80331 Munich, Germany
Tel: 49 89 290 980
Fax: 49 89 222 539
www.mandarinoriental.com

MANDARIN ORIENTAL
HOTEL DU RHÔNE
Quai Turrettini 1
1201 Geneva, Switzerland
Tel: 41 22 909 0000
Fax: 41 22 909 0010
www.mandarinoriental.com

MANDARIN ORIENTAL,
SAN FRANCISCO
222 Sansome Street
San Francisco, CA 94104 USA
Tel: 415 276 9888
Fax: 415 433 0289
www.mandarinoriental.com

THE MANSION
ON TURTLE CREEK
2821 Turtle Creek Boulevard
Dallas, TX 75219 USA
Tel: 214 559 2100
Fax: 214 528 4187
www.rosewoodhotels.com

THE MARK
25 East 77th Street
New York, NY 10021 USA
Tel: 212 744 4300
Fax: 212 744 2749
www.mandarinoriental.com

HÔTEL MARTINEZ
73 La Croisette
06406 Cannes, France
Tel: 33 4 92 98 73 00
Fax: 33 4 93 39 67 82
www.hotel-martinez.com

THE MAUNA LANI BAY
HOTEL & BUNGALOWS
68-1400 Mauna Lani Drive
Kohala Coast, HI 96743 USA
Tel: 808 885 6622
Fax: 808 885-1483
www.maunalani.com

MENA HOUSE
OBEROI
Pyramid's Road, Giza
Cairo, Egypt
Tel: 202 383 3222
Fax: 202 383 7777
www.oberoihotels.com

THE MERRION
Upper Merrion Street
Dublin 2, Ireland
Tel: 353 1 603 0600
Fax: 353 1 603 0700
www.merrionhotel.com

HOTEL METROPOLE
31, Place de Brouckere
1000 Brussels, Belgium
Tel: 32 2 217 2300
Fax: 32 2 218 0220
www.metropolehotel.be

HÔTEL MEURICE
228, rue de Rivoli
75001 Paris, France
Tel: 33 44 58 1010
Fax: 33 1 44 58 1015
www.meuricehotel.com

MIRAMONTE RESORT
45-000 Indian Wells Lane
Indian Wells, CA 92210 USA
Tel: 760 341 2200
Fax: 760 568 0541
www.miramonteresort.com

HOTEL MONASTERIO
Calle Palacio 136,
Plazoleta Nazarenas
Cusco, Peru
Tel: 51 84 24 1777
Fax: 51 84 23 7111
www.orient-express.com

MOUNT NELSON HOTEL
76 Orange Street
Cape Town 8001, South Africa
Tel: 27 21 483 1000
Fax: 27 21 424 7472
www.orient-express.com

HOTEL NASSAUER HOF
Kaiser-Friedrich-Platz 3-4
65183 Wiesbaden, Germany
Tel: 49 611 1330
Fax: 49 611 133632
www.nassauer-hof.de

THE OBEROI, BALI
Seminyak Beach, Jalan Laksmana,
Denpasar 80033, Bali, Indonesia
Tel: 62 361 730 361
Fax: 62 361 730 791
www.oberoihotels.com

THE OBEROI, BANGALORE
37-39 Mahatma Gandhi Road
Bangalore 560 001, India
Tel: 91 80 558 5858
Fax: 91 80 558 5960
www.oberoihotels.com

# HOTELS

**OBEROI GRAND**
15 Jawaharlal Nehru Road
Calcutta 700 013, India
Tel: 91 33 249 2323
Fax: 91 33 249 3229
www.oberoihotels.com

**THE OBEROI, LOMBOK**
Medana Beach, Tanjung
Lombok 83001, Indonesia
Tel: 62 370 638 444
Fax: 62 370 632 496
www.oberoihotels.com

**THE OBEROI, MAURITIUS**
Baie aux Tortues
Pointe aux Piments, Mauritius
Tel: 230 204 3600
Fax: 230 204 3625
www.oberoihotels.com

**THE OBEROI, MUMBAI**
Nariman Point
Mumbai 400 021, India
Tel: 91 22 232 5757
Fax: 91 22 204 3282
www.oberoihotels.com

**THE OBEROI, NEW DELHI**
Dr. Zakir Hussain Marg
New Delhi 110003, India
Tel: 91 11 430 3030
Fax: 91 11 436 0484
www.oberoihotels.com

**THE OBEROI, SAHL HASHEESH**
P.O. Box 117
Red Sea, Hurghada, Egypt
Tel: 20 65 440 777
Fax: 20 65 440 788
www.oberoihotels.com

**THE OBSERVATORY HOTEL**
89 Kent Street
Sydney NSW 2000, Australia
Tel: 61 2 9256 2222
Fax: 61 2 9256 2233
www.orient-express.com

**OCEAN CLUB**
P.O. Box N-4777
Nassau, Bahamas
Tel: 242 363 2501
Fax: 242 363 2424
www.oceanclub.com

**OLONANA**
Abercrombie & Kent
1520 Kensington Road
Oak Brook, IL 60523
Tel: 800 323 7308
Fax: 630 954 3324
www.abercrombiekent.com

**THE ORIENTAL, BANGKOK**
48 Oriental Avenue
Bangkok 10500, Thailand
Tel: 66 2 659 9000
Fax: 66 2 659 0000
www.mandarinoriental.com

**OUSTAU DE BAUMANIÈRE**
Les-Baux-de-Provence
13520 France
Tel: 33 4 90 54 33 07
Fax: 33 4 90 54 40 46
www.oustaudebaumaniere.com

**PALACE LUZERN**
Haldenstrasse 10
6006 Lucerne, Switzerland
Tel: 41 41 416 1616
Fax: 41 41 416 1000
www.palace-luzern.ch

**HÔTEL DU PALAIS**
1, Avenue de L'Imperatrice
64200 Biarritz, France
Tel: 33 5 59 41 64 00
Fax: 33 5 59 41 67 99
www.hotel-du-palais.com

**PALAZZO ARZAGA**
Carzago di Calvagese della Riviera
25080 Brescia, Italy
Tel: 39 030 680600
Fax: 39 030 6806168
www.palazzoarzaga.com

**PALAZZO SASSO**
Via San Giovanni del Toro, 28
84010 Ravello, Italy
Tel: 39 089 81 81 81
Fax: 39 089 85 89 00
www.palazzosasso.com

**THE PAN PACIFIC SAN FRANCISCO**
500 Post Street
San Francisco, CA 94102 USA
Tel: 415 771 8600
Fax: 415 398 0267
www.panpac.com

**LE PARC**
55-57, Avenue Raymond Poincaré
75116 Paris, France
Tel: 33 144 05 66 66
Fax: 33 144 05 66 00
www.sofitel.com

**HÔTEL DE PARIS**
Place du Casino
98000 Monte Carlo, Monaco
Tel: 377 92 16 30 00
Fax: 377 92 16 38 50
www.montecarloresort.com

**PARK HOTEL KENMARE**
County Kerry
Kenmare, Ireland
Tel: 353 64 41200
Fax: 353 64 41402
www.parkkenmare.com

**PARK HOTEL VITZNAU**
Kantonsstrasse
6354 Vitznau, Switzerland
Tel: 41 41 399 6060
Fax: 41 41 399 6070
www.parkhotel-vitznau.ch

**PARK HYATT SAN FRANCISCO**
333 Battery Street
San Francisco, CA 94111 USA
Tel: 415 392 1234
Fax: 415 421 2433
www.hyatt.com

# HOTELS

**PARROT CAY**
P.O. Box 164
Providenciales, Turks & Caicos
Tel: 649 946 7788
Fax: 649 946 7789
www.parrot-cay.com

**THE PENINSULA
BANGKOK**
333 Charoennakorn Road Klongsan
Bangkok 10600, Thailand
Tel: 66 2 861 2888
Fax: 66 2 861 1112
www.peninsula.com

**THE PENINSULA
BEVERLY HILLS**
9882 South Santa Monica Boulevard
Beverly Hills, CA 90212 USA
Tel: 310 551 2888
Fax: 310 788 2319
www.peninsula.com

**THE PENINSULA
HONG KONG**
Salisbury Road, Kowloon
Hong Kong, China
Tel: 852 2920 2888
Fax: 852 2722 4170
www.peninsula.com

**THE PENINSULA
NEW YORK**
700 Fifth Avenue at 55th Street
New York, NY 10019 USA
Tel: 212 956 2888
Fax: 212 903 3943
www.peninsula.com

**PETER ISLAND RESORT**
Road Town
Tortola, BVI
Tel: 284 495 2000
Fax: 284 495 2500
www.peterisland.com

**THE PHOENICIAN**
6000 East Camelback Road
Scottsdale, AZ 85251 USA
Tel: 602 941 8200
Fax: 602 947 4311
www.luxurycollection.com

**THE PIERRE**
Fifth Avenue at 61st Street
New York, NY 10021 USA
Tel: 212 838 8000
Fax: 212 940 8109
www.fourseasons.com

**PINK SANDS**
PO Box 87
Harbour Island, Bahamas
Tel: 242 333 2030
Fax: 242 333 2060
www.pinksandsresort.com

**HOTEL PITRIZZA**
Costa Smeralda
07020 Porto Cervo, Sardinia, Italy
Tel: 39 0789 930 111
Fax: 39 0789 930 611
www.luxurycollection.com

**HÔTEL PLAZA ATHÉNÉE**
37 East 64th Street
New York, NY 10021 USA
Tel: 212 734 9100
Fax: 212 772 0958
www.plaza-athenee.com

**HÔTEL PLAZA ATHÉNÉE**
25 Avenue Montaigne
75008 Paris, France
Tel: 33 1 53 67 66 65
Fax: 33 1 53 67 66 66
www.plaza-athenee-paris.com

**THE POINT**
HCR #1 Box 65
Saranac Lake, NY 12983 USA
Tel: 518 891 5674
Fax: 518 891 1152
www.thepointresort.com

**THE PORTMAN RITZ-CARLTON,
SHANGHAI**
Shanghai Centre,
1376 Nanjing Xi Lu
Shanghai 200040, China
Tel: 86 21 6279 8888
Fax: 86 21 6279 8999
www.ritzcarlton.com

**PRINCE DE GALLES**
33, Avenue George V
75008 Paris, France
Tel: 33 1 53 23 7777
Fax: 33 1 53 23 7878
www.luxurycollection.com

**HOTEL PRINCIPE DI SAVOIA**
Piazza della Repubblica, 17
20124 Milan, Italy
Tel: 39 02 6230 1
Fax: 39 02 653 799
www.luxurycollection.com

**HOTEL PULITZER**
Prinsengracht 315-331
1016 Amsterdam, The Netherlands
Tel: 31 20 523 5235
Fax: 31 20 627 6753
www.luxurycollection.com

**QUAIL LODGE
RESORT & GOLF CLUB**
8205 Valley Greens Drive
Carmel, CA 93923 USA
Tel: 831 624 1581
Fax: 831 624 3726
www.peninsula.com

**HOTEL QUINTA DO LAGO**
8135-024 Almancil
Algarve, Portugal
Tel: 351 289 350 350
Fax: 351 289 396 393
www.orient-express.com

**RAJVILAS**
Goner Road
Jaipur 303 012, India
Tel: 91 141 680 101
Fax: 91 141 680 202
www.oberoihotels.com

**RANCHO VALENCIA**
5921 Valencia Circle
Rancho Santa Fe, CA 92067 USA
Tel: 858 756 1123
Fax: 858 756 0165
www.ranchovalencia.com

# HOTELS

**REID'S PALACE**
Estrada Monumental 139
9000-098 Funchal, Madeira, Portugal
Tel: 351 291 71 7171
Fax: 351 291 71 7177
www.orient-express.com

**THE REGENT BEVERLY WILSHIRE**
9500 Wilshire Boulevard
Beverly Hills, CA 90212 USA
Tel: 310 275 5200
Fax: 310 274 2851
www.fourseasons.com

**THE REGENT RESORT CHIANG MAI AT MAE RIM VALLEY**
Mae Rim-Samoeng Old Road
Chiang-Mai 50180, Thailand
Tel: 66 53 298 181
Fax: 66 53 298 189
www.fourseasons.com

**THE REGENT SYDNEY**
199 George Street, Grosvenor Place
Sydney, NSW 1200, Australia
Tel: 61 2 9238 0000
Fax: 61 29251 2851
www.fourseasons.com

**LE RICHEMOND**
Jardin Brunswick
1201 Geneva, Switzerland
Tel: 41 22 715 7000
Fax: 41 22 715 7001
www.richemond.ch

**HOTEL RITZ**
Plaza de la Lealtad, 5
28014 Madrid, Spain
Tel: 34 91 701 6767
Fax: 34 91 701 6776
www.ritz.es

**THE RITZ HOTEL**
150 Piccadilly
London WIJ 9BR, England
Tel: 44 20 7493 8181
Fax: 44 20 7493 2687
www.theritzhotel.co.uk

**THE RITZ-CARLTON, AMELIA ISLAND**
4750 Amelia Island Parkway
Amelia Island, FL 32034 USA
Tel: 904 277 1100
Fax: 904 261-9063
www.ritzcarlton.com

**THE RITZ-CARLTON, BALI**
Jalan Karang Mas Sejahtera, Jimbaran
80364 Bali, Indonesia
Tel: 62 361 702 222
Fax: 62 361 702 455
www.ritzcarlton.com

**THE RITZ-CARLTON, BOSTON**
15 Arlington Street
Boston, MA 02117 USA
Tel: 617 536 5700
Fax: 617 536-1335
www.ritzcarlton.com

**THE RITZ-CARLTON, BUCKHEAD**
3434 Peachtree Rd., NE
Atlanta GA, 30326 USA
Tel: 404 237 2700
Fax: 404 239 0078
www.ritzcarlton.com

**THE RITZ-CARLTON, CANCUN**
Retorno Del Rey #36
Cancun 77500, Mexico
Tel: 52 98 81 08 08
Fax: 52 98 85 10 15
www.ritzcarlton.com

**THE RITZ-CARLTON CHICAGO**
160 East Pearson Street
at Water Tower Place
Chicago, IL 60611 USA
Tel: 312 266 1000
Fax: 312 266 1194
www.ritzcarlton.com

**THE RITZ-CARLTON, HONG KONG**
3 Connaught Road
Central, Hong Kong, China
Tel: 852 2877 6666
Fax: 852 2877 6778
www.ritzcarlton.com

**THE RITZ-CARLTON, HUNTINGTON HOTEL & SPA**
1401 South Oak Knoll Avenue
Pasadena, CA 91106 USA
Tel: 626 568 3900
Fax: 626 568 3700
www.ritzcarlton.com

**THE RITZ-CARLTON, KAPALUA**
One Ritz-Carlton Drive
Kapalua, Maui, HI 96761 USA
Tel: 808 669 6200
Fax: 808 669 1566
www.ritzcarlton.com

**THE RITZ-CARLTON, LAGUNA NIGUEL**
One Ritz-Carlton Drive
Dana Point, CA 92629 USA
Tel: 949 240 2000
Fax: 949 240 1061
www.ritzcarlton.com

**THE RITZ-CARLTON, MARINA DEL REY**
4375 Admiralty Way
Marina del Rey, CA 90292 USA
Tel: 310 823 1700
Fax: 310 823 2403
www.ritzcarlton.com

**THE RITZ-CARLTON MILLENIA, SINGAPORE**
7 Raffles Avenue
Singapore 039799
Tel: 65 337 8888
Fax: 65 338 0001
www.ritzcarlton.com

# HOTELS

**THE RITZ-CARLTON, MONTREAL**
1228 Sherbrooke Street West
Montreal, Quebec H3G 1H6, Canada
Tel: 514 842 4212
Fax: 514 842 3383
www.ritzcarlton.com

**THE RITZ-CARLTON, NAPLES**
280 Vanderbilt Road
Naples, FL 34108 USA
Tel: 941 598 3300
Fax: 941 598 6690
www.ritzcarlton.com

**THE RITZ-CARLTON, NEW ORLEANS**
921 Canal Street
New Orleans, LA 70112 USA
Tel: 504 524 1331
Fax: 504 524 7233
www.ritzcarlton.com

**THE RITZ-CARLTON, OSAKA**
2-5-25, Umeda, Kita-ku
Osaka 530-0001, Japan
Tel: 81 6 6343 7000
Fax: 81 6 6343 7001
www.ritzcarlton.com

**THE RITZ-CARLTON, PALM BEACH**
100 South Ocean Boulevard
Palm Beach, FL 33462 USA
Tel: 561 533-6000
Fax: 561 588-4202
www.ritzcarlton.com

**THE RITZ-CARLTON, PHILADELPHIA**
Ten Avenue of the Arts
Philadelphia, PA 19102 USA
Tel: 215 735 7700
Fax: 215 735 7710
www.ritzcarlton.com

**THE RITZ-CARLTON, RANCHO MIRAGE**
68-900 Frank Sinatra Drive
Rancho Mirage, CA 92270 USA
Tel: 760 321 8282
Fax: 760 321 6928
www.ritzcarlton.com

**THE RITZ-CARLTON ROSE HALL, JAMAICA**
One Ritz-Carlton Drive, Rose Hall
St. James, Jamaica, West Indies
Tel: 876 953-2800
Fax: 876 953 2501
www.ritzcarlton.com

**THE RITZ-CARLTON, SAN FRANCISCO**
600 Stockton at California Street
San Francisco, CA 94108 USA
Tel: 415 296 7465
Fax: 415 291-0288
www.ritzcarlton.com

**THE RITZ-CARLTON SAN JUAN HOTEL, SPA & CASINO**
6961 Avenue of the Governors
Carolina, Puerto Rico 00979
Tel: 787 253 1700
Fax: 787 253-3232
www.ritzcarlton.com

**THE RITZ-CARLTON SCHLOSSHOTEL, BERLIN**
Brahmsstrasse 10
14193 Berlin, Germany
Tel: 49 30 895 840
Fax: 49 30 89584 800
www.ritzcarlton.com

**THE RITZ-CARLTON, SHARM EL SHEIKH**
Om El Seed, Sharm El Sheikh
South Sinai, Egypt
Tel: 20 62 661 917
Fax: 20 62 661 785
www.ritzcarlton.com

**THE RITZ-CARLTON, ST. THOMAS**
6900 Great Bay
St. Thomas, USVI 00802
Tel: 340 775 3333
Fax: 340 775 4444
www.ritzcarlton.com

**THE RITZ-CARLTON, WASHINGTON, D.C.**
1150 22nd Street, N.W.
Washington, DC 20037 USA
Tel: 202 835 0500
Fax: 202 974-5519
www.ritzcarlton.com

**RITZ PARIS**
15 Place Vendôme
75001 Paris, France
Tel: 33 1 43 16 30 30
Fax: 33 1 43 16 36 68
www.ritzparis.com

**HOTEL ROMAZZINO**
Costa Smeralda
07020 Porto Cervo, Sardinia, Italy
Tel: 39 0789 977111
Fax: 39 0789 96258
www.luxurycollection.com

**ROSARIO RESORT & SPA**
1400 Rosario Road
Eastsound, WA 98245 USA
Tel: 360 376 2222
Fax: 360 376 2289
www.rockresorts.com

**ROUND HILL HOTEL & VILLAS**
P. O. Box 64
Montego Bay, Jamaica
Tel: 876 956 7050
Fax: 876 956 7505
www.roundhilljamaica.com

**ROYAL PALMS HOTEL & CASITAS**
5200 East Camelback Road
Phoenix, AZ 85018 USA
Tel: 602 840 3610
Fax: 602 840 6927
www.royalpalmshotel.com

**ROYAL PARC EVIAN HOTEL ROYAL**
South Bank of Lake Geneva
74500 Evian, France
Tel: 33 4 50 26 85 00
Fax: 33 4 50 75 38 40
www.royalparcevian.com

**HOTEL DE RUSSIE**
Via del Babuino 9
00187 Rome, Italy
Tel: 39 06 32 8881
Fax: 39 06 32 888 888
www.rfhotels.com

# HOTELS

**HOTEL SACHER**
Philharmonikerstrasse 4
1010 Vienna, Austria
Tel: 43 1 51 456
Fax: 43 1 51 456 810
www.sacher.com

**HOTEL SACHER SALZBURG
ÖSTERREICHISCHER HOF**
Schwarzstrasse 5-7
5020 Salzburg, Austria
Tel: 43 662 88 9 77
Fax: 43 662 88 9 77 14
www.sacher.com

**SALISH LODGE & SPA**
6501 Railroad Avenue SE
Snoqualmie, WA 98065 USA
Tel: 425 888 2556
Fax: 425 888 2420
www.salishlodge.com

**SANDY LANE**
St. James, Barbados
Tel: 246 444 2000
Fax: 246 432 5430
www.sandylane.com

**HOTEL SAVOY**
Piazza della Repubblica, 7
50123 Florence, Italy
Tel: 39 055 27351
Fax: 39 055 273 5888
www.rfhotels.com

**THE SAVOY**
The Strand
London WC2R OEU, England
Tel: 44 207 836 4343
Fax: 44 207 240 6040
www.savoy-group.co.uk

**SAXON**
36 Saxon Road
Sandhurst, Johannesburg,
Saxonwold 2132, South Africa
Tel: 27 11 292 6000
Fax: 27 11 292 6001
www.thesaxon.com

**HOTEL SCHLOSS FUSCHL**
Hof bei Salzburg
5322 Salzburg, Austria
Tel: 43 6229 22530
Fax: 43 6229 2253 531
www.luxurycollection.com

**LE SIRENUSE**
Via Cristoforo Colombo, 30
84017 Positano, Italy
Tel: 39 089 875066
Fax: 39 089 811798
www.lesirenuse.com

**SONEVA FUSHI**
Malé
Republic of the Maldives
Tel: 960 230 3045
Fax: 960 230 374
www.sixsenses/sonevafushi

**SONOMA MISSION
INN & SPA**
100 Boyes Boulevard
Sonoma, CA 95476 USA
Tel: 707 938-9000
Fax: 707 938-4250
www.sonomamissioninn.com

**HOTEL SPLENDIDO
& SPLENDIDO MARE**
Salita Baratta, 16
16034 Portofino, Italy
Tel: 390 185 267 801
Fax: 390 185 267 806
www.orient-express.com

**SPRING CREEK RANCH**
1800 Spirit Dance Road
Jackson, WY 83001 USA
Tel: 307 733 8833
Fax: 307 733 1524
www.springcreekranch.com

**THE ST. DAVID'S
HOTEL & SPA**
Havannah Street
Cardiff 10 5SD, Wales
Tel: 29 2045 4045
Fax: 29 2031 3075
www.rfhotels.com

**THE ST. REGIS BEIJING**
No 21, Jian Guo Men Wai Da Jie
Beijing 100020, China
Tel: 86 10 6460 6688
Fax: 86 10 6460 3299
www.stregis.com

**THE ST. REGIS GRAND**
Via Vittorio Emanuele Orlando 3
00185 Rome, Italy
Tel: 39 06 47091
Fax: 39 06 474 7307
www.stregis.com

**THE ST. REGIS LOS ANGELES**
2055 Avenue of the Stars
Los Angeles, CA 90067 USA
Tel: 310 277 6111
Fax: 310 277 3711
www.stregis.com

**THE ST. REGIS NEW YORK**
Two East 55th Street
New York, NY 10022 USA
Tel: 212 753 4500
Fax: 212 787 3447
www.stregis.com

**THE ST. REGIS
WASHINGTON, D.C.**
923 16th Street, N.W.
Washington, D.C. 2006 USA
Tel: 202 638 2626
Fax: 202 638 4231
www.stregis.com

**STAPLEFORD PARK**
Near Melton Mowbray
Leicestershire LE14 2EF, England
Tel: 44 1572 787522
Fax: 44 1572 787651
www.stapleford.co.uk

**THE STAFFORD**
St. James's Place
London SW1A 1NJ, England
Tel: 44 207 493 0111
Fax: 44 207 493 7121
www.thestaffordhotel.co.uk

# HOTELS

**STEIGENBERGER FRANKFURTER HOF**
Am Kaiserplatz 17
60311 Frankfurt, Germany
Tel: 49 69 215 02
Fax: 49 69 215 900
www.steigenberger.com

**STOKE PARK CLUB**
Park Road, Stoke Poges,
Buckinghamshire SL2 4PG, England
Tel: 44 1753 717 171
Fax: 44 1753 717 181
www.stokeparkclub.com

**THE SUKHOTHAI**
13/3 South Sathron Road
Bangkok 10120, Thailand
Tel: 66 2 287 0222
Fax: 66 2 287 4980
www.sukhothai.com

**THE TIDES**
1220 Ocean Drive
Miami, FL 33139 USA
Tel: 305 604 5070
Fax: 305 604 5180
www.thetideshotel.com

**LE TOINY**
Anse de Toiny
97133 Saint-Barthélemy
Tel: 0590 27 88 88
Fax: 0590 27 89 30
www.letoiny.com

**THE TRYALL CLUB**
P.O. Box 1206
Montego Bay, Jamaica
Tel: 876 956 5660
Fax: 876 956 5673
www.tryallclub.com

**TURNBERRY ISLE RESORT & CLUB**
19999 W. Country Club Drive
Aventura, FL 33180 USA
Tel: 305 932 6200
Fax: 305 933 6560
www.mandarinoriental.com

**UDAIVILÄS**
Haridasji Ki Magri
Udaipur 31300, India
Tel: 91 11 3890505
Fax: 91 11 3890568
www.oberoihotels.com

**VANYAVILÄS**
Ranthambor Road,
Sawai Madhopur
Ranthambor, India
Tel: 91 11 3890505
Fax: 91 11 3890568
www.oberoihotels.com

**VATULELE ISLAND RESORT**
Vatulele Island, Fiji
Tel: 61 2 9665 8700
Fax: 61 2 9665 7833
www.vatulele.com

**VENTANA INN & SPA**
Highway One
Big Sur, CA 93920 USA
Tel: 831 667 2331
Fax: 831 667 2419
www.ventanainn.com

**VICTORIA-JUNGFRAU GRAND HOTEL & SPA**
3800 Interlaken, Switzerland
Tel: 41 33 828 28 28
Fax: 41 33 828 28 80
www.victoria-jungfrau.ch

**VILLA D'ESTE**
Via Regina 40, Lake Como
22012 Cernobbio, Italy
Tel: 39 031 3481
Fax: 39 031 348 844
www.villadeste.it

**VILLA LA MASSA**
Villa della Massa 24
Candeli Bagno a Ripoli
50012 Florence, Italy
Tel: 39 055 62 611
Fax: 39 055 63 3102
www.villalamassa.com

**VILLA SAN MICHELE**
Via di Doccia, 4
50014 Fiesole, Florence, Italy
Tel: 390 55 567 8200
Fax: 390 55 567 8250
www.orient-express.com

**THE VINEYARD AT STOCKCROSS**
Newbury, Berkshire
RG20 8JU, England
Tel: 44 1635 528770
Fax: 44 1635 528398
www.the-vineyard.co.uk

**THE WALDORF TOWERS**
100 East 50th Street
New York, NY 10022 USA
Tel: 212 355 3100
Fax: 212 872 4799
www.waldorf-towers.com

**THE WESTCLIFF**
67 Jan Smuts Avenue
Westcliff 2193,
Johannesburg, South Africa
Tel: 27 11 646 2400
Fax: 27 11 646 3500
www.orient-express.com

**WILDFLOWER HALL, MASHOBRA**
Charabra
Shimla 171012, India
Tel: 91 177 480808
Fax: 91 177 480909
www.oberoihotels.com

**THE WINDSOR**
103 Spring Street
Melbourne 3000, Australia
Tel: 61 3 9633 6000
Fax: 61 3 9633 6001
www.oberoihotels.com

**WINDSOR COURT HOTEL**
300 Gravier Street
New Orleans, LA 70130 USA
Tel: 504 523 6000
Fax: 504 596 4513
www.orient-express.com